ETHNOLOGY

OF THE

UNGAVA DISTRICT,
HUDSON BAY TERRITORY

LUCIEN M. TURNER

INTRODUCTION BY STEPHEN LORING

SMITHSONIAN INSTITUTION PRESS
Washington and London

Published in association with Makivik Corporation and the Avataq Cultural Institute

Publisher's note: Lucien Turner's research was originally published in 1894 in the Smithsonian Institution's *Eleventh Annual Report of the Bureau of Ethnology*. This reissue is now part of the Classics of Smithsonian Anthropology Series.

All photographs in the gallery immediately following the "Introduction to Lucien M. Turner and the Beginnings of Smithsonain Anthropology in the North" are courtesy of the National Anthropological Archives, National Museum of Natural History, Smithsonian Institution.

Production editor: E. Anne Bolen

Library of Congress Cataloging-in-Publication Data
Turner, Lucien M. (Lucien McShan)
   Ethnology of the Ungava district, Hudson Bay territory/
     Lucien M. Turner
     p. cm.— (Classics of Smithsonian anthropology)
   "Originally published in 1894 in the Smithsonian Institution's
   Eleventh Annual Report of the Bureau of Ethnology"—T.p. verso.
     ISBN 1-56098-965-3 (alk. paper)
   1. Indians of North America—Québec (Province) —Social life and
   customs. 2. Inuit—Québec (Province)—Ungava Peninsula—Social life
   and customs. 3. Indians of North America—Québec (Province)—Ungava
   Peninsula—Folklore. I. Title. II. Series.
E78.Q3 T9 2001
971.4'1700497—dc21   2001020345

British Library Cataloguing-in-Publication Data available

Manufactured in the United States of America
08 07 06 05 04 03 02 01 5 4 3 2 1

♾ The paper used in this publication meets the minimum requirements of the American National Standard for Information Sciences—Permanence of Paper for Printed Library Materials ANSI Z39.48-1984

Makivik Corporation is honored to participate in this special reissue of Lucien McShan Turner's nineteenth-century account of life in southern Ungava Bay. His observations, documented in writing, illustrations, and the collection of artifacts, provide a tangible link to a past that has been eclipsed by a modernity that must have been unimaginable in the 1880s.

Makivik is part of the modern story of the Inuit whom Turner chronicled. Created following the signing of the James Bay and Northern Quebec Agreement in 1975, Makivik is an economic development company owned by the Inuit of Nunavik in northern Quebec. Its head office is located across the river from where Turner drew his illustrations and obtained his numerous artifacts.

Part of the mandate of Makivik Corporation is to promote the Inuit way of life, values, and traditions. To this end it is a pleasure to work in stride with the Avataq Cultural Institute, whose mandate is focused wholly on cultural preservation, and with the Arctic Studies Center of the Smithsonian Institution's National Museum of Natural History.

This edition is distinguished by the inclusion of rare photographs that have never been published. It is thanks in part to these photographs, snapped so carefully over a century ago by Lucien Turner, that this joint publishing venture saw the light of day. At a photography exhibition held at the British Museum in London in the spring of 1996, then-Makivik President Zebedee Nungak met with Stephen Loring, museum anthropologist with the Arctic Studies Center, and the idea for this reissue was sparked.

FOREWORD

The collaboration between the Smithsonian Institution, Makivik Corporation, and Avataq Cultural Institute to publish this edition of Lucien Turner's work began in 1996. Consequently, this book has occupied my thoughts for quite some time and I would like to share a few important remarks at its outset. As a thoroughly modern Inuk (Eskimo), I view this edition as a hundred-year-old pent-up comment waiting to be told.

Turner's observations of the Inuit who lived in the southernmost point of Ungava Bay from 1884 to 1886 compose an invaluable snapshot of our people. These observations are documented through his writings, superb illustrations, and priceless photographs, and of course the numerous artifacts he collected while in Old Fort Chimo. So this book is actually a bit of a catalogue, or a primer, of a remarkable collection of Inuit artifacts.

When Avataq representatives visited the Smithsonian Institution in September of 1999, we were utterly delighted to see century-old parkas perfectly preserved. Their flawless stitching that would protect very well against the elements awed us. We marveled at the waterproof kayak gear and the winter kamiks, boots with grip soles clearly made for an elder.

If you were to bring the *amautik*—the women's parka—that Turner obtained while in Fort Chimo to modern Kuujjuaq to compare it with a parka made by an Inuk today, the basic pattern would be the same. Inuit passed these designs down orally from generation to generation. Girls learned to sew from their mothers without the aid of diagrams or illustrations. When Turner was gathering artifacts, the Smithsonian had proper archives in which to conserve these rare items for future generations. However, preserving, conserving, or even passing material things on from one generation to the next was not part of our culture; our heirlooms are our traditional Inuit knowledge preserved through our oral tradition. Turner's collective portrait of life in Nunavik a century ago validates our oral tradition. I look forward to working with the Smithsonian Institution in the not-too-distant future to take the parkas out of the drawers and display them in the showcases.

Although I have some reservations about Turner's written observations, notably with regards to the origin of dominoes and the descriptions of gambling activities, the artifacts he collected breathe authenticity. For example, no Inuit carvings as are known in the art world today appear in the collection; these did not exist at the time, as they are a product of a market that developed in the 1950s. Turner, commissioned by the Smithsonian, acquired items then of everyday use that are now extraordinary!

In preparing to write this foreword, I was joking with some colleagues about what the women who sold the items to Turner may have thought. I doubt if they were thinking "Oh, we'd better sew the seams perfectly on this *amautik* because Lucien Turner is bringing it back to the Smithsonian Institution and a hundred years from now people will have to see that they are perfect." Instead they might have thought, "Why do you want to buy my old parka, Lucien?"

In a sense, Avataq picked up the recording of our culture about one hundred years after Turner left off. Our archaeologists, language specialists, and curators continue to document and distribute knowledge of our cultural heritage in all its richness. A counterpoint to Turner's observations is a growing collection of illustrated texts and essays the Avataq Cultural Institute lovingly publishes as *Tumivut* magazine. If you were to read through these issues, you would get a sense of the history of the Inuit of Nunavik from our perspective and the value of this edition of Turner's work would become more evident.

In addition, after a quarter century of rapid development in our region, we are as wired and wireless as anyone, as plugged in and Webified as those Aussie fishermen selling their catch over the Internet before they reach shore. The municipality of Kuujjuaq—across the river from where Turner observed our people—may soon have a convention center with museum-quality space able to showcase artifacts from the Turner collection. You will be able to visit it in person or take a virtual Web tour.

However, lest you be left with the impression that modern technology has had the effect of ridding us of our traditions, let me assure that technology helps us be more Inuit, not less. Today we can hunt seals in the daytime and be home in time to watch the television program *West Wing*. We hunt for seal and caribou more efficiently now, but we still hunt. Our parkas are made with textile and sewn with machines, but they are made from the same pattern as those Turner collected in 1886 and are still trimmed in fur. Our group dynamics are remarkably similar to those of ancient times. While our organizations hold annual, executive, and board meetings, these meetings are conducted in our native language of Inuktitut, with less and less being translated into English or French.

In fact, we recently launched an updated version of an Inuktitut computer font that will work on the Apple Macintosh platform, the PC platform, and the Web. The new font, called AiPaiNunavik, will reintroduce a row of syllabic characters lost when our language was adapted to an IBM electric typewriter in the 1970s. We are collaborating with our colleagues at Makivik Corporation, the Kativik School Board, the Kativik Regional Government, and the Nunavik Regional Board of Health and Social Services to continue to bolster our language.

So read this book with a keen, critical spirit. Turner's contribution is vital in that he collected artifacts at a time when we did not do so. More than a century later, his work validates our very real sense of being Inuit in modern times.

In closing, I wish to thank Stephen Loring at the Arctic Studies Center of the Smithsonian Institution for being such a gracious host to visitors from our organizations while we were in Washington, for his sensitivity to the important issues of cultural preservation, and for carefully preserving the numerous artifacts that provide important pieces of our story's puzzle. Thanks as well to Scott Mahler at the Smithsonian Institution Press for forging ahead with this special reprint edition. Finally, thanks to Makivik Corporation and its president, Pita Aatami, for believing in this project and supporting it with a contribution to ensure that it saw the light of day.

Nakurmiimarialuk. (Thank you very much.)

Robert Watt
President, Avataq Cultural Institute
Nunavik, Québec, Canada

INTRODUCTION TO LUCIEN M. TURNER AND THE BEGINNINGS OF SMITHSONIAN ANTHROPOLOGY IN THE NORTH

This reissue of Lucien McShan Turner's *Ethnology of the Ungava District, Hudson Bay Territory* (1894) completes a trio of historic northern ethnologies that are the intellectual bedrock of North American arctic anthropology. Turner's research, Edward William Nelson's *The Eskimo About Bering Strait* (1899, reprinted in 1983), and John Murdoch's *Ethnological Results of the Point Barrow Expedition* (1892, reprinted in 1988) were originally published in the Bureau of American Ethnology's annual reports and are now reissued as part of the Smithsonian Institution Press's Classics of Smithsonian Anthropology Series. In 1888 the bureau published a fourth volume, *The Central Eskimo* by Franz Boas, which presents the results of Boas's work with the Inuit of Baffin Island. While this research was neither initiated nor sponsored by the Smithsonian, it is strikingly similar in scope and methodology to the work of the Smithsonian naturalists. In fact, it may have been the template that John Wesley Powell, the founder and first director of the Bureau of American Ethnology, later applied to the other volumes in this series.

EARLY SMITHSONIAN ANTHROPOLOGY

Established in 1846 by an act of Congress, the Smithsonian Institution was the legacy of the eccentric English scientist James Smithson. He left his considerable family fortune to the U.S. government with the stipulation that it be used to create "an institution devoted to the increase and diffusion of knowledge." Under the leadership of its first secretary, Joseph Henry, the fledgling Institution began investigating the origins and status of Native Americans through studies of ethnography, linguistics, and archaeology (Hinsley 1981). In fact, the first official publication in the Smithsonian Contributions to Knowledge series was the prodigious *Ancient Monuments of the Mississippi Valley* by Ephraim Squier and Edwin Davis (1848). This book sought to shed light on the origins and antiquity of the earthen monuments found throughout the eastern United States as well as the relationship of the "Moundbuilders" to the extant Native American tribal peoples. Clearly an interest in all aspects of Native American history and culture has been at the core of the Institution's intellectual identity since its inception.

Smithsonian anthropology and its study of Native American culture evolved from an initial period of unstructured, haphazardly acquired ethnographic objects and observations that included material gathered by the Lewis and Clark Expedition, the United States Exploring Expedition (1838–1842), and other government-sponsored expeditions, as well as donations from citizens and scholars. The ethnographic objects were housed in the Smithsonian galleries and storage rooms alongside ever-expanding collections of fossils, plants, birds, mollusks, and rocks.

In 1850 Secretary Henry appointed Spencer F. Baird as his assistant secretary. Among the leading naturalists of his day, Baird arrived in Washington accompanied by two railroad boxcars full of his own collections of natural history specimens. Baird attracted a remarkable cadre of young students and scientists, a group of gifted naturalists with a broad set of interests and experiences who conducted fieldwork and acquired collections throughout much of North America. Although Baird's researchers were mostly ornithologists and invertebrate zoologists and none were trained ethnologists, all of them understood the importance of collecting cultural materials. Baird became the Institution's second secretary in 1878 and continued in this position until his death in 1887.

Under Baird's inspired leadership, the Smithsonian expanded rapidly in the years after the Civil War and emerged as one of the world's greatest natural history research facilities. As an arm of the U.S. government, the Smithsonian Institution was closely allied to the national agenda, and its growth not surprisingly coincided with the ascension of the United States as an international power. The federal government sought to further national interests, territorial expansion, and economic development through the acquisition and management of western lands and resources. While the growth of the United States as a world entity never included a declared colonialist foreign policy, closer to home, government policy increasingly sought control over the indigenous peoples of North America. Therefore, growth of Smithsonian anthropology also served to further the economic interests of the federal government. Increasingly, as military and economic resources were brought to bear against the remaining land-holding Indian groups, the indigenous way of life was profoundly altered. Recognizing this and fearing the disappearance of Indian groups, Smithsonian Institution officials desired to preserve knowledge of Indian cultures and so established the Bureau of American Ethnology (1879–1965)—the predecessor of the current Department of

Anthropology in the National Museum of Natural History—as part of the Smithsonian's United States National Museum.

THE FIELD OF NATURAL HISTORY IN THE UNITED STATES

Toward the end of the nineteenth century, most Americans realized that Native American cultures were likely to vanish beneath the onslaught of expanding commercial and political interests, the so-called tides of progress. In this climate of the "disappearing Indian," many of the vast holdings of anthropological museums worldwide were created as a result of the efforts of "salvage" anthropologists who scoured the countryside for what traces of Indian culture could be saved. These collections had a strong materialistic bias, but they also included folklore, language, and later, Indian bones—all of which were collected, cataloged, and stored with little concern for the fate of the communities or the individuals from which they were acquired. The need to address this troubling legacy has become ever greater, especially within the context of repatriation as the descendants of the Native Americans who refused to disappear have become increasingly aware and concerned for the fate of their patrimony residing within museum walls (Loring 2001).

THE SMITHSONIAN'S NORTHERN AGENDA

Spencer Baird was a man of uncommon vision and unbounded interests. With Baird's support and enthusiasm, the Smithsonian supported northern exploration almost from its inception. For example, it loaned materials and equipment to Charles Francis Hall for his eastern Arctic expeditions to Baffin Island and Greenland (Hall 1864). But Baird's influence was most pronounced in extreme northwest Canada, in the MacKenzie River country, and in adjacent Alaska (Fitzhugh 1988; Fitzhugh and Selig 1981). In 1858 Baird sent Robert Kennicott (from Chicago) to British North America (northwestern Canada). Kennicott was the epitome of the type of Smithsonian naturalist Baird recruited and sponsored. In addition to acquiring a wide range of natural history specimens, Kennicott arranged for the first systematic collections of ethnographic materials from the north to be assembled and shipped to Washington. These collections from Inuvialuit and Dene villages along the lower MacKenzie River had been assembled with the assistance of a pair of remarkable Hudson's Bay Company factors, Bernard R. Ross and Roderick MacFarlane, who became important collectors for Baird (Lindsay 1993).

In 1865 Kennicott accepted the position of director of the Western Union Telegraph Survey, an enterprise that sought to extend a telegraph route through Alaska and Siberia to the capitals of Europe. Kennicott, then with the Chicago Academy of Sciences, arranged with Baird to assemble an eclectic group of naturalists and surveyors called the "Scientific Corps" to conduct natural history research and collect specimens for the Smithsonian. Kennicott's tragic death in 1866 and the success of the transatlantic cable terminated the Alaskan initiative. Dall took over the organization of the Scientific Corps and consequently sending the collections to Washington. The tide of collections astonished even Baird and was instrumental in bringing about an awareness of the potential resources of Alaska. These collections and Baird's aggressive lobbying were crucial to stimulating the U.S. Congress to acquire the Russian territory of Alaska in 1867 (Fitzhugh and Selig 1981; James 1942). Soon thereafter, Dall's book *Alaska and Its Resources* (1870) was instrumental in bringing to an English-speaking, North American audience knowledge of the Alaska territory (Sherwood 1965).

Dall was the first of four intrepid researchers associated with the Smithsonian who were assigned to work in Alaska. Under the aegis of the U.S. Coast Survey and the U.S. Geological Survey, he was instrumental in developing a government association with the Smithsonian. His protégés included Lucien Turner, Edward Nelson, and John Murdoch, the three luminaries of the Smithsonian northern ethnologies previously mentioned.

THE LIFE OF LUCIEN TURNER

Lucien McShan Turner has been called "one of the ablest field naturalists in North America" (Barr 1985:204). He is also one of the most obscure. Little biographic information has emerged beyond the inferences derived from his few published works. Beyond a few details gleaned from archival sources (Barr 1985; Harper 1964:99–107), next to nothing is known about his private life, including his marriage and family, or his professional career and interests following his Smithsonian association. Turner was born in Ohio in 1848 and then his family moved to Illinois soon after. From a young age, Turner delighted in exploring nearby forests and fields. His keen interest in birds brought him to the attention of neighbor Robert Ridgway, a leading ornithologist and later curator of birds at the Smithsonian's United States National Museum under the direction of Spencer Baird. Ridgway figured significantly in Turner's career. A lifelong friend, Ridgway taught the younger man the rudiments of ornithology and taxidermy and paved Turner's way for his association with the Smithsonian.

As a young man of modest means, Turner worked as a farmhand, bricklayer, and teacher. He married in 1869 and fathered two sons. What prompted the rural schoolteacher and family man to seek employment in the field of natural history is unknown. However, his gift to the

Smithsonian of more than a thousand bird specimens collected from the vicinity of his home in Mt. Carmel, Illinois, indicates that Turner remained a devoted amateur naturalist. Turner's dedication did not go unrecognized by Ridgway, his former mentor. When the United States acquired Alaska in 1867, the opportunity arose for the Smithsonian to influence the selection of personnel to staff positions in the U.S. Army's Signal Corps at posts throughout the former Russian territory (Brodhead 1995). Although the Signal Corps employees' primary duties were the rigorous, systematic reading and recording of meteorological, atmospheric, and tidal data, Smithsonian officials hoped the scientists would be able to conduct research and collect specimens to ship back to the Institution in their free time. This expedition was a dream come true for Turner, and it marked the beginning of the aspiring naturalist's extraordinary decade of northern research.

TURNER IN ALASKA

Turner's first Alaskan tour of duty (from May 1874 to August 1877) was at the former Russian trading post at St. Michael on Norton Sound north of the Yukon Delta (Turner 1886:5). An environment that contrasted more with the Midwest's forests and farmlands is hard to imagine. The region surrounding St. Michael was one of low relief and sparse vegetation, with a poorly drained maze of rivers, sloughs, and ponds underlain by deep permafrost deposits. In the depth of winter, the frozen ocean blurred the boundary between land and sea, and a succession of blizzards and fiercely cold weather brought most appearances of life to a standstill. Yet in the summer months, the seemingly barren arctic lands in the St. Michael environs hosted an extraordinary pageant of life as the air filled with noxious insect pests; the tundra bloomed; rivers swelled with a succession of anadromous fish runs; lakes and ponds were home for vast flocks of nesting waterfowl, including swans, geese, and ducks; and the adjacent ocean waters teemed with beluga whales and seals. It was a wild and fabulous region for an aspiring naturalist to explore. With the exception of the pioneering investigations of the Smithsonian's Scientific Corps a few years earlier, the region had remained unknown to science. As fascinating as the exotic landscape filled with undiscovered plants, fishes, and birds was to the young naturalist, Turner recognized as he stepped off the boat at St. Michael that this land was also home to native Yup'ik villagers who had crafted an extraordinarily rich social and spiritual landscape from the land's and seas' bounties.

Russian fur traders established the St. Michael trading post in 1833 (Ray 1983). It rapidly became the nexus of far-flung social and economic activities as Yup'ik and Inupiat from the Bering Strait region and Athabaskan traders from the interior brought furs and other items to the post. In spite of the inroads made by the traders, at the time of Turner's visit these native cultures were still remarkably intact; they had a rich tradition of village life, ceremonies, and subsistence practices. The ability to recognize the significant opportunity to make observations and collections among relatively undisturbed native cultures was a distinguishing hallmark of the naturalists Spencer Baird sent to Alaska. Although his researchers were trained in other areas and they had to make other interests paramount, Baird's directions to his scientists emphasized the importance he placed on collecting ethnological materials. To Turner's credit, he not only followed but eagerly embraced these instructions.

With the meteorological station completed and the daily routine of observation and recording established, Turner avidly turned to his naturalist pursuits. He wrote in the introduction to his Alaskan report, "During my leisure time I was employed in obtaining such objects pertaining to the natural history of that region as could be done. The collection embraced specimens of plants, insects, fishes, birds, mammals, and a great quantity of ethnological matter, together with extensive vocabularies of the Unálēt, Malémūt, Nulato, Ingálēt, and Aleut languages" (Turner 1886:5). Where this gift for languages was acquired is a mystery. At St. Michael as well as at his subsequent postings in the Aleutians and in Ungava, Turner applied himself to mastering native languages with a surprising alacrity and determination. While in the Aleutians, he set out to learn to speak and write Russian (Dunbar 1983), a task he parodies in a letter to Ridgway: "My teeth chatter over the sesquipedalian polysyllabic conglomerations of this fearfully compound language" (Harper 1964:101–102).

The pursuit of specimens and their collection, documentation, and preservation must have been daunting under the primitive conditions at St. Michael. In the introduction to his book on Alaska's natural history, Turner (1886) laments the lack of necessary preservative materials and the challenges the notoriously inclement weather of the region posed. He reports that, on more than one occasion, moisture and mold ruined an entire summer's work of collecting, drying, and pressing plant specimens. Turner was further frustrated because he was not able to aggressively pursue his ethnographic and biological research far from the Signal Corps' meteorological instruments, which required an exact recording regime. And although the actual reading of the instruments was not especially taxing, he was unable to recruit local people with the dedication and skill to conduct the work in his absence. His inability to range far from the station was partially offset by his interest in the language and culture of the Yup'ik residing in the vicinity of St. Michael, several of whom became quite skilled in capturing birds and other species for him.

Turner's first tour of duty in Alaska lasted more than three years. Whether this was of uninterrupted duration is not known, but by the winter of 1876–1877 Turner probably desired to return to his known civilization and the opportunity to renew himself with his family and friends. He was relieved of his official duties for the Signal Corps by Edward W. Nelson, another of Baird's intrepid young naturalists, to whom Turner turned over his responsibilities and the government property under his supervision. It is interesting to speculate on the relationship between these two young men and the role that Turner may have played in channeling Nelson's considerable collecting zeal toward cultural matters. Surviving correspondence with Baird clearly indicates that at least Nelson's initial shipments of specimens to the Institution were a result of his collaboration with Turner (S.I. Archives 1877). Nelson, whose Yup'ik name was "the man who collects the good for nothing [*sic*] things," carried ethnological collecting in Alaska to new heights (Nelson 1899; Fitzhugh and Kaplan 1982; Lantis 1954; Fitzhugh 1983). His introduction to the Yup'ik world probably came through Turner's connections, and presumably a significant portion of the ethnological materials collected by Turner were subsequently attributed to Nelson. Between 1877 and 1881 Nelson made a series of epic sled and kayak journeys throughout the Yukon–Kuskokwim region as well as to Point Barrow and Siberia, where he amassed the single largest collection of native Alaskan objects for the Smithsonian. The results of this herculean labor are documented in his *The Eskimo About Bering Strait* (Nelson 1899), the companion volume to Turner's subsequent ethnological work in Ungava.

Back in Washington, with the support of Baird and Smithsonian staff, Turner immersed himself in preparing and describing the biological specimens he had recovered and in writing a report on his observations and collections. Turner's sojourn in Washington turned out to be short-lived. However eager he had been to take a break from his work in Alaska, he needed only a winter in Washington before he accepted a second term of employment with the Signal Corps so that he could return to Alaska.

Turner's second stint of Alaskan research, between 1878 and 1881, was centered in the Aleutian Islands, where he was instructed to establish and staff a series of meteorological stations throughout the region. In May 1878 he arrived in Unalaska, the former Russian territory's western administrative and commercial center, and soon had a meteorological station running. He subsequently established stations at Fort Alexander on Bristol Bay, at Belkofski on the Alaskan Peninsula, on St. Paul Island in the Pribilofs, and in the western Aleutians on Atka and Attu islands. The most remote of these far-flung stations would have been on Attu. More than a thousand miles west of the Alaskan mainland, this small mountainous island was home to a hardy, self-sufficient group of Aleut families with whom Turner lived for a year beginning in June 1880. The following summer Turner returned to Unalaska, where he received instructions to return to Washington to organize his notes and research for publication.

The most significant outcome of Turner's tenure in Alaska was his 1886 publication *Contributions to the Natural History of Alaska,* the second of five volumes of arctic research published as a result of meteorological investigations conducted for the Signal Service (also referred to as the Signal Corps) of the U.S. Army. Turner's volume provides a brief description of the physical geography of western Alaska, a lengthy distillation of his meteorological findings, and a compilation of his observations on the region's botany, fish, birds, and mammals. The section on the birds of Alaska, obviously the material closest to Turner's heart, is beautifully illustrated with a gorgeous set of chromolithographies, eleven colored plates of drawings by his mentor and friend Robert Ridgway. The volume's detailed descriptions and nomenclature typify the broad interdisciplinary approach characteristic of Baird's naturalists. Unlike today's scientific researchers who have distinct research areas, Baird's naturalists were eclectic generalists who often made significant discoveries in a number of disciplines. Their research formed the foundation for a broad range of subsequent fieldwork.

Unfortunately, Turner never produced a companion ethnological work to his Alaskan natural history volume. However, a careful reading of his Alaska book reveals numerous ethnographic details about the importance of different plant and animal species to Aleut and Yup'ik economies as well as occasional references to oral traditions and folklore. Turner's discussion of Native Alaskan plant use is an early and significant source of ethnobotanical and ethnopharmaceutical knowledge.

Regrettably, Turner also never prepared a published report on his observations of life on Attu, the distant Aleutian outpost where he spent a year. Perhaps because of the impression that much of the traditional life of the Aleuts had been eroded after more than a century of Russian economic and ecclesiastical domination, nineteenth-century ethnologists did not closely scrutinize the western Aleutian communities. Turner did produce a preliminary manuscript resulting from his research into Attuan life and folkways that is based on some archaeological materials he acquired from Attu (Turner n.d. a)

TURNER IN THE QUÉBEC–LABRADOR PENINSULA

The curtain of Turner's private life pulled close about him upon his return from Alaska. After he collectively spent more than six and a half years stationed at remote posts in western Alaska and the Aleutian Islands, Turner might have taken a lengthy sojourn from his northern peregrinations. But such was not to be. Something inexplicable about the freedom and adventure of northern fieldwork has proved infectious for innumerable scientists, explorers, and adventurers—an intangible magnetic pull at the heartstrings, the intellect, and the imagination. Exactly what combination of professional interests, family dynamics, employment opportunities, and personalities conspired to send Lucien Turner north once again is now impossible to tell. Nevertheless, Turner had barely settled into his Washington quarters and begun assembling the fruits of his Alaskan labors when he accepted Baird's invitation to conduct fieldwork at Ungava Bay on the northern portion of the Québec–Labrador peninsula.

This region was terra incognita to the field of science, even more so than Alaska. At the boundary between the boreal spruce forest and the arctic tundra, the region surrounding Ungava Bay was home to a wide array of arctic plant and animal species that had never been investigated or described by a trained scientist. It was also the homeland of the Inuit (Eskimo) and the Innu (Montagnais–Naskapi Indians, whom Turner refers to in his volume as the Nenenot or the "true, ideal people"). Only the scattered Hudson's Bay Company personnel and Moravian missionaries whose posts and settlements circled the peninsula's perimeter knew of these peoples' shadowy existence. For one such as Turner, the chance to conduct pioneering research in the natural sciences and ethnology of the eastern Arctic may simply have been too enticing to resist.

Turner's opportunity to travel to northern Québec came about through the U.S. government's participation in the first International Polar Year. The International Polar Year was an ambitious experiment designed to conduct coordinated international scientific research at observatories distributed around the circumpolar world (Barr 1985). Fourteen expeditions from eleven countries were sent into the polar regions to acquire precise simultaneous observations of meteorological and magnetic phenomena between August 1882 and September 1883. While their primary task was geophysical research, personnel accompanying these expeditions made valuable contributions to the knowledge of polar ecosystems, geology, and oceanography. The International Polar Year initiated the first professional anthropological research in the eastern Canadian Arctic by facilitating Franz Boas's access to Baffin Island in 1883–1884 to conduct his geographical and anthropological research (Cole and Muller-Wille 1984). It was also the reason for Turner's posting at Fort Chimo: to obtain meteorological records for the Signal Corps. The Smithsonian provided men and scientific equipment to two other International Polar Year Expeditions: one to Point Barrow, Alaska, the other to Lady Franklin Bay in northern Ellesmere Island. While the Point Barrow program was a great success, the expedition to northern Ellesmere under the direction of Lt. Adolphus Greely was tragically mismanaged; it resulted in the deaths of eighteen men from starvation, drowning, exposure, disease, and execution (Guttridge 2000).

Turner left Washington late in May 1882, traveling overland to Québec in order to rendezvous with a Hudson's Bay Company schooner called the *Labrador* on which he had arranged passage to Fort Chimo in Ungava Bay. Turner was delivered to the Hudson's Bay Company post at Rigolet in Hamilton Inlet on the central Labrador coast, where he immersed himself in a flurry of ornithological collecting while awaiting the arrival of the supply ship. The trip along the north Labrador coast included a stop at Davis Inlet, where Turner had his first opportunity to learn about the Innu. The stay at Davis Inlet afforded Turner the first opportunity to experiment with his photographic equipment, and a number of images still exist of the Post's manager, his family, Inuit servants, and local "Settlers," former Hudson's Bay Company employees who married Inuit women and became independent fishermen and trappers.

Under way again, the ship battled the contrary tides, thick fog, and ice in Ungava Bay for weeks. Drifting masses of pack ice twice beset the *Labrador*, so it was required to anchor off the mouth of the George River and await open water to approach the Koksoak River on which the post at Fort Chimo was situated. Ungava Bay, having some of the most treacherous tides in the world, coupled with the perils imposed by fog, ice, and the lack of decent charts, posed a daunting challenge to the captain and crew of the company supply vessels. The vessel grounded on a rocky reef that was exposed at low tide in the Koksoak River estuary, enabling Turner an opportunity to collect mollusks. Fortunately the ship was undamaged, floated free on the following tide, and subsequently arrived soon after at Fort Chimo to the great relief of the post personnel who anxiously awaited the annual supply vessel.

The Hudson's Bay Company post at Fort Chimo (where the community of Kuujjuaq is located today) had been founded in 1830 in an attempt to entice the Innu into participating in the lucrative fur trade (Cooke 1964, 1969, 1979). Unfortunately, the difficulties of supplying the post and the resistance of the Innu, who were cautious about abandoning their caribou subsistence practices in favor of trapping animals only for their fur, precluded success and the post was abandoned soon after. The fort operated intermittently during the next few decades until 1866, when the innovation of auxiliary steam-powered vessels that could maneuver in ice-choked northern waters enabled Fort Chimo to gain some semblance of permanence. By 1870 the Hudson's Bay Company had solidified its position with a ring of widely scattered posts surrounding the Québec–Labrador peninsula. Assured a virtual monopoly on economic transactions with the Innu, the company withdrew its last posts from the interior, forcing the Innu to bring their trade out to the coast. At the northern posts and at Fort Chimo especially, company factors sought to involve the Inuit in their trading arrangements and therefore expand their markets to include baleen, oil, fish, and seal skins.

At the time of Turner's visit, Fort Chimo was a solid outpost of the far-flung economic web that was the Hudson's Bay Company's empire in British North America. It was home to a contingent of post employees, the manager, his family, and a small cadre of assistants and servants. The only trading establishment in hundreds of miles, the post was regularly frequented by small groups of Inuit from throughout the region, including from western Québec and northern Labrador, and by the Innu, who made their way to the shores of the Koksoak River from distant encampments in the Labrador interior.

Arriving in this small enclave, Turner suddenly found himself the odd man out. Although negotiations between Smithsonian and Hudson's Bay Company officials had provided for Turner's board and lodging and for use of one of the company's outbuildings as an observatory, conveying these plans prior to Turner's arrival had not been possible. Life at the post was hard and pragmatic at best. Considerable dissension reigned among the employees, who showed little interest or enthusiasm regarding Turner or his work. The junior chief trader at Fort Chimo, Keith McKenzie, clearly defined the company's position: "Further I may say that as long as you keep entirely to your own legitimate business and do not in any way interfere with the Company's affairs or with any of the work or servants under my charge, I will be most happy to render you any assistance in my power to make your stay at Ungava a successful and a pleasant one" (Hudson's Bay Company Archives B.38/b/5, fos. 142–143).

Accepting the sullen climate of the post, Turner quickly erected his observatory and settled into the daily routine of making observations and measurements. Once the observatory was operational, Turner began to explore the surrounding countryside in pursuit of biological specimens. Unfortunately, he had a short tether. As in Alaska, his obligations to read instruments and maintain continual records tied him to the post, and he lamented the lost opportunity to conduct fieldwork more in line with his aspirations and inclinations. These disappointments were partially assuaged by the arrival in the late winter through early spring of small bands of Inuit and Innu families who camped near the post. He was also able to make several small journeys during his tenure at Fort Chimo. He traveled upriver from the post to where the Kaniapiskau and Larch rivers joined to form the Koksoak and where he had the opportunity to witness a huge congregation of caribou. During the summer of 1883 post officials loaned Turner a whaleboat that had been retrieved from a second Ungava Bay post at George River. Rigged with a small jib sail and accompanied by two Indian guides, Sescumounagan and Kanawabano, he was able to pursue "an egg hunting expidition [sic]" (Hudson's Bay Company Archives B.38/a/20).

Unfortunately, most of Turner's original manuscripts and whatever journals and records pertaining to his Ungava adventure he might have kept have been misplaced or lost, so only the bare bones of his sojourn at Fort Chimo can be discerned (Barr 1985; Dunbar 1983; Harper 1964; Turner n.d. b). The one surviving manuscript of Turner's Ungava report indicates that he developed a meaningful rapport with the Innu and Inuit who visited the post (Turner n.d. b). Most of the evidence for this rapport has been edited out of the published version, but judging from the information he gathered, his conversations with both Innu and Inuit visitors must have been deep and wide-ranging. Turner's broad interests in the various aspects of the natural world that they knew intimately must have intrigued the natives. Unlike the Hudson's Bay traders' interest in economic gain, Turner's passionate curiosity about native language, stories, and mythology and his insights into the behavior of birds and animals must have seemed extraordinary. He bought almost everything they cared to sell, employed their children to catch bugs and birds, and spent long, attentive hours listening to their stories. In letters sent to his Smithsonian mentor Robert Ridgway, Turner complains of suffering writer's cramp from trying to record the legends and stories that Inuit and Innu visitors to the post conveyed (Harper 1964:103). He also laments the passing of the wife of the post's cooper, Mrs. Maggie Brown, who was of mixed English and Indian descent and who had served as Turner's translator and teacher. Mrs. Brown, who spoke both Inuktitut and Innuaimun, had intimate conversations with both the Innu and Inuit visitors and was able to acquire objects for Turner that whites were not normally allowed to handle.

As weather and circumstances allowed, Turner spent his time compiling vocabularies and ethnological materials and collecting birds, nests, and eggs, as well as a vast array of invertebrate, mollusk, plant, fish, and mammal specimens that were carefully prepared and subsequently shipped to the Smithsonian. His collection of several hundred ethnographic specimens acquired from the Innu and Inuit at Fort Chimo and their extensive annotations and documentation remain his most lasting legacy. With few exceptions—Inuit shamanistic paraphernalia and Innu hunting charms—the majority of the materials Turner collected were artifacts and clothing used in day-to-day activities. The passage of time and the miracle of conservation have transformed these ethnographic minutiae, these objects and materials of relatively minor significance in the past, into treasured cultural icons.

In addition to the objects and stories that Turner collected, Inuit and Innu culture has been further preserved through his use of photography. (See the photo gallery following this introduction.) The value of photography for documenting the progress and the nature of scientific investigations in the American West had become readily apparent during the U.S. government's geographic and topographic surveys in the years after the Civil War, including work under the direction of John Wesley Powell. Powell was deeply interested in the condition and future of Native Americans and aware how significant photography was for documenting a native way of life on the cusp of tremendous change. A hallmark of the fieldwork conducted by Smithsonian naturalists and ethnologists under Powell's and Baird's supervision is their use of photographic apparatus in their research agenda (Fitzhugh 1998). The earliest extant photographs of many northern peoples and localities were apparently derived from Edward Nelson while in Alaska (1877–1881) and Lucien Turner while in northern Québec (1882–1884). The bulky camera equipment of the day, the process of preparing and developing wet glass-plate negatives, and the environmental constraints (including subzero temperatures, too little light indoors and too much light on the snow-covered landscape, and the onslaughts of biting insect hordes) proved to be awesome challenges. In spite of these difficulties, Turner persevered and created a unique photographic record of his stay at Fort Chimo, including a number of images of the post, its environs, and scenes at nearby Innu and Inuit camps, as well as a series of formal portraits, mostly of Inuit but a few of Innu.

When the Hudson's Bay Company annual supply vessel arrived in Ungava Bay in September 1884, Turner packed up his equipment, collections, documents, and records and left for Washington. According to a surviving manifest in the Smithsonian's accession files, Turner's shipment from Ungava consisted of twenty-six barrels, tanks (for shipping wet specimens in alcohol), and boxes and one salted shark. Turner's stay at Fort Chimo was his last northern expedition. What his thoughts were at the time of his departure—his aspirations and future intentions—remain unknown.

REPORTING THE QUÉBEC–LABRADOR RESEARCH

Back in Washington for the winter of 1884–1885, Turner resided near the National Museum and applied himself to bringing his Alaskan and Ungava manuscripts to press. By then he had nearly a decade of northern fieldwork behind him but little beyond the support of his Smithsonian colleagues to show for it. As previously mentioned, the partial results of his Alaskan work were published in 1886 as *Contributions to the Natural History of Alaska*. Turner then worked dutifully toward publication of his Ungava manuscript, some portions of which were read before the Royal Society of Canada in 1887 (Turner 1887a, 1887b) and others that appeared as brief papers in anthropological journals (1888a, 1888b). *Ethnology of the Ungava District, Hudson Bay Territory* as it is now known was published in 1894.

Whether or not Turner was disappointed by the editing his manuscript had received is not known. He had hoped that the results of his Ungava research would be published in a collection of papers similar to the treatment his collections from Alaska had received. His unpublished manuscripts on the birds, mammals, and fishes of the Ungava District are stored in the Smithsonian's archives (Turner n.d. b). They are perhaps the most lasting testament to his prowess as a naturalist. His descriptions of animal and bird species invariably include details about their economic significance and the means employed to catch them. They also record Inuu and Inuit vocabularies as well as detailed descriptions of plants, insects, moths, mollusks, crustacea, and fish. Turner weaves a web of the relations between animals and human beings, transcending the notion of an environment apart from human influence. In addition, based mostly on the testimony of Inuit and Innu hunters, his accounts of species in the Québec-Labrador peninsula that are now extinct (including the barren-ground grizzly bear and the wolverine) offer a valuable contribution to understanding the historical biological diversity of the region. The existence of grizzly bears in Labrador, long known by the Innu and by the Hudson's Bay Company traders with whom they traded, was the subject of much debate prior to the recovery of a grizzly bear skull from an eighteenth-century Labrador Eskimo midden at Okak on the Labrador coast (Spiess 1976; Spiess and Cox 1976). Similarly, Turner's observations on capelin and cod at Fort Chimo have proved invaluable to fisheries researchers and climatologists (Dunbar 1983). Many of these descriptions, however, did not appear in the much-edited final version of the manuscript.

Turner had the natural historian's penchant for detailed descriptive analyses of the objects he chose to scrutinize, and if the published work could be faulted at all it would be for this strong materialistic perspective. Because Turner mostly relied upon interviews conducted at the post at Fort Chimo, his perceptions of Indian and Inuit life were constrained by the information acquired about the artifacts he bought. How tools were obtained and manufactured and the context in which they were used structured his perception of native adaptations. So while his account features detailed information about aspects of hunting, subsistence technologies, and settlement patterns, it contains little about the dynamics of social interaction at either a local or regional scale.

Therefore, in the less-tangible realm of social affiliations, kinship, and group organization, Turner's observations seem disappointingly shallow today. In his defense, no overt social or economic theoretical notions hampered his pervasive materialist paradigm. His interest in ethnology emerged out of his other naturalist pursuits that were dominated by classificatory schemes and organizational methodology. Also, his exposure to the Inuit and the Innu was limited to their late winter through early spring and summer camps in the vicinity of the trading post. Therefore, he had little opportunity to witness the composition of hunting bands throughout most of the year or the dynamics of decision making and planning.

The other ethnologist working in the eastern Arctic during the International Polar Year was Franz Boas, one of the father figures of American anthropology. Like Turner, Boas came to anthropology only tangentially, his training having primarily been in geography. He was eager to map the unexplored shorelines of northern and western Baffin Island. Likewise, Turner's first love remained ornithology, even though his most significant contributions were to be to the field of ethnology. Despite their varied agendas and disparate backgrounds, their subsequent ethnological monographs, Boas's *The Central Eskimo* (1888) and Turner's *Ethnology of the Ungava District* (1894), were the first major scientific treatises on the Canadian Inuit and subarctic Indian peoples. Their endeavor to understand the native Inuit and Indian groups' adaptation to an environment that European and American scholars perceived as inhospitable initiated a new perspective on northern native populations.

Turner saw the Innu and Inuit at Fort Chimo as having been molded by their environment. John Wesley Powell summarized their successful adaptation in the preface to Turner's volume (1894:xliii): "It is shown that they are not an abnormal part of mankind, and that their peculiarities chiefly arise from their environment." Devoid of any awareness of how historical events may have impacted the groups he met, Turner presented an image of the arctic–subarctic environment and the Innu and Inuit social systems as stable and immutable. In fact, the belief that northern cultural systems represented ancient, time-honored adaptations to the arctic and subarctic environment, hardy relics of a former Stone Age existence, formed the prevailing view of most nineteenth-century Europeans and Americans. Turner's depiction of the seasonal round for the Innu and Inuit families at Fort Chimo adopts this limited perspective in assuming a rather rigid and static series of responses to the resources available in the region. In spite of these limitations, Turner's ethnography remains a classic introduction to the lifeways and culture of the Innu and Inuit people of the northern Québec–Labrador peninsula.

TURNER'S LATER YEARS AND LEGACY

Little is known of Turner's later years. Why his apparently successful career as a field naturalist was cut short remains conjectural. In his enthusiasm to expand the Smithsonian collections, Spencer Baird had been highly successful at pairing his naturalists with other official government agencies to help defray the costs of fieldwork. However, support for staff to analyze and curate collections has always been a budgetary constraint, and so long-term support for Turner might not have been available.

After leaving Washington, Turner returned to the Midwest, where he apparently worked as an accountant with Department of the Interior in Indiana. By 1888, he was in Washington State pursuing various business and mining initiatives. Turner retained his association with the U.S. National Museum and offered to make mineral and ethnological collections from the Pacific Northwest for the Institution. He remained a devoted collector of birds throughout his life, supplementing his income by selling specimens of western birds to Harvard University and the Smithsonian.

When Spencer Baird died in 1887, Turner lost his strongest Smithsonian ally. Intrigued about the possibility of coffee and rubber production, Turner attempted to interest the Smithsonian in sponsoring a natural history collecting expedition to the Philippines in 1898, but nothing apparently came of this venture. Turner died in San Francisco in 1909. Francis Harper, a naturalist who followed in Turner's footsteps conducting biological and cultural studies in the Québec–Labrador peninsula in the 1960s and the sleuth who ferreted out many of the details of Turner's personal history, concluded, "The history of American zoology and ethnology during the past hundred years can furnish few examples of such a distinguished and at the same time such an elusive personality as Lucien M. Turner" (Harper 1964:105).

SUBSEQUENT ANTHROPOLOGICAL RESEARCH IN NORTHERN QUÉBEC–LABRADOR

Anthropological research in the northern Québec–Labrador peninsula took a hiatus following Turner's departure in 1884. Prior to the advent of aerial transport, the region remained nearly inaccessible to outsiders. The annual supply vessels that stocked the Moravian mission stations on the Labrador coast and the Hudson's Bay Company posts in the Ungava and eastern Hudson bays were the only sure means of access. Ostensibly these missionary and mercantile establishments created an infrastructure that could facilitate access to native communities, but for the most part the missionaries and traders had little contact with scientists, adventurers, or government administrators. The regions' scattered Inuit and Innu bands gradually allied with the different posts and mission stations, as they came to appreciate the advantages of increasingly reliable trading relations.

The only significant anthropological studies that focused on the Inuit of the Ungava region prior to World War II were brief investigations in the summers conducted by Bernhard Hantzsch (1931 [1909], 1932 [1909]) in 1906 and by Ernest W. Hawkes (1916) in 1914. A more detailed review of the history of anthropological research in Ungava can be found in summaries by Saladin d'Anglure (1984a, 1984b), Malurie and Rousseau (1964), and Vézinet (1982).

During this period anthropologists were considerably more interested in the Innu, who adhered to a subsistence-based lifestyle predicated on caribou and whose hunting range of the forested interior and northern barren grounds of the Québec–Labrador peninsula remained practically unknown. William Brooks Cabot was a prosperous civil engineer from Boston who had a propensity for wilderness travel and a keen interest in the language and culture of the Indians of New England and eastern Canada (Loring 1986–1987, 1987). Inspired by the prospect of exploration and of meeting with the mysterious Innu, arguably the most "traditional" group of extant Indian hunters in North America, Cabot made a number of trips to the "Indian country" of northern Labrador. His book (Cabot 1920)—a curious blend of anthropological insight and the romance of wilderness wandering—provides the only detailed, eyewitness account of the Innu as they were living in the interior at the heyday of their specialized caribou-hunting economy. Cabot's unpublished journals also contain a wealth of detail and miscellanea about Innu beliefs, language, and customs (Cabot n.d.). In addition, Cabot was an amateur photographer, and the photographs from his various expeditions provide unique and compelling insights into Innu culture (Loring 1997). These photographs and unpublished manuscripts elaborate on the very aspects of Indian life that Turner knew only from vague accounts and provide a poignant window on Innu culture beyond the confines of the trading posts at a time of relative caribou abundance.

The Rawson–MacMillan subarctic expedition to northern Labrador in 1926–1927 provided the opportunity for William Duncan Strong, a young anthropologist from Chicago's Field Museum of Natural History, to make the first avowed ethnological study of the Innu (Strong 1929; Leacock and Rothschild 1994; VanStone 1985). Strong, as Cabot had been before him, was attracted by the possibilities of observing a traditional nomadic northern hunting society, "one of the most primitive of extant peoples." Strong spent the winter with a small Innu band inland from Davis Inlet. Since Cabot's day the Innu settlement and subsistence patterns had changed significantly, almost entirely because of the demise and finally the disappearance of the large caribou herds on which life in the interior was predicated. The cessation of the caribou migration, probably resulting from a major population crash, was apparent in 1916 when the Indians who hunted around Indian House Lake abandoned the barren grounds for the coast. Other Indian bands in the northern interior only narrowly escaped starvation (Todd 1963:30–31).

The Innu abandoned year-round occupation in the interior for a winter residence in a near-coastal setting and increased their dependence on a trading economy and "beggary" (Strong 1929:284). In the end, they altered their settlement–subsistence pattern to take advantage of coastal resources, including seal hunting, cod fishing, and sustained interaction with traders, settlers, and missionaries. Innu trading out of the Hudson's Bay Company post at Davis Inlet befriended an independent trader, Richard White, who had posts in Voisey's Bay and near Nain. White later provided anthropologist Frank Speck information for much of his influential work on the Innu (Speck 1931, 1935; Speck and Eiseley 1942). In the mid-1960s and early 1970s, Alika Podolinsky Webber made a number of short visits to Innu communities in the course of her research on Innu material culture (Webber 1983). While hunting and fishing activities remained at the center of the Innu economy and values (Henriksen 1973), articulation with Canadian and provincial governmental policies substantially altered and eventually disrupted many of their land use patterns of old.

The Innu have lost significant portions of their former territory to large-scale economic development programs, including massive iron-ore mining in the Schefferville region and hydroelectric development at Churchill Falls. Both of these areas have interdependent infrastructures of towns, roads, transmission lines, and railroads as well as an influx of non-Innu workers. The disruptions to the social fabric and the physical environment in the wake of industrial development have had profound influences on the Innu, whose struggle to adapt to village life has been both tragic and transformative.

CONTEMPORARY POLITICAL DEVELOPMENTS

Archaeological research in northern Québec and Labrador has exposed the fallacy that Inuit and Innu cultures were static backwaters of humanity, isolated populations frozen in time and doomed to eke out an existence in a barren, inhospitable land. Nothing could be further from the truth. Inuit and Innu ancestors had developed a remarkable set of technologies, social strategies, and spiritual beliefs that enabled them to access resources throughout a huge territory and proved exceptionally resilient and adaptable to changes in both the physical and sociopolitical environments. Inuit and Innu cultures have always thrived on challenge and change; their heritage, language, customs, and attachment to their land and its animals, birds, and fishes have provided a deep, abiding source of strength and inspiration. The north that Turner knew, that nearly inaccessible scattering of isolated trading establishments frequented by nomadic bands of hunters and their families, may be no more. But the people, the descendants of those with whom he bartered for artifacts and information, continue to reside there.

At first change came gradually: the Hudson's Bay Company monopoly on trade was challenged, creating additional opportunities for the Innu and Inuit to participate in the market economy; missionary activities increased; and the Canadian government, in an effort to assert sovereignty, posted a Royal Canadian Mounted Police detachment to the region. During World War II the U.S. Air Force constructed air bases at Fort Chimo and Goose Bay in Labrador, facilities that continued to expand in the postwar years (Wadden 1991). The geopolitical significance of the Canadian Arctic during the Cold War era saw the further militarization of the area with the construction of distant early warning line stations. And in an effort to expand social services, the Candian and provincial governments encouraged a policy of village consolidation. Although still firmly rooted to a subsistence-based economy, with many families spending extended periods of time at hunting and fishing camps, most of the Innu and Inuit of northern Québec and Labrador had adopted village life by 1965.

To European eyes the Ungava country has always appeared bleak and inhospitable. Other than for a few fishermen, an occasional whaling crew, and a smattering of itinerant prospectors, hunters, and explorers, the land long held few inducements for development and commerce. Technological difficulties prevented bringing the region's known resources to distant markets. Today, however, the economic potential of the region's vast mineral and energy resources has transformed its political and physical landscapes. The development of extraction technologies and communication and transportation infrastructures have the potential to reach even the formerly most inaccessible locations.

The hydroelectric development and mining operations beginning in the 1950s had serious economic implications for the provincial governments of Newfoundland–Labrador and Québec (Geren and McCullogh 1990). Equally profound were the implications to the Innu, whose land rights had been abrogated without consideration or compensation. In the early 1970s further hydroelectric development in the James Bay region was the catalyst behind the implementation of the James Bay and Northern Québec Agreement with the Cree and Inuit nations. In exchange for surrendering their title to the land, the native groups were granted substantial economic incentives and political authority. The Inuit of northern Québec formed the Makivik Corporation to manage this financial compensation. The corporation is involved with a host of business arrangements, school and social service agencies, heritage concerns, and public policies, indicating the increasingly sophisticated involvement of the Québec Inuit in all aspects of their own lives.

At the time of this writing, the Inuit (under the auspices of the Labrador Inuit Association and Makivik) and the Innu (represented by the Innu Nation) are negotiating with the Canadian and the Newfoundland–Labrador provincial governments to regain some authority to manage their lands and resources. Land claims resolution in northern Québec–Labrador, while endowing the Inuit and Innu with certain rights, privileges, and self-autonomy, carries with it the sobering real-ization that invading Europeans have completed their land acquisitions in North America. Ironically, the first portion of the New World to be visited by voyaging Europeans—intrepid Norse adventurers who arrived about a thousand years ago—was the last whose indigenous title was sur-rendered.

RESURGENCE OF INTEREST IN NORTHERN CANADIAN CULTURES

Circles of rocks, the ringed imprints of Inuit tents, and the timeworn portage trails the Innu left behind are ubiquitous all across the country that Turner called the Ungava District of British North America. Such traces are physical reminders that the country, which the Inuit called Nunavik and the Innu called Nitassinan, has been their homeland for eons. The gifts of hospitality, shelter, and food are often freely given to newcomers in the north. Prior to the advent of television and video, strangers were a welcome source of diversion and a potential resource to be carefully weighed and assessed. Brought together by inclement weather and the long winter nights, both guest and host could explore each other's memories and learn more about the world they both occupied.

It is clear from Turner's edited manuscript and his few surviving letters that he enjoyed a close companionship with the Inuit and the Innu who came to trade at the post. Although it is impossible to know what the natives thought of him, clearly he greatly respected their knowl-edge and valued his association with them. It is a poor guest who leaves without some tangible expression of appreciation for the host. We can only speculate who thought they got the best of the trade: old clothes, pipes, and hunting equipment for tea, tobacco, ammunition, knives, and flour. Could Turner or any of the people with whom he traded have envi-sioned the value that time and preservation would add to the daily objects he acquired? Could they imagine the capacity of these everyday things to astonish and delight distant generations of the men and women who crafted them more than a century ago? Turner's dedication to acquiring and documenting the collection he assembled at Fort Chimo was the first step in a process that has led to their preservation. Preservation, in its vicarious fashion, becomes the means to acknowledge and thank the people who once manufactured the items in the collec-tion—items that today provide a powerful testament to the ingenuity, tenacity, and success of Innu and Inuit land tenure in northern Québec and adjacent Labrador.

If we are to fault Lucien Turner at all, it is only because his written records have made us greedy for more intimate detail. Those days when the Inuit and Innu were still in the thrall of their shamans and intimate with spiritual beliefs about the land and its resources are over. Turner was an enigmatic, pragmatic American scientist whose penchant for stolid description rarely allowed him to plumb beneath the surface of his discussions of the objects in the collection. Still, we are grateful for the preservation of the material that Turner acquired. It is to such odds and ends that we look to derive inspiration about the past for the celebration of the future. Turner's tome remains a classic work of late nineteenth-century Smithsonian anthropology; it is both a product of its time and timeless.

ACKNOWLEDGMENTS

Every book has its story. This publication's trail began more than a century ago with Lucien Turner's tribulations on the shores of Ungava Bay and leads to the Smithsonian Institution Archives, where I spent the spring of 1987 reading Turner's surviving manuscripts and correspondence. Time stands still in old museum archives, or perhaps the concentration needed to read the elongated cursive script of nineteenth-century scribes is such that it holds time in abeyance. I often found my eyes wandering to descriptions of the places in the north where I had traversed Turner's trail, and I wondered what the Innu and Inuit youth I knew would make of Turner's observations about their great-great grandparents. From this, the idea was hatched and now the book's trail has ended with its republication through Smithsonian Institution Press.

For help in ferreting out old records and their dedication to preserving the paper treasures in their trust, an enormous debt of acknowledgment and appreciation is due to Alan Bain, archives division director of the Smithsonian Institution Archives, as well as his competent staff, past and present. Herman Viola, Paula Fleming, and James Glenn facilitated access to Turner materials in the National Anthropological Archives, a division of the Anthropology Department in the Smithsonian's National Museum of Natural History.

My fellowship at the Smithsonian came about after more than a decade of archaeological and ethnohistorical research conducted in northern Labrador. This research owed its inception, implementation, and continuity to the unfailing support and inspiration of William Fitzhugh, curator of North American archaeology and director of the Arctic Studies Center at the National Museum of Natural History. His commitment to unraveling the history of human occupations in northern Québec–Labrador has never wavered. He pioneered an anthropology that was responsive to the needs and interests of Inuit communities with reports in support of land-claim negotiations (Fitzhugh 1977), museum workshops, and traveling exhibits. His endorsement of this publishing project now makes Turner's work accessible to a new generation of Innu and Inuit students, scholars, and educators.

Plans to reissue Turner's *Ethnology of the Ungava District* might have languished indefinitely but for my fortuitous meeting with Zebedee Nungak, then president of Makivik Corporation, and Stephen Hendrie, communications officer of Makivik, at a conference on the history of photography in the Arctic held at the British Museum in London in 1996. Nungak's knowledge of and passion for the history of the eastern Arctic are unbounded. At a subsequent visit to Washington, D.C., he had the opportunity to examine the Turner collection (now carefully stored in the National Museum of Natural History's Museum Support Center in Suitland, Maryland) and to see the original prints of the photographs Turner took (located in the National Anthropological Archives). From that moment to this, Nungak's and Hendrie's determination to help produce this volume has never wavered, and they arranged for a grant from the Makivik Corporation to help offset the production costs. A special thanks is due to Taqralik Partridge at Avataq—the cultural and educational arm of Makivik—who brought much-needed youthful ebullience and support to the project.

Finally, gratitude is due to the staff at the Smithsonian Institution Press, especially Scott Mahler, acquisitions editor in anthropology and archaeology, and E. Anne Bolen, production editor.

BIBLIOGRAPHY

Barr, William
    1985   *The Expeditions of the First International Polar Year, 1882–1883.* Technical Paper No. 29. Calgary, Alberta: The Arctic Institute of North America, University of Calgary.

Boas, Franz
    1888   The Central Eskimo. In *Sixth Annual Report of the Bureau of Ethnology, 1884–85.* J. W. Powell, ed. Pp. 399–669. Washington, D.C.: Government Printing Office.

Brodhead, Michael J.
    1995   The United States Army Signal Service and Natural History in Alaska, 1874–1883. *Pacific Northwest Quarterly* 86 (2): 72–82.

Cabot, William Brooks
    1920   *Labrador.* Boston: Small, Maynard & Co.
    n.d.   Journals, photographs, letters and notes. William Brooks Cabot collection, National Anthropological Archives, Smithsonian Institution, Washington, D.C.

Cole, Douglas and Ludger Muller-Wille
    1984   Franz Boas' Expedition to Baffin Island. *Études Inuit* 8:37–63.

Cooke, Alan
    1964   The Exploration of New Québec. Le Nouveau-Québec, Contribution a L'Étude de L'Occupation Humaine. Jean Malaurie and Jacques Rousseau, eds. *École Pratique de Hautes Études-Sorbonne* 2:137-179.

1969   The Ungava Venture of the Hudson's Bay Company, 1830–1843. Unpublished Ph.D. dissertation, Cambridge University.

1979   L'Independence des Naskapis et le Caribou. Dossier Caribou, Ecologie et Exploitation de Caribou au Québec–Labrador. Francois Trudel and Jean Huot, eds. *Recherches Amérindiennes au Québec* 9:99–104.

Dall, William H.

1870   *Alaska and Its Resources.* Boston: Lee and Shepard.

Dunbar, M. J.

1983   A Unique International Polar Year Contribution: Lucien Turner, Capelin and Climatic Change. *Arctic* 36 (2): 204–205.

Fitzhugh, William W.

1977   Indian and Eskimo/Inuit Settlement History in Labrador: An Archaeological View. In *Our Footsteps Are Everywhere.* Carol Brice-Bennett, ed. Pp. 1–41. Nain: Labrador Inuit Association.

1983   Introduction. In *The Eskimo About Bering Strait.* Washington, D.C.: Smithsonian Institution Press. [Reprint of 1899 Edward W. Nelson.]

1988   Baird's naturalists: Smithsonian collectors in Alaska. In *Crossroads of Continents: Cultures of Siberia and Alaska.* W. W. Fitzhugh and A. C. Crowell, eds. Pp. 89–96. Washington, D.C.: Smithsonian Institution Press.

1998   The Alaska Photographs of Edward W. Nelson, 1877–81. In *Imaging the Arctic.* J. C. H. King and Henrietta Lidchi, eds. Pp. 125–142. Seattle: University of Washington Press.

Fitzhugh, William W., and Susan A. Kaplan

1982   *Inua: Spirit World of the Bering Sea Eskimo.* Washington, D.C.: Smithsonian Institution Press.

Fitzhugh, William W., and Ruth Selig

1981   The Smithsonian's Alaska Connection: Nineteenth-Century Explorers and Anthropologists. In *The Alaska Journal: 1981 Collection.* V. McKinley, ed. Pp. 193–208. Anchorage: Alaska Northwest Publishing Company.

Geren, Richard, and Blake McCullogh

1990   *Cain's Legacy: The Building of Iron Ore Company of Canada.* Sept-Îles, Québec: Iron Ore Company of Canada.

Guttridge, Leonard F.

2000   *Ghosts of Cape Sabine: The Harrowing True Story of the Greely Expedition.* New York: G. P. Putnam's Sons.

Hall, Charles Francis

1864   *Life with the Esquimaux.* 2 vols. London: Sampson Low, Son and Marston.

Hantzsch, Bernhard

1931   Contributions to the Knowledge of Extreme Northeastern Labrador.
[1909] *The Canadian Field-Naturalist* 45:49–55, 85–90, 115–118, 143–146, 169–174, 194–198, 222–224.

1932   Contributions to the Knowledge of Extreme Northeastern Labrador.
[1909] *The Canadian Field-Naturalist* 46:7–12, 34–36, 56–63, 84–89, 112–116, 143–145, 153–162.

Harper, Francis
  1964   *The Friendly Montagnais and their Neighbors in the Ungava
            Peninsula*. Museum of Natural History Miscellaneous Publication 37.
            Lawrence: University of Kansas.
Hawkes, Ernest W.
  1916   *The Labrador Eskimo*. Geological Survey Memoir 91, Anthropological
            Series 14. Ottawa, Canada: Department of Mines.
Henriksen, Georg
  1973   *Hunters in the Barrens, The Naskapi on the Edge of the White
            Man's World*. St. John's, Newfoundland: Institute of Social and
            Economic Research, Memorial University of Newfoundland.
Hinsley, Curtis M.
  1981   *The Smithsonian and the American Indian*. Washington, D.C.:
            Smithsonian Institution Press.
Hudson's Bay Company Archives
  pre-1870 Fort Chimo post outward correspondence copy books. London,
            England: Hudson's Bay Company Archives.
James, James Alton
  1942   The First Scientific Exploration of Russian America and the
            Purchase of Alaska. *Northwestern University Studies in the Social
            Sciences*, No. 4. Evanston, Illinois: Northwestern University.
Lantis, Margaret
  1954   *Edward William Nelson*. Anthropological Papers of the University of
            Alaska 3 (1): 5–16. Fairbanks, Alaska: University of Alaska.
Leacock, Eleanor B., and Nan Rothschild, eds.
  1994   *Labrador Winter: The Ethnographic Journals of William Duncan
            Strong*. Washington D.C.: Smithsonian Institution Press.
Lindsay, Debra
  1993   *Science in the Subarctic: Trappers, Traders, and the Smithsonian
            Institution*. Washington, D.C.: Smithsonian Institution Press.
Loring, Stephen
  1986–   O Darkly Bright: the Labrador Journeys of William Brooks Cabot.
  1987   *Appalachia* 46 (2): 60–73.
  1987   Arctic Profiles: William Brooks Cabot (1858–1949). *Arctic* 40 (2):
            168–169.
  1997   On the Trail to the Caribou House: Some Reflections on Innu Caribou
            Hunters in Northern Ntessinan (Labrador). In *Caribou and Reindeer
            Hunters of the Northern Hemisphere*. Lawrence Jackson and Paul
            Thacker, eds. Pp. 185–220. Avebury, Great Britain: Aldershot.
  2001   Repatriation and Community Anthropology: The Smithsonian
            Institution's Arctic Studies Center. In *The Future of the Past:
            Archaeologists, Native Americans, and Repatriation*. Tamara Bray,
            ed. Pp. 185–200. New York: Garland.
Malaurie, Jean, and Jacques Rousseau, eds.
  1964   Le Nouveau–Québec. *Contribution a L'Étude de L'Occupation
            Humaine*. Paris: École Pratique de Hautes Études–Sorbonne.

Murdoch, John
　1892　Ethnological Results of the Point Barrow Expedition. In *Ninth Annual Report of the Bureau of Ethnology 1887–88*. J.W. Powell, ed. Pp. 19–441. Washington, D.C.: Government Printing Office.
Nelson, Edward W.
　1899　The Eskimo About Bering Strait. In *Eighteenth Annual Report of the Bureau of American Ethnology 1896–97*, part 1. J. W. Powell, ed. Pp. 3–518. Washington, D.C.: Government Printing Office.
Ray, Dorothy Jean
　1983　*Ethnohistory in the Arctic: The Bering Strait Eskimo*. Kingston, Ontario: Limestone Press.
Saladin d'Anglure, Bernard
　1984a　Arctic: Inuit of Québec. In *Handbook of North American Indians*, vol. 5. David Damas, ed. Pp. 476–507, Washington, D.C.: Smithsonian Institution.
　1984b　Arctic: Contemporary Inuit of Québec. In *Handbook of North American Indians,* vol. 5. David Damas, ed. Pp. 683–688. Washington, D.C.: Smithsonian Institution.
Sherwood, Morgan
　1965　*Exploration of Alaska, 1865–1900*. New Haven: Yale University Press.
Smithsonian Institution Archives
　1877　Letters 345–383, Book No. 207, Spencer F. Baird Papers. Smithsonian Institution Archives, Washington, D.C.
Speck, Frank. G.
　1931　Montagnais–Naskapi Bands and Early Eskimo Distribution in the Labrador Peninsula. *American Anthropologist* 33 (4): 557–600.
　1935　*Naskapi: The Savage Hunters of the Labrador Peninsula*. Norman: University of Oklahoma Press.
Speck, Frank G., and Loren Eiseley
　1942　Montagnais–Naskapi Bands and Family Hunting Districts of the Central and Southeastern Labrador Peninsula. *Proceedings of the American Philosophical Society* 85 (2): 215–242.
Spiess, Arthur
　1976　Labrador Grizzly (*Ursus Arctos L.*): First Skeletal Evidence. *Journal of Mammalogy* 57:787–790.
Spiess, Arthur, and Steven Cox
　1976　Discovery of the Skull of a Grizzly Bear in Labrador. *Arctic* 29:194–200.
Squier, Ephraim G., and Edwin H. Davis
　1848　Ancient Monuments of the Mississippi Valley. *Smithsonian Contributions to Knowledge 1*. Washington, D.C.: Smithsonian Institution.
Strong, William Duncan
　1929　Cross-cousin Marriage and the Culture of the Northeastern Algonkian. *American Anthropologist* 31:277–288.

Todd, W. E. Clyde
1963 *Birds of the Labrador Peninsula.* Toronto: University of Toronto Press.

Turner, Lucien M.
n.d. a Descriptive catalogue of ethnological specimens collected by Lucien M. Turner in Alaska. Lucien Turner papers, Bureau of American Ethnology collection, National Anthropological Archives, National Museum of Natural History, Smithsonian Institution, Washington, D.C., unpublished MS.

n.d. b Lucien Turner Ungava manuscript, Record Group 7192, Box.1., Smithsonian Institution Archives, Washington, D.C., unpublished MS.

1882– *Language of the "Koksoagmyut" Eskimo at Fort Chimo, Ungava,*
1884 *Labrador Peninsula.* 3 vols. Manuscript No. 2505–a. National Anthropological Archives, National Museum of Natural History, Smithsonian Institution, Washington, D.C., unpublished MS.

1886 *Contributions to the Natural History of Alaska.* Washington, D.C.: Government Printing Office.

1887a On the Indians and Eskimos of the Ungava District, Labrador, section II, vol. 5. In *Proceedings and Transactions of the Royal Society of Canada for the Year 1887.* Pp. 99–119. Montreal, Canada: Royal Society of Canada.

1887b The Physical and Zoological Character of the Ungava District, Labrador. *Transactions of the Royal Society of Canada, Proceedings* 5 (IV): 79–83.

1888a Scraper of the Nascopie. *American Anthropologist* 1: 186–188.

1888b The Single Headed Drum of the Naskopie. *Proceedings of the U.S. National Museum* II:433–434.

1894 Ethnology of the Ungava District, Hudson Bay Territory. In *Eleventh Annual Report of the Bureau of Ethnology, 1889-90.* J. W. Powell, ed. Pp. 159–350. Washington, D.C.: Government Printing Office.

VanStone, James W.
1985 Material Culture of the Davis Inlet and Barren Ground Naskapi: The William Duncan Strong Collection. *Fieldiana: Anthropology New Series* 7. Chicago: Field Museum of Natural History.

Vézinet, Monique
1982 *Occupation Humaine de l'Ungava.* Perspective Ethnohistorique et Écologique. Paléo–Québec 14. Montreal: Les Presses de l'Université du Québec.

Wadden, Marie
1991 *Nitassinan, the Innu Struggle to Reclaim Their Homeland.* Vancouver: Douglas & McIntyre.

Webber, Alika Podolinsky
1983 Ceremonial Robes and Atikwish. *American Indian Art Magazine* 9:60–77.

Above: Lucien McShan Turner in his observatory at Fort Chimo, 1883–1884. (SI 6968)

Right: Turner employed children of some of the Hudson's Bay Company employees to collect specimens for him in the vicinity of the post. His notation on the back of this photograph was: "Kakik, Harriet, Kittie Gordon and Jennie Brown, my bug catchers at Ft. Chimo." (SI 3208)

Numbers in parentheses are National Anthropological Archives negative numbers.

Above: The Hudson's Bay Company post at Fort Chimo on the Koksoak River, 1883–1884. (SI 6971)

Opposite: Inuit kayaks (foreground) and the moored Hudson's Bay Company whaleboat (background) that Turner used on his collecting outings, Koksoak River at Fort Chimo, June 1883. (SI 3218)

3271

Opposite: Inuit visitor to
Lucien Turner's observa-
tory at Fort Chimo,
1883–1884. (SI 3271)

Below: Inuit visitor to
Lucien Turner's observa-
tory at Fort Chimo,
1883–1884. The small,
circular beaded patch on
the man's parka is an
unusual feature on some
men's clothing in the
Ungava region. (SI 6966)

Above: Innu crooked canoe at Fort Chimo. A triumph of ingenuity and craftsmanship, the Innu crooked canoe was admirably suited for coastal navigation in the treacherous waters of Ungava Bay and Hudson Bay. (SI 3202)

Opposite, above: Innu lodge and cache of food and equipment raised off the ground, east of Fort Chimo, April 1883. (SI 3241)

Opposite, below: Innu men, women, and children poising for Turner's camera at their late winter–early spring camp east of Fort Chimo, April 1883. An Innu toboggan appears in the foreground and raised cache scaffolds, lodges, and piles of poles for firewood are arranged in the background. (NAA 75-6009)

Above, left: Innu woman and children photographed in Lucien Turner's observatory at Fort Chimo, 1883–1884. (SI 6977)

Above, right: Innu woman, a "Mountaineer Nascope" from the Québec North Shore at Fort Chimo, 1883–1884. Lucien Turner identifies her as "Mistashuna" or "Big Susan." (SI 3239)

Below: Hudson's Bay Company employees at the Davis Inlet post, Labrador, 1882. (SI 3284)

SMITHSONIAN INSTITUTION—BUREAU OF ETHNOLOGY.

ETHNOLOGY

OF THE

UNGAVA DISTRICT, HUDSON BAY TERRITORY.

By LUCIEN M. TURNER.

CONTENTS.

ILLUSTRATIONS.

ETHNOLOGY OF THE UNGAVA DISTRICT, HUDSON BAY TERRITORY.

By Lucien M. Turner.

(Edited by John Murdoch.)

INTRODUCTION.

Ungava bay is on the northern coast of old Labrador—the last great bight of the strait between the ocean and the mouth of Hudson bay. Its chief affluent is Koksoak or South river, which is several hundred miles long and takes its rise in a picturesque festoonery of lakes looped through the highlands half way down to Quebec.

FORT CHIMO AND THE SURROUNDING REGION.

Fort Chimo is in longitude 68° 16' west of Greenwich and latitude 58° 8' north. The post is on the right bank of the Koksoak river, about 27 miles from its mouth. The elevation of the level tract on which the houses are situated is but a few feet above high-water mark. The location was selected on account of its comparative dryness, and also because the river affords a safer anchorage in that vicinity than lower down.

The early Moravian missionaries, long before established on the Atlantic coast, desired to extend their labors for the conversion of the Eskimo to their teachings. About the year 1825 a vessel ascended the Koksoak river for the purpose of selecting a new missionary station. Nearly opposite Fort Chimo is a beacon, yet standing, erected by the people of that vessel. Their reception among the natives was such that they gave a glowing account of it on their return. The Hudson Bay Company immediately took steps to erect a trading post upon the river, and a small party was sent in the year 1831 from Moose Factory to establish a trading post where the trade would appear to promise future development. The men remained there, obtaining a precarious subsistence, as the vessel delivering them supplies visited that place only once in two years. Their houses were simple, consisting of a single structure for the official in charge, another for the servants, and two more for the storage of goods. A palisade was erected around the houses to prevent the intrusion of the natives, Indians and Eskimo, who were so lately at war with each other that the rancorous feeling had not subsided and might break out afresh at any moment without warning. The remnants of the palisade were yet visible in 1882. The establishment of this trading post had a pacifying influence upon the natives, who soon found they could do better by procuring the many valuable fur-bearing animals than by engaging in a bloody strife, which the traders always deprecate and endeavor to prevent or suppress. After many trials to establish an overland communication with the stations on Hamilton inlet, it was found to be impracticable, and in 1843 the station was abandoned.

John M'Lean, in a work entitled "Twenty-five Years in the Hudson's Bay Territory,"[1] gives an account of that portion of the country that came under his knowledge from the year 1838 to 1843.

In the year 1866 the steamer *Labrador* was built and sent with a party to reestablish the post at Fort Chimo. Since 1866 the post has been a paying station, and in later years a good profit has been made.

Fort Chimo is the chief trading station of the Ungava district. The Ungava district proper is the area embraced by the watershed whose outflow drains into Ungava bay. The eastern boundary is formed by the foothills on the west side of the coast range, which is the western limit of Labrador. This range has a trend northwest and southeast to latitude 60°, where it makes a somewhat abrupt angle and pursues a nearly north course, terminating with Cape Chidley and the Buttons, the latter a low group of islets some 7 miles north of the cape. The southern boundary is the "Height of Land," near latitude 55°. This region is estimated to be from 1,000 to 3,000 feet above sea level. The greater portion of it is comparatively level, and on its surface are innumerable lakes of various sizes, some of which are quite large. The western boundary is not so well known in the southern part of the region, as it has been seldom traversed. It seems to be a high elevation extending toward the north-northwest, as numerous streams run from the southwest and west toward the central or Koksoak valley. Eskimo who have traversed the region many times report that the elevated land abruptly ends near 58° 30', and that there is formed a wide swampy tract, estimated to be about 80 miles wide, which opens to the northeast and southwest. The northwestern portion of the district is a great area abounding in abrupt hills and precipitous mountains of various heights. These heights, estimated to range no higher than 2,600 feet, terminate abruptly on the western end of the strait, and the numerous islands in that portion of the water are, doubtless, peaks of this same range continuing to the northwest.

It will be thus seen that the district of Ungava is a huge amphitheater opening to the north. The interior of the district is excessively varied by ridges and spurs of greater or less elevation. The

---

[1] Two vols. in one. London, 1849.

farther south one travels, the higher and more irregularly disposed are the hills and mountains. These spurs are usually parallel to the main ranges, although isolated spurs occur which extend at right angles to the main range. The tops of the higher elevations are covered with snow for the entire year. The summits of the lower ones are shrouded with snow as early as the 1st of September, and by the 1st of October the snow line descends nearly to their bases. The lower lands are full of swampy tracts, lakes, and ponds.

The more elevated regions are totally destitute of vegetation, except the tripe des roches, which gives to the hills a somber color, anything but inspiring. Fully three-fourths of the more elevated region is, with the exception of black lichens, barren rock. Everywhere is the evidence of long continued glacial action. The southern exposures of all the hills show the same character of wearing, and, in many instances, a fine polish on the rocks forming their bases. This smoothness extends nearly to the summits of the higher peaks. These again are somewhat rougher and often broken into jagged, angular fragments, frequently of immense size. The more moderate elevations are usually rounded summits on whose higher portions may be found huge bowlders of rock having a different character from that upon which they rest, proving that they were carried there by masses of ice in the glacial ages. The northern extremity of all the ridges and spurs indicate that the glacial sheet moved to the north-northwest, for these portions of the rocks are so jagged and sharp edged as to appear to have been broken but yesterday.

The rivers of this district are numerous and several are of great size, although but two of them are navigable for more than 100 miles, and this only for boats of light draft.

The river usually known as George's river (Kan'gûk¢lua'luksoak) is the largest on the eastern side. This stream takes its rise about latitude 55° and pursues a moderately tortuous course nearly northward and falls into the eastern side of Ungava Bay. It has a wide bay-like mouth narrowing rapidly at the mouth proper. Swift rapids are formed here on account of an island near the center. Beyond this the river expands and has an average width of half a mile for a distance of about 18 miles where the river bends eastward and forms rapids for over 2 miles. It is navigable for the steamer *Labrador* only about 12 miles. Beyond the rapids it runs tolerably smooth and deep for nearly 40 miles and thence to the source is a series of rapids and falls, rendering portages frequent, and making it utterly impracticable for even a heavy skiff to ascend beyond 70 miles from the mouth. Indians assert that high falls occur about 150 miles from the mouth of the George's river. The water is said to fall from a terrific height, almost perpendicularly, and it causes the ground to tremble so that the thundering noise may be heard for more than a day's journey from it.

The tide at the mouth of George's river rises 53 feet, and at the

Anchorage, opposite the newly established station of Fort George, some 12 miles from its mouth, 42 feet.

Whale river is the next important river toward the east. Off the mouth of this river is a huge island, locally known as Big island. This high island extends parallel to the course of the river, and a reef, connecting its upper end with the mainland, becomes dry at low water. The course of Whale river is not well known. About 40 miles up this stream it suddenly contracts and becomes a mere creek, forming the outlet of a large lake, whose position is not satisfactorily determined. It is to the banks of this lake that certain families of the Indians repair for summer fishing.

The next large river is the Koksoak. This stream is the largest in the district. It takes its rise from lakes situated on the plateau—the "Height of Land,"—and pursues a course having a general direction north-northeast. On emerging from the lake it is rather small, but forks and unites again about 40 miles below. The current is is sluggish at the upper end, and the eastern branch is so narrow that the Indians have to part the overhanging alders and willows to afford their canoes a passage. This branch is said to be the shorter way to the lake and is not so difficult to ascend, the eastern branch being shallow and containing a number of rapids.

Below the junction of the branches the river rapidly becomes larger and contains several very high falls, below which the river flows northwest for a couple of hundred yards and then curves to the north-northeast for a distance of 5 miles. This portion is only about 700 feet wide. It then turns abruptly westward and rushes swiftly through a narrow gorge only 200 feet wide for a distance of about 7 miles. This course is noted for several rapids, through which a boat can not make its way without great difficulty. At the end of this 7-mile run the river again bends abruptly to the east, and continues that course with little northing until the last bend, some 65 miles below, is reached. At the lower end of the 7-mile run the ledges and reefs are too numerous to count. From this place to the mouth of the Larch river the Koksoak is obstructed by islands, bars, and shoals. Below these, however, it becomes quite broad, until nearly opposite the high point or promontory below the mouth of the Larch (Pl. XXXVI). From this locality it is monotonous till the last bend is reached, some 4 miles above Fort Chimo, where it suddenly turns to the north and pursues that direction to the sea with little variation. At the last bend, however, a large island, locally known as Big island, not only obstructs but ends navigation for boats drawing over 6 feet. Small boats, such as skiffs and native boats, ascend to the lower end of 7-mile run. The principal obstruction to travel in any kind of vessel in the Koksoak from Big island to the mouth of the Larch river is the presence of two falls or rapids about 40 miles from Fort Chimo.

The extreme rise and fall of the tide at the mouth of the river is 62

VIEW ON KOKSOAK RIVER.

feet 3 inches. The usual rise and fall is from 8 to 12 feet less, depending on the stage of the river. At Fort Chimo the tide rises as much as 31 feet. The backwater is held in check as far as the upper rapids in a common stage of water, and during a high rise in the month of June the water is "backed" some 3 miles beyond the upper rapids.

The branches of the Koksoak river are few and unimportant. The larger tributary is the Larch river. It is a rapid and almost unnavigable stream of variable depth, mostly shallow, and 100 to nearly 400 yards wide.

At about 40 miles from its mouth the Larch forks, the lower or southwest fork draining the eastern sides of the same mountains whose western slopes are drained by the Little Whale river. This southwest fork of the Larch river is quite small and scarely capable of being ascended, although it may, with great caution, be descended. This is the course followed by the Little Whale river Indians when they traverse the country to join the Naskopies of the Koksoak valley. The northwest branch of the Larch is still smaller and is reported to issue from the swampy tract of land in about latitude 58° 30′.

The next large river is the Leaf. Its mouth is about 34 miles northwest of Fort Chimo, and it flows into a peculiarly shaped bay named Tass′iyak, or "like a lake." The length of the river proper is estimated to be but 40 miles, flowing from a very long and narrow lake, having its longer axis extending southwestward and draining the greater part of the swampy tract lying in latitude 58° 30′. The southwestern portion of this tract is merely an area covered with innumerable small lakes so intimately connected by short water courses that it is difficult to determine whether water or land constitutes the greater part of the area. The rivers to the west are of less importance and drain the rugged area forming the northwestern portion of the district, or that part lying under the western third of Hudson strait.

The principal portion of Hudson strait that came under my observation is Ungava bay. This bay is a pocket-shaped body of water lying south of the strait and toward its eastern end. Soundings in various portions of this bay indicate a depth of 28 to 70 fathoms for the central area. The bottom appears to be uniformly the washings from the fresh-water streams. The extreme tides of Hudson strait tend to produce the most violent currents in this bay. Opposite the entrance of Leaf river bay is a whirlpool of considerable size, which causes much trouble to navigation. It is safe enough at high water but very dangerous at half-tide.

The large island known as Akpatok lies in such a position as to break much of the current along the south side of the middle of the strait, but to give additional force to the currents at either end. This island is about 100 miles long and has an average width of 18 miles. It is the largest island in the strait proper.

The coast line of the northwest portion of the mainland is imperfectly known, as is the western coast forming the eastern shore of Hudson bay. Navigation in any portion of Hudson strait is attended with much danger, not alone from the tremendous energy of the tides but also from the quantity of ice to be found at all times. During the months of August and September the strait is comparatively free from large fields of ice, but after that date the harbors, coves, and other anchorages are apt to be frozen up in a single night.

CLIMATE.

The temperature is controlled by the direction of the wind. The warmest winds are southeast, south, and southwest during the summer. The northeast winds bring (if backing) fog, rain, or snow; the north wind is usually cold and disposed to disperse the clouds. The northwest wind is always very cold in winter and chilly in summer. Westerly winds are moderate in winter and summer. The southerly winds are warm at all seasons if blowing hard, but very cold if blowing lightly in winter. I think the coldest light winds of the winter are from a point little west of south. They are doubtless due to the cold from the elevated region—the Height of Land.

The greatest amount of cloudiness occurs in the spring and fall; rather less in July and August, and least during December, January, and February. The average cloudiness for the entire year is not less than eighty-two hundredths of the visible sky.

Sleet falls mostly from the middle of September to the beginning of December. Snow then succeeds it and continues to be the only form of precipitation until the middle of April, when sleet and snow fall until the first rain sets in. The season of rain is very erratic. It may rain by the first of May, but rarely does. Snow falls every month in the year; the 2d of July and the 6th of August were the dates farthest apart for this form of precipitation. The character of the rain is usually moderate to hard for the summer showers; although several notable exceptions of abundant dashes occur during late June and all of July. The August and September rains are usually light to moderate, but often persistent for several days. The snowfalls are light to heavy in character, rarely, however, lasting more than twenty-four hours. The sleet is usually precipitated in severe squalls. The lower grounds are permanently covered with snow by the 1st of December, this covering remaining until the 10th of June. At the latter date only the heavier drifts and the snow of the ravines remain. It entirely disappears by the last of July at all elevations no higher than that of Fort Chimo.

The higher hills retain snow until the last of August, but none is to be seen in the vicinity of Fort Chimo after that date. By the middle of September snow again covers the tops of the distant high hills.

Fogs rarely occur so far inland as Fort Chimo. Those occurring are in July and August. At times they are very dense; and, as they form during the earliest hours of the day, they are usually dissipated by 4 to 7 a. m. While the ice is setting in the river, and driven back and forth by the tides, huge volumes of steam arise from the inky water and are spread over the land by the light winds prevailing at that season. This moisture deposited on the bushes and trees forms a most beautiful sight.

AURORAS.

Auroras may be seen on most of the clear nights of the year. The month of June is, on account of its light nights, the only month in which an aurora is not observable.

VEGETATION.

The northern limit of trees on the Labrador coast is in latitude 57°. Here the conifers are stunted and straggling. Beyond the coast range they attain a slightly higher altitude and thence continue to a point about thirty miles north of the mouth of George's river. On the western side of the mouth of this river the trees are pushed back 15 to 20 miles from the sea. At the mouth of Whale river, the trees attain a height of 30 to 50 feet on the eastern (right) bank and within 2 miles of the shore. On the left bank the trees do not approach to within 10 to 15 miles of the coast. At the mouth of False river they form a triangular extension and attain considerable size, due in great measure to the peculiar formation of a huge amphitheater whose north wall serves as an admirable protection against the cold winds from the bay. On the western side of False river the tree line extends in a southwesterly direction across the Koksoak and to the banks of the Leaf river nearly at its source from the large lake. From the south side of this lake the trees are very much scattered and attain inconsiderable size, scarcely fitted for other uses than fuel.

A line from this lake southwest to the eastern shore of Hudson bay forms the northern limit of trees for the northwest portion of the region. The people (Eskimo only) who dwell north of this line are dependent upon the stunted willows and alders, growing in the deeper ravines and valleys having a southern exposure. Large pieces of wood are much sought for by the Eskimo of the northwest portion, for use in constructing their kaiaks, umiaks and paddles, as well as spear shafts and smaller requirements for which the distorted stems of willow and alder will not suffice.

South of the line given as the northern limit of trees the growth slowly attains greater size and extension of area. The timber north of the Height of Land is comparatively small, the spruce and larch rarely attaining a size greater than 12 to 15 inches at the ground and rapidly tapering up for 2 feet or so above the surface. Above the height of 2 feet the stems slowly taper and, in a few instances, produce symmetrical stems for more than 15 feet. The trees growing within 40 miles of Fort Chimo seldom exceed 10 inches in diameter, and of the larger trunks the logs are selected to form the material from which the walls of all the buildings at that place are constructed.

The alders, willows, and a few other bushes attain a greater or less size, depending upon the situation and amount of protection afforded. I have seen as large stems of these shrubs growing within a mile of Fort Chimo as I have seen at either Davis inlet or Rigolet.

The flowering plants are sparsely scattered over the northern areas, and then only in most suitable soils. The ground remains frozen from the last of October—earlier some seasons—to the last of May, or even into the middle of June. The appearance of the annuals is sudden, and they rapidly attain their full size and quickly fall before the chilling winds of autumn.

ANIMAL LIFE.

MAMMALS.

The marine mammals alone appear to be well known, but the number of cetaceans can certainly be increased above the number usually reported inhabiting the waters immediately bordering upon the region.

The phocids are best known for the reason that off the shores of southeast Labrador the pursuit of species of this family is carried on each spring to an extent probably surpassing that anywhere else on the face of the globe.

At the mouth of Little Whale river, the white whale is taken to the number of 500 each year, although the capture is steadily decreasing. The Indians here do the greater part of the labor of driving, killing, flaying, and preserving them. At Fort Chimo another station for the pursuit of white whales is carried on. Here the Eskimo do the driving and killing, while the Indians perform the labor of removing the blubber and rendering it fit for the oil tanks into which it is placed to put it beyond the action of the weather. The skin of the white whale is tanned and converted into a leather of remarkably good quality, especially noted for being nearly waterproof.

Of the land mammals, the reindeer is probably the most abundant of all. It is found in immense numbers in certain localities, and forms for many of the inhabitants the principal source of subsistence, while to nearly all the residents its skins are absolutely necessary to protect them from the severity of the winter.

The black, white and brown bears are common enough in their respective areas. The former rarely ranges beyond the woodlands, never being found so far north as Fort Chimo. The white bear is common in the northern portions bordering the sea and is occasionally found as far south as the strait of Belleisle, to which it has been carried on icebergs or fields of ice. Akpatok island and the vicinity of Cape Chidley are reported to be localities infested with these brutes. The brown or barren-ground bear appears to be restricted to a narrow area and is not plentiful, yet is common enough to keep the Indian in wholsome dread of its vicious disposition when enraged.

The smaller mammals occur in greater or less abundance according to the quality and quantity of food to be obtained. The wolves, foxes, and wolverines are pretty evenly distributed throughout the region. The hares are found in the wooded tracts for the smaller species and on the barren regions for the larger species.

BIRDS.

The actual residents were ascertained to be less than twenty species for the northern portion of the Ungava district.

Of the actual residents the two species of the genus *Lagopus* are the most abundant of all birds in the region, and form an important article of food for all classes of people inhabiting the district. The winter exerts an important influence on the smaller resident species. During the winter of 1882–'83 the number of the four species obtained of the genus *Acanthis* was almost incredible. Their notes might be heard at any time during that season, which was cold, though regularly so, and not specially stormy. In the winter of 1883–'84 not a single individual was observed from the middle of November to the last of March. The same remarks may well apply to the white-winged crossbill (*Loxia leucoptera*), which was very abundant the first winter, but during the last winter a very small flock only was observed and these were apparently vagrants.

Among the water birds, certain species which were expected to occur were conspicuously absent. The character of the country forbids them rearing their young, as there is little to feed upon; and only a few breed in the immediate vicinity of Fort Chimo. Among the gulls, *Larus argentatus smithsonianus* is certainly the only one breeding in abundance within Ungava bay. Of the terns, the Arctic tern (*Sterna paradiseœ*) was the only one ascertained to breed in Hudson strait. I am not certain that they do breed there every year. Although I saw them in early July, 1883, under conditions that led me to believe that they were on their way to their nests, yet it was not until 1884 that a number of eggs were secured near that locality.

Of the smaller waders, but two species were actually ascertained to breed in the vicinity of Fort Chimo, yet two or three other species were observed under such circumstances as to leave no doubt that they also breed there.

THE NATIVE INHABITANTS OF THE COUNTRY—GENERAL SKETCH.

THE ESKIMO.

The northern portions of the coast of the region under consideration are inhabited by the Eskimo, who designate themselves, as usual, by the term "Innuit," people (plural of innuls, "a person"). That they have been much modified by contact with the whites is not to be doubted, and it is equally certain that their language is constantly undergoing modifications to suit the purposes of the missionary and trader, who, not being able to pronounce the difficult guttural speech of these people, require them to conform to their own pronunciation. The region inhabited by the Innuit is strictly littoral. Their distribution falls properly into three subdivisions, due to the three subtribal distinctions which they maintain among themselves. The first subdivision embraces all the Innuit dwelling on the Labrador coast proper and along the south side of Hudson strait to the mouth of Leaf river, which flows into Ungava bay.

These people apply the term Sû hi′ nĭ myut to themselves and are thus known by the other subdivisions. This term is derived from Sû hi′ nûk, the sun, and the latter part of the word, meaning people (literally "those that dwell at or in"); hence, people of the sun, sunny side, because the sun shines on them first. At the present time these people are confined to the seashore and the adjacent islands, to which they repair for seals and other food. South of Hamilton inlet I could learn of but one of these people.

The Innuit of pure blood do not begin to appear until the missionary station of Hopedale is reached. Here a number of families dwell, although mostly at the instigation of the missionaries. Between this station and Hebron are several other Moravian missionary stations, at each of which dwell a greater or less number of pure Innuit. North of Hebron to Cape Chidley there are but few families, some seven in all, embracing a population of less than 40 souls. On the west side of Cape Chidley, as far as the mouth of George's river, only about eight families live. These with the George's river Innuit comprise less than 50 individuals. There is a stretch of coast bordering Ungava bay, from George's river to the Koksoak river, which is uninhabited.

The Koksoak river people include only four or five families and number less than 30 souls. The next people are those dwelling at the mouth of Leaf river, but they are more properly to be considered under the next subdivision.

The exact number of the Sûhĭnĭmyut could not be definitely determined. They are subdivided into a number of small communities, each bearing a name compounded of the name of their home and myut, "the people of."

The inhabitants of Cape Chidley are known as Ki lĭn′ĭg myut, from the word ki lĭn′ĭk, wounded, cut, incised, lacerated; hence, serrated, on account of the character of the rough rocks and mountains.

The natives of George's river are known as Kan′gûk¢lua′luksoagmyut; those of the Koksoak river are known as Koksoagmyut.

The second subdivision includes the Innuit dwelling on the area lying between the mouth of Leaf river, thence northward, and along the south side of Hudson strait. Their western and southern limit extends to about latitude 60°.

These Innuit are known by the other subdivisions as Ta hág myut. They apply the same term to themselves. The word is derived from Tá hak, a shadow; hence people of the shade or shadow as distinguished from the Sû hĭ′ nĭ myut, or people of the light or sunshine. These people are but little influenced by contact with the white traders, who apply to them the term " Northerners." Their habits and customs are primitive, and many appear to be entirely distinct from the customs of their neighbors south and east. The character of the region in which they dwell is very rugged. Huge mountain spurs and short ranges ramify in every direction, forming deep valleys and ravines, along which these people must travel to reach the trading station of Fort Chimo of the Ungava district, or else to Fort George of the Moose district.

The distance to the former is so great that only three, four, or five sledges are annually sent to the trading post for the purpose of conveying the furs and other more valuable commodities to be bartered for ammunition, guns, knives, files and other kinds of hardware, and tobacco. Certain persons are selected from the various camps who have personally made the trip and know the trail. These are commissioned to barter the furs of each individual for special articles, which are mentioned and impressed upon the mind of the man who is to effect the trade. The principal furs are those of the various foxes. Among them are to be found the best class of silver foxes, and wolverenes and wolves. Those to be sent are procured the previous winter, and when the snow falls in November or early December the line of sleds starts out for the trading post. The sled which represents the wants of the more western of these Innuit speeds to where the second may be, and they repair to the place of meeting with the third, and thus by traversing the line of coast the arctic caravan is made up. Provisions are supplied by the wayside, and when all is in readiness a southern course is traveled until the frozen morasses on the south of the hills are reached. Thence the course is toward Leaf river and across to Fort Chimo. By the last week of April or the first week of May the visitors are expected at the trading post. They usually bring with them about two-fifths of all the furs obtained in the district; indeed, the quantity often exceeds this amount. They seldom remain longer than the time needed to complete their bartering, as the rapidly melting snow warns them that each day of delay adds to their labor in returning.

The homeward journey is more frequently made along the coast, as there the snow is certain to remain longer upon the ground. It is not infrequent that these travelers experience warm weather, which detains them so long that they do not reach the end of their journey until the middle of the summer or even until the beginning of the next winter. Many of the Innuit who accompany these parties have never seen white men until they arrive at Fort Chimo; women are often of the party. These people are usually tall and of fine physique. The men are larger than the average white man, while the women compare favorably in stature with the women of medium height in other countries.

They have quite different customs from those of their present neighbors. Their language is dialectically distinct; about as much so as the Malimyut differ from the Kaviagmyut of Norton Sound, Alaska. The Tahagmyut have a rather harsh tone; their gutturals are deeper and the vowels usually rather more prolonged. They are much given to amusement and still retain many of the old games, which the Sûhĭ′nĭmyut have forgotten or no longer engage in. Their dead are treated with no ceremony. They simply lash the limbs of the deceased to the body and expose the corpse to the elements, removing it, however, from immediate sight of the camp. Old and infirm people are treated with severity, and when dependent upon others for their food they are summarily disposed of by strangulation or left to perish when the camp is moved.

Women are held in little respect, although the men are very jealous of the favors of their wives, and incontinence on the part of the latter is certain to be more or less severely punished. The male offender, if notoriously persistent in his efforts to obtain forbidden favors, is usually killed by the injured lover or husband.

Gambling is carried on to such a degree among both sexes that even their own lives are staked upon the issue of a game. The winner often obtains the wife of his opponent, and holds her until some tempting offer is made for her return. The only article they possess is frequently wagered, and when they lose they are greeted with derision. The women, especially, stake their only garment rather than be without opportunity to play. The usual game is played with a number of flattened pieces of walrus ivory. On one side are a number of dots forming various crude designs, which have received names from their fancied resemblance to other objects. These must be matched. The game somewhat resembles dominoes, and whether it is original with these Innuit I was unable to conclude. They stoutly maintain that it originated with themselves. I suspect, however, it had its origin in the imitation of some one who had observed the playing of dominoes on board of some of the whaling vessels visiting these waters.

For other amusements these Innuit indulge in a number of tests of personal strength, such as wrestling and leaping.

Feasts are held at stated times in huge structures built of snow blocks. The exact signification of these feasts was not learned, owing to the limited stay these people made each year at Fort Chimo. Their dress consists of the skins of seals and reindeer. The sealskins are worn during rainy weather and by those who are in the canoe or kaiak. The skirts of their garments are ornamented with an edging of ivory pieces cut into a pear-shape, having a small hole pierced through the smaller end.

These pieces of ivory, often to the number of many scores, give a peculiar rattle as the wearer walks along. Their boots are noticeably different from those made by the Koksoak river people, inasmuch as the soles are often made with strips of sealskin thongs sewed on a false sole, which is attached to the under surface of the sole proper. The strips of thong are tacked on by a stout stitch, then a short loop is taken up, and another stitch sews a portion of the remainder of the strip. This is continued until the entire under surface consists of a series of short loops, which, when in contact with the smooth ice, prevents the foot from slipping. This sort of footgear is not made in any other portion of the district.

The third subdivision comprises the Innuit dwelling on the eastern shore of Hudson bay, between latitudes 53° and 58°.

The number of these Innuit could not be definitely ascertained, as they trade, for the most part, at Fort George, belonging to the Moose district. Each year, however, a party of less than a dozen indiviuals journey to Fort Chimo for the purpose of bartering furs and other valuables. Those who come to Fort Chimo are usually the same each year. In language they differ greatly from the Koksoak Innuit, inasmuch as their speech is very rapid and much harsher. Many of the words are quite dissimilar, and even where the word has the same sound it is not unusual that it has a meaning more or less different from that used by the Koksoak Innuit. As these people have been long under the advice and teachings of the missionary society of London, it is to be expected that they, especially those nearer the trading station, are more or less influenced by its teachings. Their customs differ somewhat from the other Innuit, though this is due in a great measure to the impossibility of procuring the necessary food, and skins for garments, unless they are constantly scouring the plains and hills for reindeer or the shore for seals and other marine creatures.

These people are called by their neighbors and themselves I'tivi' myut, Iti'vûk signifies the other, farther, distant side (of a portion of land); hence, the word Itivimyut means people of the other side. The northern Itivimyut are probably the most superstitious of all the Innuit dwelling in the region under consideration.

Although the missionaries have devoted considerable energy to the work of converting these people, and though many of them profess Christianity, these professions prove on examination to be merely nominal. As soon as the converts are beyond the teacher's influence, they return to the shaman for guidance.

In the spring of 1883 a party of these people visited Fort Chimo. A great number of the Koksoak people were ill, some 30 miles above the station. The visitors had among them a shaman renowned throughout the land. He, with the connivance of two or three of the people with whom he stopped, began some of the most astonishing intrigues to dispel the evil spirit afflicting the people. Several men were parted from their wives, and these were compelled to dwell with other men who were at the bottom of the conspiracy. Other couples had to flee from that place to prevent being divorced, at least temporarily. After a time the visitors descended to Fort Chimo, and while the bartering was going on the shaman announced his conversion to Christianity, and vowed never again to return to practicing shamanism. On the return of the harried fugitives they passed the camp of the Koksoak river people, where they had a few days before been the guests, and stole their supplies of reindeer meat and other valuable property, even attempting to purloin a kaiak; and they had proceeded many miles thence before they were overtaken and compelled to relinquish the stolen property. They were seen some months after by some Tahagmyut, to whom they stated their fear of returning among the Koksoak people. A more plausible scamp does not dwell in those regions than this shaman, whose name is Sápa. His power over the spirit controlling the reindeer is widely believed in and invoked by the other shamans, who feel incapable of turning the heads of the deer and thus compelling them to wander in the desired direction.

Among these people only have I heard of a son who took his mother as a wife, and when the sentiment of the community compelled him to discard her he took two other women, who were so persecuted by the mother that they believed themselves to be wholly under her influence. She even caused them to believe they were ill, and when they actually did become so they both died.

In former years the Innuit extended entirely around the shore of Hudson bay. Now there is a very wide gap, extending from the vicinity of Fort George, on the eastern coast, to the vicinity of Fort Churchill, on the western coast. At the present time the Innuit occupy the areas designated in these remarks. That they formerly extended along the Atlantic coast far to the south of their present limit is attested by an abundance of facts.

The Innuit of the eastern shore of Hudson bay, the Itivimyut, informed me that the Innuit dwelling on the islands of Hudson bay, more or less remote from the mainland to the east, are termed Ki'gĭktag'myut, or island people. They relate that those islanders have quite different customs from the mainland people, inasmuch as their clothing consists of the skins of seals and dogs, rarely of reindeer skins, as the latter are procurable only when one of their number comes to the shore to trade for such articles as can not be obtained on his locality. The spear, kaiak, bow and arrow are used, and they have but little knowledge of firearms. These people are represented as often being driven to greatest extremity for food. It is said that their language differs considerably from that of their neighbors.

The Innuit, as a rule, are peaceful and mild-tempered, except when aroused by jealousy. They are, however, quick enough to resent an insult or avenge an injury. They form a permanent attachment for the white man who deals honestly and truthfully with them, but if he attempts any deception or trickery they are certain to be ever suspicious of him, and it is difficult to regain their favor.

Their courage and ability are not to be doubted, and when they are given a due amount of encouragement they will perform the most arduous tasks without complaint.

THE INDIANS.

The Indian inhabitants of this region may be divided into three groups, differing but slightly in speech, and even less in habits.

(1) The Mountaineers, "Montagnais" of the early Jesuit missionaries, roam over the areas south of the Hamilton inlet and as far as the Gulf of St. Lawrence. Their western limits are imperfectly known. They trade at all the stations along the accessible coast. Many of them barter at Rigolet and Northwest river.

In customs they differ little from the Indians to the north of them. Their means of subsistence are the flesh of reindeer, porcupines, and various birds, such as geese, ducks, ptarmigan, and grouse.

The habits of the reindeer in this portion of the country are very erratic. They are often absent from large tracts for several years, and appearing in abundance when little expected. The scarcity of the reindeer renders the food supply quite precarious; hence, the Indians rely much upon the flesh of the porcupine, hare and birds for their principal food.

Their clothing is of the tanned skin of the deer when they are able to procure it. As nearly all the skins of the reindeer are used for garments, few are prepared for other purposes; hence the northern stations (Fort Chimo) furnish great numbers of these skins in the parchment condition to be purchased by the Mountaineers, who cut them into fine lines for snowshoe netting and other purposes.

They procure the furs of marten, mink, fur beaver, muskrats, lynxes, wolverines, wolves, and foxes. A considerable number of black bears are also obtained by these Indians. By the barter of these furs they procure the articles made necessary by the advent of the white people among them. They are quiet and peaceable. Many of them profess a regard for the teachings of the Roman missionaries, who have visited them more or less frequently for over a hundred and fifty years. I was unable to obtain the term by which they distinguish themselves from their neighbors. That they are later comers in the region than the Innuit is attested by the bloody warfare formerly carried on between them, of which many proofs yet exist. The Mountaineers applied to the more northern Indians the term of reproach, "Naskopie." This word denotes the contempt the Mountaineers felt for the Naskopies when the latter failed to fulfill their promise to assist in driving the Innuit from the country.

It was impossible to obtain a satisfactory estimate of the numbers of the Mountaineers. My stay in their vicinity was too short to learn as much about them as was desired.

(2) The Indians dwelling to the southwest of the Ungava district differ rather more than the Mountaineers, in their speech, from the Indians of the Ungava district. They average, for both sexes, slightly taller than the Naskopies. The men are spare, and have small limbs and extremities. The cheek bones are also more prominent, although this is partly due to the thin visage. The women are disposed to be stout, and in the older women there is a decided tendency to corpulence. The complexion, too, is considerably darker. The men wear long hair, usually cut so as to fall just upon the shoulders. The hair of the women is quite heavy, and is worn either in braids or done up in folds upon the side of the head.

In their personal habits they are much more tidy than their eastern relations. Their dress differs but little from that of their neighbors. The women dress in cloth made of material procured from the traders, and some of these appear respectable enough when so dressed. They have been so long in contact with the white people at Moose Factory, some of whom had brought their wives from home with them, that the women have imitated the dress of the latter. Certain of these women are skillful in working fancy articles. The men occupy their time in hunting and fishing. The reindeer have in recent years become so scarce in the vicinity of Fort George that many of the Indians have left that locality and journeyed to the eastward, dwelling in proximity to the Naskopies, or even with them.

Both sexes are mild and sedate, although the women are exceedingly garrulous when well acquainted.

These Indians are often employed to assist in the capture of the white whale, which ascends the lower portions of the larger streams of that district. They are the only Indians whom I have seen eating the flesh and blubber of these whales. The Naskopies will not touch it, declaring it to be too fat. The fins and tail are portions highly prized while they are helping render out the blubber of these whales at Fort Chimo.

A point of great dissimilarity between the Naskopies and the Little Whale river Indians is that the birch-bark canoe of the latter is much more turned up at each end, producing a craft well adapted to the swift currents of the rivers. The occupants are skillful boatmen, and will fearlessly face wind and wave that would appall the heart of the Naskopie. Sails are sometimes erected in a single canoe. At times two canoes are lashed together and a sail spread from a single mast. This double boat is very convenient for the traveler. These people are strongly addicted to the practice of polygamy; and while they are Christians externally, they are so only as long as they are within the reach of the missionary.

Among those who had come to dwell in the Ungava district were several who had, because of the opportunity, taken two wives. The missionary, E. J. Peck, suddenly appeared among them as he was on his way to London. On learning of the conduct of the people he gave them a sound rating and besought them to relinquish the practice. They assented, and sent the second wives away until the missionary was out of the country, and then they took them back.

Girls are often taken as wives before they attain puberty, and for this reason they seldom have large families. Two, three, or four children form the usual number for each family. They are satisfied if the first child is a male; and to the mother who delivers only female children a term of contempt is often applied. The women appear to be well treated, and occasional laxity of morals is not noticed among them so long as it is not notorious.

Their beliefs and traditions were not learned by me, on account of the presence of these people at Fort Chimo when other labors occupied my entire time.

Their purchases are made with furs of the same kinds as those procured in the Ungava district. The black bear is procured in great numbers by these Indians. They preserve the under lip, dressed and ornamented with beads and strips of cloth, as a trophy of their prowess.

The harpoon used in striking the white whale of their rivers is an implement doubtless peculiar to those people, and much resembles that of the Innuit.

(3) The third division of Indians includes those dwelling for the most part in the Ungava district. The total number of these Indians is about 350. They apply the term Ne né not—true, ideal men—to themselves, although known by the epithet Naskopie, which was applied to them by the Mountaineers of the southeastern portion of the region.

They differ slightly in customs from their neighbors, but their speech is somewhat different, being very rapidly uttered and with most singular inflections of the voice. A conversation may be begun in the usual tone, and in a moment changed to that of a whining or petulant child. It is impossible for the white man to imitate this abrupt inflection, which appears to be more common among the males than the females. During ordinary conversation one would erroneously suppose, from the vehemence of gesture, that the speaker was angry. They are much more demonstrative than their neighbors, often shouting at the full strength of their voices when an ordinary tone would apparently suffice. That their voice is penetrating may be inferred from the fact that during quiet days it is not unusual for parties to converse from opposite sides of the Koksoak river, at Fort Chimo, where the river is nearly a mile and a half wide.

As certain words are spoken in a voice scarcely louder than a whisper, I did not believe it possible that they could understand each other at so great a distance, until I saw the people on the opposite shore doing what they were bidden by those with me.

When the women get together it is amusing to observe the eagerness of the old crones endeavoring to make their voices heard above the rest. The clerk, while trading with them, often teases them until the entire number turn their voices on him, and the only relief he has is to expel them all from the store and admit one or two at a time, while the remainder throng the windows and shout at the top of their voices.

During the spring, when flocks of Canada geese are winging their way northward, the Indians will imitate their notes so closely that the birds do not discover the source until too late. Some of the party make one note, while the others imitate the other note. It seldom fails to beguile the geese to the spot.

Owing to the impossibility of getting a reliable person to teach me the language of these people I was able to procure but few words. The number obtained, however, is sufficient to prove that the people of this region, excluding the Innuit and whites, belong to the Cree branch. The Mountaineers and Little Whale river Indians belong to the same stock, and the difference in their language is due wholly to environment.

The Indians and Innuit of this region are more or less directly in contact. At Fort Chimo it is especially so. Here, as elsewhere, they do not intermix, an Indian never taking an Innuit wife or the Innuit taking a squaw for a wife. I knew of one instance where a Naskopie went to dwell with some Innuit camped near the mouth of the Koksoak, but after remaining away for a few days he returned to his own people.

SPECIAL ACCOUNT OF THE PEOPLE AROUND FORT CHIMO.

THE KOKSOAGMYUT.

The Eskimo with whom I was brought in contact at Fort Chimo were those belonging to that immediate vicinity. They term themselves Koksoagmyut, or people of the Koksoak or Big river.

The people who apply this name to themselves do not number more than a score and a half. There are but four families, and among these are some who belong to other localities, but now dwell with the Kok soagmyut. They consider themselves a part of the people dwelling as far to the north as the western end of Akpatok island, and to the east as far as George's river. The Eskimo dwelling between those points have similar habits, and range indiscriminately over the hunting grounds of that locality, seldom going farther southward than the confluence of the Larch river or the North river with the Koksoak.

Among these few natives now inhabiting the Koksoak valley we find the men to be above the stature usually ascribed to the Eskimo. All but one of the adult males are above 5 feet 8 inches. The smallest man is little more than 5½ feet tall. All are well proportioned and present an exceptionally good physique. The females are also well proportioned, and, in fact, appear to compare well with females of civilized countries as far as their stature is concerned. The lower extremities of both sexes really are shorter than the general appearance would indicate, and thus the body is somewhat longer. The great individual variation in the proportional length of the legs is doubtless the result of the way infants are carried in the hood on the backs of the mothers. In this constrained position the limbs were obliged to conform to the shape of the body on which the child, in a manner, grew. While the limbs are not decidedly curved, yet they are not so nearly under the body as those of the whites. In walking, the inner edges of the feet often touch each other, and, in a manner, tend to cause the boots to slip outward on the feet.

The head, hands, and feet appear fairly proportioned; although, as a rule, they have small hands and feet. The females have proportionally smaller feet than hands. The head may seem larger than it really is, on account of the flattened features of the face.

The average nose is large and flat, and the prominence of this organ is often diminished by the wide cheeks and overhanging forehead. In most cases the chin projects less than the nose. The average face is round and flat, but there are exceptions, as I have seen one or two persons whose faces were a regular oval, and with the exception of the flat front, seen from a side view, were as well formed as one will meet among other people.

The skin has the same differences of color as among white people. The greater number of people are moderately dark, but this depends very greatly on the season of the year. I have not seen any white people so much changed as these are by the exposure to the summer sunshine. In the winter they are confined to their huts and bleach to a lighter color. A couple of weeks' exposure renders them scarcely recognizable as the same persons. The young children are usually lighter than the adults, although some are quite dark. The hair is coarse, long and abundant, and always straight.

The few half-breeds seen at Fort Chimo are the young children of the male servants of the company, who have in two instances taken full-blooded Eskimo women for wives and who were married by the agent of the company. These children are quite pretty, the male favoring the mother and the girl resembling the father. With these, as with the children of natives, much depends on the cleanliness of the person. The soot and other filth accumulating on their faces and hands, seldom washed, of course modifies the appearance of the exposed portions of the body. Some of the girls would be attractive enough if a copious amount of water was used to remove the ridges of dirt which are too plainly visible. The hands are often much disfigured from numerous cuts and bruises, which, when healed over, leave a heightened scar of a whitish color quite different in color from the surrounding tissue and often presenting an unsightly appearance.

By the time puberty is attained the girls quickly change, and in a few years begin to show the result of their arduous life by the appearance of wrinkles, haggardness, and general breaking down, which, although it may progress slowly, is seldom recovered from.

Like the rest of the Innuit, the Koksoagmyut are usually peaceful and mild tempered. Among themselves affrays are of rare occurrence. Jealousy arouses the worst passions, and the murder of the offender is generally the result. When a person becomes so bad in character that the community will no longer tolerate his presence he is forbidden to enter the huts, partake of food, or hold any intercourse with the rest. Nevertheless, as long as he threatens no one's life, but little attention is paid to him. Should he be guilty of a murder, several men watch their opportunity to surprise him and put him to death, usually by stoning. The executioners make no concealment of their action. and are supported by public opinion in the community.

In the case of a premeditated murder, it is the duty of the next of kin to avenge the deed, though years may pass, while the murderer pursues his usual occupations undisturbed, before an opportunity occurs to the relative for taking him by surprise. Sometimes the victim is not overcome and turns upon the assailant and kills him. The man, now guilty of two murders, is suffered to live only at the pleasure of the people, who soon decree his death. That murder is not approved, either by the individual or the community, is well attested by the fact that the island of Akpatok is now tabooed since the murder of part of the crew of a wrecked vessel, who camped on that island. Such a terrible scene was too much, even for them; and now not a soul visits that locality, lest the ghosts of the victims should appear and supplicate relief from the natives, who have not the proper offerings to make to appease them.

Aged people who have no relatives on whom they may depend for subsistence are often quietly put to death. When an old woman, for instance, becomes a burden to the community it is usual for her to be neglected until so weak from want of food that she will be unable to keep up with the people, who suddenly are seized with a desire to remove to a distant locality. If she regains their camp, well for her; otherwise, she struggles along until exhausted and soon perishes. Sometimes three or four of the males retrace their steps to recover a lost whip or a forgotten ammunition bag. They rarely go farther than where they find the helpless person, and if their track be followed it will be found that the corpse has stones piled around it and is bound with thongs.

An old woman at Fort Chimo had but one eye, and this was continually sore and very annoying to the people with whom she lived. They proposed to strangle her to relieve her from her misery. The next morning the eye was much better and the proposed cure was postponed.

Cases of suicide are not rare, considering the few people of that locality. Pitching themselves from a cliff or producing strangulation are the usual methods. Sometimes a gun is used. Remorse and disappointed love are the only causes of suicide.

A man discovered, during a period of great scarcity or food, that while he went in quest of food his wife had secretly stored away a quantity of fish and ate of them during his absence only. Coming home unexpectedly, he caught her eating and she endeavored to secrete the remainder. He quietly went out of the snow hut and blocked up the entrance. She inquired why he did so. His reply was for her to come out and she would discover why it was done. His tone was not at all reassuring. She remained within the hut and perished from starvation, knowing she would be killed if she went out.

Instances are reported where, in times of great scarcity, families have been driven to cannibalism after eating their dogs and the clothing and other articles made of skins. Unlucky or disliked women are often driven from the camp, and such must journey until they find relief or perish by the wayside.

DISEASES.

The principal diseases from which these people suffer are pulmonary troubles, chiefly arising from their filthy manner of living in crowded huts, too ill ventilated to allow the escape of the odors emanating from their own bodies and from accumulations of slowly decomposing animal food. All openings must be closed as quickly as possible in order to economize the heat within, for when once chilled it is difficult to restore the house to the proper degree of warmth. An Eskimo would always prefer to erect a new hut of snow rather than pass the night in one which has been deserted for only a single night if the doorway has not been tightly closed with a block of snow.

Within the walls, reeking with the exhalations of various putrid matters, the people breathe and rebreathe the air filled with poisonous gases; so fully one-half of the Eskimo die of pulmonary troubles. The other prevailing diseases are those causing devitalization of the blood, such as scurvy. Sores break out on the shoulders, elbows, knees, and ankles. The ravages of these diseases proceed at an astonishing rate, soon carrying off the afflicted person.

The means of relief usually employed are those which the shaman (or conjurer, as he is locally known) is able to effect by working on the imagination of the sick, who is in this condition easily influenced. The will power of both the patient and shaman is stretched to its utmost tension, and as faith with them, as with many others of fairer skins, often produces more of the relief than the ministrations of drugs or drafts, the cure is effected, or else the shaman, like the physician, has not the devil on his side.

The magnitude of the disease is generally measured by the amount of the patient's worldly wealth.

MARRIAGE.

A woman is married as soon after puberty as a male comes along who has the requisite physical strength to force her to become his wife. Many of the females are taken before that period, and the result is that few children are born to such unions and the children are generally weakly.

The ceremony between the couples is quite simple. The sanction of the parents is sometimes obtained by favor or else bought by making certain presents of skins, furs, and other valuables to the father and mother. The girl is sometimes asked for her consent, and, if unwilling, often enlists the sympathy of the mother, and the affair is postponed to a more favorable opportunity, or till the suitor becomes disgusted with her and takes somebody else.

If the parents are not living, the brothers or sisters must be favorable to the union. There is often so much intriguing in these matters that the exact truth can seldom be ascertained.

Where all obstacles are removed and only the girl refuses, it is not long before she disappears mysteriously to remain out for two or three nights with her best female friend, who thoroughly sympathizes with her. They return, and before long she is abducted by her lover, and they remain away until she proves to be thoroughly subjected to his will. I knew of an instance where a girl was tied in a snow house for a period of two weeks, and not allowed to go out. She finally submitted, and they returned with the other couple, who were less obstreperous, and doubtless went along to help their male friend and companion. The woman left her husband in the course of two or three weeks, and when he was asked about it he acknowledged that she had pulled nearly all the hair from his head and showed numerous bruises where she had struck him. This same woman was afterward tied to a sled to make her accompany the man she subsequently chose as her husband, who wished her to go to another part of the country. It was a lively time, some of the old women pushing her and persuading, the younger ones doing all in their power to obstruct her. Children are often mated at an early age, and I have known of several instances where two friends, desirous of cementing their ties of fellowship, engage that their children yet unborn shall be mated. In such instances the children are always recognized as married, and they are allowed by the parents to be so called. I knew a small boy of less than seven years who always addressed a girl of apparently a year older as his wife.

The marriageable age of the female varies greatly, although puberty takes place early. I have known of a child of fourteen having children. I heard of a half-breed girl, on the Labrador coast, who became a mother a few months after the age of thirteen.

Monogamy is generally the rule, but as there are so many counteracting influences it is seldom that a man keeps a wife for a number of years. Jealousy resulting from a laxity of morals produces so much disagreement that one or the other of the parties usually leave with little ceremony.

In rare instances, where there is a compatibility of temper and a disposition to continence, the pair remain together for life.

Many of the girls bear children before they are taken for wives, but as such incidents do not destroy the respectability of the mother the girl does not experience any difficulty in procuring a husband. Illegitimate children are usually taken care of by some aged woman, who devotes to it all her energies and affections.

The number of children born varies greatly, for, although these Eskimos are not a prolific race, a couple may occasionally claim parentage of as many as ten children. Two or three is the usual number, and many die in early childhood.

When the family is prosperous the husband often takes a second wife, either with or without the approval of the first, who knows that her household duties will be lessened, but knows also that the favors of her husband will have to be divided with the second wife. The second wife is often the cause of the first wife's leaving, though sometimes she is sent away herself. Three or four wives are sometimes attained by a prosperous man, and one instance was known where the head of the family had no less than five wives. The occupation of a single snow house by two or three wives brings them into close intimacy and often produces quarreling. The man hears but little of it, as he is strong enough to settle their difficulties without ceremony, and in a manner better adapted to create respect for brute strength than affection for him.

The females outnumber the males, but the relationship among the Koksoagmyut is now so close that many of the males seek their wives from other localities. This, of course, connects distant people, and interchange of the natives of both sexes is common.

Separation of couples is effected in a simple manner. The one who so desires leaves with little ceremony, but is sometimes sought for and compelled to return. Wives are often taken for a period, and an exchange of wives is frequent, either party being often happy to be released for a time, and returning without concern. There is so much intriguing and scandal-mongering among these people that a woman is often compelled by the sentiment of the community to relinquish her choice and join another who has bribed a conjurer to decide that until she comes to live with him a certain person will not be relieved from the evil spirit now tormenting him with disease.

The only way for the couple against whom such a plot has been laid to escape separation is for them to flee to another locality and remain there until the person gets well or dies, whereupon the conjurer declares it was their cohabitation as man and wife which afflicted the invalid. A designing woman will often cause a man to cast off the legal wife to whom he is much attached and come and live with her. In such instances the former wife seldom resents the intrusion upon her affections and rights but occasionally gives the other a severe thrashing and an injunction to look to herself lest she be discarded also. The children of the cast-off woman are frequently taken by her and they go to live with her relatives as menials on whom devolve the labor of severest kinds, she being glad to obtain the refuse of the hovel to support her life in order that her children may be well taken care of.

Some wives are considered as very "unlucky" and a ɘr trial are cast off to shift for themselves. A woman who has obtained the reputation of being unlucky for her husband is eschewed by all the men lest she work some charm on them.

In social relations the head of the family comes first, and the oldest son second, the other sons following according to respective ages.

The sons of the first wife, if there be more than one wife, take precedence over those of the second or third wife. It may be that a man has lost his first wife and takes another. The sons of these two are considered as those of one wife so far as their relation to each other is concerned. When the father becomes superanuated or his sons are old enough to enable him to live without exertion, the management of affairs devolves on the eldest son, and to the second is delegated the second place. Each may be occupied in different affairs, but the elder alone chooses what he himself shall do.

If the father live to a great age, and some of the men certainly attain the age of more than 80 years, he may have great grandchildren about him, and these never fail to show respect for their ancestor.

All this family may dwell in a single tent, or in two or more tents. Where the leader directs, there they all repair, although each one who is at the head of a family may be left to employ himself as he may prefer. These sons, with their wives and children, form a community, which may have other persons added to it, namely, the persons who are related to the wives of the sons. There may be but one community in a locality, and this is locally known to the white people as the "gang" of the head man.

Families whose members have decreased in number by death or by marriage may seek the companionship of one of these communities for protection. The new arrival at once acknowledges his dependence and is, in a manner, under the influence, if not control, of the leader of the community which he joins.

DREN.

A new born babe must not be washed until six or eight hours have elapsed. It is then placed to the breast and rarely gets any water to drink until old enough to help itself to it.

The child may be named while yet in utero. There being no distinctions for sex in names the appellation can scarcely be amiss. Several names may be acquired from the most trivial circumstances. Old names may be discarded and new names substituted or certain names applied by certain people and not used by others.

Love for offspring is of the deepest and purest character. I have never seen a disrespectful Eskimo child. Mothers and fathers never inflict corporal punishment on their children, for these are early taught to obey, or rather they are quick to perceive that their parents are their protectors and to them they must go for assistance. Orphan girls are taken as nurses for small children, and the nurse so employed has seldom any trouble in controlling the child.

Among young children at play the greatest harmony prevails. An accident resulting in sufficient harm to cause tears obtains the sympathy of all, who strive to appease the injured child by offers of the greatest share of the game, the little fellow often smiling with the prospective pleasure while the tears yet course down his begrimed cheeks. In a moment all is forgotten and joyous shouts sound merrily as the chubby youngsters of both sexes redouble their exertion in playing football or building toy houses in the newly fallen snow, where, on the bed of snow within the wall of the hut, the doll of ivory, wood or rags rolled into its semblance, plays the part of hostess whom they pretend to visit and with whom they converse.

Among the younger boys and girls, of 10 or 12, there is a great spirit of cheerful rivalry, to prove their ability to secure such food as they are able to capture. If they can procure enough to purchase some ammunition with which to kill ptarmigan they soon have a certain amount of credit. This enables them to provide some coveted luxury for their parents, who, of course, aid and encourage them to become successful hunters. Within the huts the girls display their skill by sewing fragments of cloth into garments for dolls or striving to patch their tattered clothes.

The older boys look with contempt upon these childish occupations and, to show their superiority, often torment the younger ones until the father or mother compels them to desist. Pranks of various kinds are played upon each other and they often exhibit great cunning in their devices to annoy. These boys are able to accompany their elders on hunting trips and run ahead of the team of dogs attached to the sled-

BURIAL CUSTOMS.

When a person dies the body is prepared by binding it with cords, the knees being drawn up and the heels placed against the body. The arms are tied down, and a covering of deerskin or sealskin is wrapped around the body and fastened. The nearest relatives on approach of death remove the invalid to the outside of the house, for if he should die within he must not be carried out of the door but through a hole cut in the side wall, and it must then be carefully closed to prevent the spirit of the person from returning. The body is exposed in the open air along the side of a large rock, or taken to the shore or hilltop, where stones of different sizes are piled around it to prevent the birds and animals from getting at it. (See Fig. 21.) It is considered a great offense if a dog be seen eating the flesh from a body. In case of a beloved child dying it is sometimes taken with the people to whom it belonged if they start for another locality before decomposition has progressed too far.

FIG. 21. Eskimo grave.

The dying person resigns himself to fate with great calmness. During illness, even though it be of most painful character, complaint is seldom heard; and so great is fortitude that the severest paroxysms of pain rarely produce even a movement of the muscles of the countenance.

The friends often exhibit an excessive amount of grief, but only in exceptional instances is much weeping indulged in. The loss of a husband often entails great hardships on the wife and small children, who eke out a scanty living by the aid of others who are scarcely able to maintain themselves.

These people have an idea of a future state and believe that death is merely the separation of the soul and the material body. The spirits of the soul go either up to the sky, "keluk," when they are called Kelugmyut, or down into the earth, "Nuna," and are called "Nunamyut." These two classes of spirits can hold communication with each other.

The place to which the soul goes depends on the conduct of the person on earth and especially on the manner of his death. Those who have died by violence or starvation and women who die in childbirth are supposed to go to the region above, where, though not absolutely in want, they still lack many of the luxuries enjoyed by the Nunamyut. All desire to go to the lower region and afterwards enjoy the pleasure of communicating with the living, which privilege is denied to those who go above.

If death result from natural causes the spirit is supposed to dwell on the earth after having undergone a probation of four years rest in the grave. During this time the grave may be visited and food offered and songs sung, and the offering, consisting of oil and flesh, with tobacco for smoking and chewing, is consumed by the living at the grave. Articles of clothing may also be deposited near the grave for the spirit to clothe itself after the garments have disappeared in the process of decay. It is customary to place such articles as may be deemed of immediate use for the departed soul in the grave at the time the body is interred. Ammunition, gun, kaiak and its appurtenances, with a shirt, gloves, knife, and a cup from which to drink are usually so deposited. The spirit of the dead man appropriates the spirits of these articles as soon as they decay. It is often said when an article becomes lost that so-and-so (mentioning his name), has taken it.

Some of the people prefer to expose their dead on the flat top of a high point extending into the water. The remains of others are placed along the shore and covered with rocks, while still others are taken to the smooth ridges on which may nearly always be found a huge bowlder carried by glacial action and deposited there. Here generally on the south side the body is placed on the bare rocky ridge and stones are piled around and upon it.

While these people have but little fear of the dead man's bones they do not approve of their being disturbed by others. The Indians, however, are known to rifle the graves of Eskimo to obtain the guns, clothing, etc., which the relatives of the deceased have placed there.

There are no such elaborate ceremonies pertaining to the festivals of the dead among the people of Hudson strait as obtain among the Eskimo of Alaska.

RELIGION.

Among these people there is no such person as chief; yet there is a recognized leader who is influenced by another, and this last is the conjurer or medicine-man. These two persons determine among themselves what shall be done. It sometimes happens that slight differences of opinion on the proper course to pursue collectively will cause them to go in different directions to meet after a few months' separation, by which time all is forgotten and former relations are resumed.

All the affairs of life are supposed to be under the control of spirits, each of which rules over a certain element, and all of which are under the direction of a greater spirit. Each person is supposed to be attended by a special guardian who is malignant in character, ever ready to seize upon the least occasion to work harm upon the individual whom it accompanies. As this is an evil spirit its good offices and assistance can be obtained by propitiation only. The person strives to keep the good will of the evil spirit by offerings of food, water, and clothing.

The spirit is often in a material form in the shape of a doll, carried somewhere about the person. If it is wanted to insure success in the chase, it is carried in the bag containing the ammunition.

When an individual fails to overcome the obstacles in his path the misfortune is attributed to the evil wrought by his attending spirit, whose good will must be invoked. If the spirit prove stubborn and reluctant to grant the needed assistance the person sometimes becomes angry with it and inflicts a serious chastisement upon it, deprives it of food, or strips it of its garments, until after a time it proves less refractory and yields obedience to its master. It often happens that the person is unable to control the influence of the evil-disposed spirit and the only way is to give it to some person without his knowledge. The latter becomes immediately under the control of the spirit, and the former, released from its baleful effects, is able successfully to prosecute the affairs of life. In the course of time the person generally relents and takes back the spirit he gave to another. The person on whom the spirit has been imposed should know nothing of it lest he should refuse to accept it. It is often given in the form of a bundle of clothing. It is supposed that if in hunting somebody merely takes the bag to hang it up the influence will pass to him. The spirit is supposed to be able to exert its influence only when carried by some object having life. Hence the person may cast it away for a time, and during that period it remains inert.

Besides this class of spirits, there are the spirits of the sea, the land, the sky (for be it understood that the Eskimo know nothing of the air), the winds, the clouds, and everything in nature. Every cove of the seashore, every point, island, and prominent rock has its guardian spirit. All are of the malignant type and to be propitiated only by acceptable offerings from persons who desire to visit the locality where it is supposed to reside. Of course some of the spirits are more powerful than others, and these are more to be dreaded than those able to inflict less harm.

These minor spirits are under the control of the great spirit, whose name is "Tung ak." This one great spirit is more powerful than all the rest besides. The lesser spirits are immediately under his control and ever ready to obey his command. The shaman (or conjurer) alone is supposed to be able to deal with the Tung ak. While the shaman does not profess to be superior to the Tung ak, he is able to enlist his assistance and thus be able to control all the undertakings his profession may call for.

This Tung ak is nothing more or less than death, which ever seeks to torment and harass the lives of people that their spirits may go to dwell with him.

A legend related of the origin of the Tung ak is as follows: A father had a son and daughter whom he loved very much. The children fell ill and at last died, although the father did all in his power to alleviate their sufferings, showing his kindness and attentions to the last moment. At their death the father became changed to a vicious spirit, roaming the world to destroy any person whom he might meet, determined that, as his dear children died, none others should live.

Tung ak visits people of all ages, constantly placing obstacles in their pathway to prevent the accomplishment of their desires, and provoking them beyond endurance so as to cause them to become ill and die and go to live with him. Tung ak no longer knows his own children and imagines all persons that he meets to be his children. Famine, disease, and death are sent abroad to search for these lost children.

People at last began to devise some means of thwarting the designs of Tung ak and discovered that a period of fasting and abstinence from contact with other people endowed a person with supernatural powers and enabled him to learn the secrets of Tung ak. This is accomplished by repairing to some lonely spot, where for a greater or less period the hermit abstains from food or water until the imagination is so worked upon that he believes himself imbued with the power to heal the sick and control all the destinies of life. Tung ak is supposed to stand near and reveal these things while the person is undergoing the test. When the person sees the evil one ready to seize upon him if he fails in the self-imposed task to become an "Angekok" or great one, he is much frightened and beseeches the terrible visitor to spare his life and give him the power to relieve his people from misfortune. Tung ak then takes pity on him, and imparts to him the secret of preserving life, or driving out the evil which causes death.

This is still the process by which the would-be shaman fits himself for his supernatural duties.

The newly fledged angekok returns to his people and relates what he has seen and what he has done. The listeners are awed by the recitals of the sufferings and ordeal, and he is now ready to accomplish his mission. When his services are required he is crafty enough to demand sufficient compensation, and frankly states that the greater the pay the greater the good bestowed. A native racked with pain will gladly part with all of his worldly possessions in order to be restored to health.

The shaman is blindfolded, or else has a covering thrown over his head to prevent his countenance from being seen during the incantation. The patient lies on the ground before him and when the shaman is worked up to the proper state of frenzy he prostrates himself upon the afflicted person and begins to chase the evil from its seat. The patient often receives blows and jerks sufficiently hard to dislocate the joints. As the spell progresses the shaman utters the most hideous noises, shouting here and there as the evil flees to another portion of the body, seeking a retreat from which the shaman shall be unable to dislodge it. After a time victory is declared; the operator claims to have the disease under his control, and although it should escape and make itself again felt in the patient, the shaman continues until the person either gets well or dies. If the former, the reputation of the shaman is increased proportionally to the payment bestowed by the afflicted one. If he dies, however, the conjurer simply refers his failure to the interference of something which was beyond his control. This may have been the influence of anything the shaman may at the moment think of, such as a sudden appearance in the changing auroras, a fall of snow, or a dog knocking down something outside of the house. If the people deny that the dog did the act, the shaman replies that the dog was the instrument in the hands of a spirit which escaped him. Any little incident is sufficient to thwart the success of his manipulations. If any person be the subject of the shaman's displeasure he or she must undergo some sort of punishment or do an act of penance for the interference. It is not unusual to see a person with the harness of a dog on his back. This is worn to relieve him or somebody else of a spell of the evil spirit. The tail of a living dog is often cut from its body in order that the fresh blood may be cast upon the ground to be seen by the spirit who has caused the harm, and thus he may be appeased. Numerous mutilations are inflicted upon animals at the command of the conjurer, who must be consulted on nearly all the important undertakings of life in order that he may manage the spirits which will insure success.

The implicit belief in these personages is wonderful. Almost every person who can do anything not fully understood by others has more or less reputation as a shaman.

Some men, by observation, become skilled in weather lore, and get a great reputation for supernatural knowledge of the future weather. Others again are famous for suggesting charms to insure success in hunting, and, in fact, the occasions for consulting the conjurer are practically innumerable. One special qualification of a good shaman is the ability to attract large numbers of deer or other game into the region where he and his friends are hunting.

Some of these shamans are superior hunters and, as their experience teaches them the habits of the deer, they know at any season exactly where the animals are and can anticipate their future movements, influenced greatly by the weather. Thus the prophet is able to estimate the proximity or remoteness of the various herds of stragglers from the main body of deer which were in the locality during the preceding fall months. These hunters have not only a local reputation but are known as far as the people have any means of communication.

In order to cause the deer to move toward the locality where they may be desired the shaman will erect, on a pole placed in a favorable position, an image of some famous hunter and conjurer. The image will represent the power of the person as conjurer and the various paraphernalia attached to the image assist in controlling the movements of the animals.

I obtained one of these objects at Fort Chimo. (Fig. 22.) It is quite elaborate and requires a detailed description. It is intended to repre-

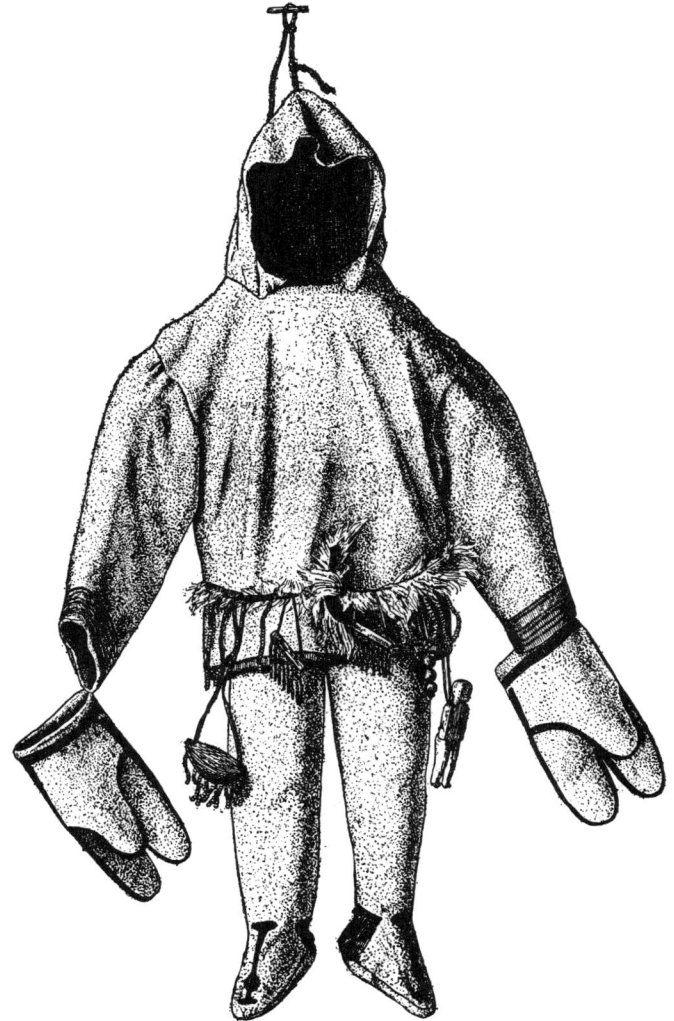

FIG. 22. Magic doll.

sent a celebrated conjurer living on the eastern shore of Hudson bay. He occasionally visited Fort Chimo where his reputation as a hunter had preceded him. His name is Sa'pa.

He is dressed in a complete suit of the woolen stuff called "strouds" at Fort Chimo, trimmed with black and with fancy tartan gartering. In the belt of polar-bear skin (kak-cung'-unt) (Fig. 23) are hung strings of colored beads and various amulets. These are, first, a wooden doll (Fig. 24) (ĭnug'-wak, a little man) hung to the belt so that he faces outward and is always on the alert; then, two bits of wood (agówak) (Fig. 25) to which hang strands of beads and lead drops; next, a string of three bullets (Fig. 26) to symbolize the readiness of the hunter when game approaches; and, last, a semicircular piece of wood ornamented with strings of beads (Fig. 27).

This last is called the tu-a'-vi-tok, or hastener. The hunter holds it in his hand when he sights the game, and the tighter he grasps it the

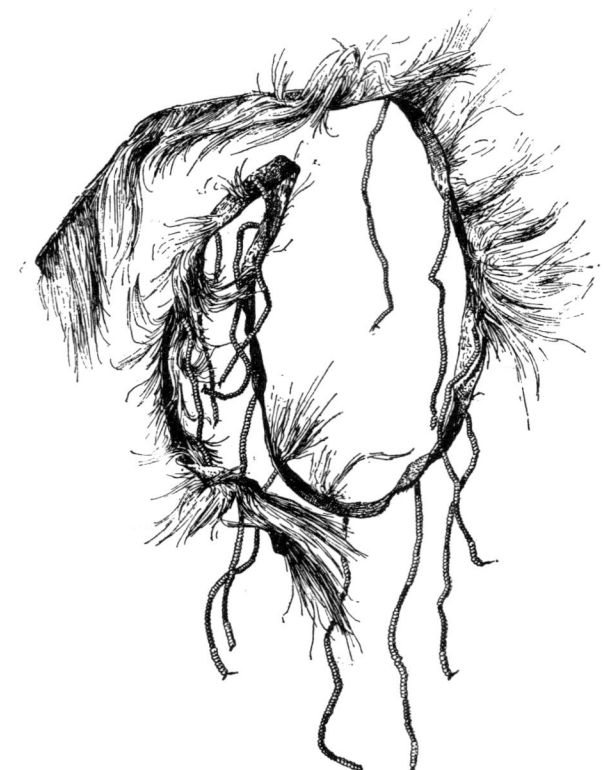

FIG. 23. Belt of magic doll.

faster he is supposed to get over the ground. It is supposed that by the use of this one may be able to travel faster than the wind and not even touch the earth over which he passes with such incredible speed that he overtakes the deer in a moment. The entire affair, as it hung on the pole, was called tung wa'gn e'nog ang', or a materialization of a Tung ak.

This object hung there for several days until I thought it had served its purpose and could now afford to change ownership. The local conjurer was thus compelled to invoke the assistance of another. I am happy to add that the deer did come, and in thousands, actually running among the houses of the station.

The shaman of the community possesses great influence over its members. He very frequently decides the course to be pursued by man and wife in their relations with each other, and, conspiring with some evil old woman who loves to show preference for a young man, he often decrees that husband or wife shall be cast off.

If the person become ill the wife is often accused of working some charm on her husband in order that she may enjoy the favors of another.

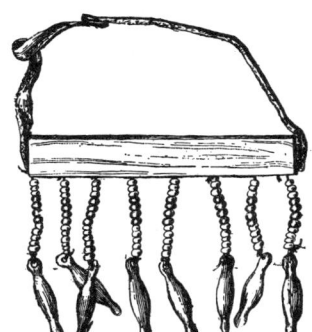

FIG. 25. Talisman.

FIG. 24. Talisman attached
to magic doll.

FIG. 26. Talisman.

A woman whose husband had recently died was espoused by another who soon after became violently ill. She nursed him with the greatest assiduity until he convalesced. At this period his mother, with the advice of some old hags, decreed that she had been the sole cause of her husband's illness and must leave the tent. Her things were pitched out and she was compelled to journey in quest of her relatives.

Another illustration came under my notice.

A widow was taken to wife by a Koksoak Eskimo. He was soon taken violently ill and she was accused by the shaman of being the cause of it, as the spirit of her deceased husband was jealous. Unless she were cast off the Koksoak man would never recover. It was then also found that unless the wife of another man should desert him and become the wife of a man who already had two of this woman's sisters as wives the sick man would die. The woman and her husband escaped divorce by fleeing from the camp.

The shaman may do about as he pleases with the marriage ties, which oftener consist of sealskin thongs than respect and love. Many

old hags have acquired great reputations for being able to interpret dreams. An instance of dream interpretation, which also illustrates how a person may acquire a new name, came under my observation. A woman, sitting alone, heard a noise like the rapping of someone at the door desiring admittance. She said, " Come in." No one appeared, and she inquired of the girl who acted as nurse for her child if anyone had knocked at the door. A negative answer was given. Further questioning of a white man, who was asleep near by, revealed that he had made no such sound. The woman knew

FIG. 27. Talisman.

that no man had died within the place and so his spirit could not be seeking admittance. She went to an old woman and related the affair, and was informed that it was the rapping of her brother, who had died suddenly some two years before. She must go home and prepare a cup of tea, with a slice of bread, and give it to the nurse, as her brother, Nakvak (the one who died) was hungry and wanted food. She especially enjoined upon the woman that the girl must now be known as Nakvak (meaning "found") and that through her the dead would procure the food which, although it subserves a good purpose in nourishing the living, tends, by its accompanying spirit, to allay the pangs of hunger in the dead.

As I have already said, everything in the world is believed to have its attendant spirit. The spirits of the lower animals are like those of men, but of an inferior order. As these spirits, of course, can not be destroyed by killing the animals, the Eskimo believe that no amount of slaughter can realy decrease the numbers of the game.

A great spirit controls the reindeer. He dwells in a huge cavern near the end of Cape Chidley. He obtains and controls the spirit of every deer which is slain or dies, and it depends on his good will whether the people shall obtain future supplies. The form of the spirit is that of a huge white bear. The shaman has the power to prevail upon the spirit to send the deer to the people who are represented as suffering

for want of food.   The spirit is informed that the people have in no way
offended him, as the shaman, as a mediator between the spirit and the
people, has taken great care that the past food was all eaten and that
last spring, when the female deer were returning to him to be delivered
of their young, none of the young (or fœtal) deer were devoured by the
dogs.   After much incantation the shaman announces that the spirit
condescends to supply the people with spirits of the deer in a material
form and that soon an abundance will be in the land.   He enjoins upon
the people to slay and thus obtain the approval of the spirit, which loves
to see good people enjoy an abundance, knowing that so long as the
people refrain from feeding their dogs with the unborn young, the
spirits of the deer will in time return again to his guardianship.

Certain parts of the first deer killed must be eaten raw, others discarded, and others must be eaten cooked.   The dogs must not be allowed to taste of the flesh, and not until an abundance has been obtained must they be allowed to gnaw at the leg bones, lest the guardian
spirit of the deer be offended and refuse to send further supplies.   If
by some misfortune the dogs get at the meat, a piece of the offending
dog's tail is cut off or his ear is cropped to allow a flow of blood.

Ceremonies of some kind attend the capture of the first slain animal
of all the more important kinds.   I unfortunately had no opportunity
of witnessing many of these ceremonies.

As a natural consequence of the superstitious beliefs that I have described, the use of amulets is universal.   Some charms are worn to
ward off the attacks of evil-disposed spirits.   Other charms are worn as
remembrances of deceased relatives.   These have the form of a headless doll depending from some portion of the garment worn on the upper part of the body.

As many of their personal names are derived from
natural objects, it is usual for the person to wear a
little image of the object for which he is named or a
portion of it; for example, a wing of the bird, or a bit
of the animal's skin.   This is supposed to gratify the
spirit of the object.   Strange or curious objects never
before seen are sometimes considered to bring success to the finder

Two articles selected from my collection will illus-
trate different forms of amulets.   The first, No. 3018,
is a little wooden model of a kaiak.   The other (3090,
Fig. 28) was worn on the back of a woman's coat.   It
is a small block of wood carved into four human
heads.   These heads represent four famous conjurers
noted for their skill in driving away diseases.   The
woman, who came from the eastern shore of Hudson's

Fig. 28. Eskimo wo-
man's amulet.

bay, was troubled with rheumatism and wore this charm from time to
time as she felt the twinges of pain.   She assured me that the pain

always disappeared in a few hours when she wore it. It was with the greatest difficulty that I persuaded her to part with it. She was, however, about to return home, and could get another there.

OUTDOOR LIFE.

The Eskimo acquire an extended knowledge of the country by early accompanying their parents on hunting trips, and as they have to rely upon memory alone, they must be observant and carefully mark the surroundings from all the views afforded. The faculty of memory is thus cultivated to an astonishing degree, and seldom fails, even in the most severe weather, to insure safety for the individual. I knew a native stick his ramrod in the ground among scattered stalks of grass which attained the height of the rod, yet after several hours he found the spot again without the least hesitation. Every rise of land, every curve of a stream, every cove in the seashore, has a name descriptive of something connected with it, and these names are known to all who have occasion to visit the place. Though the aspect of the land is entirely changed by the mantle of snow which covers all the smaller objects, a hunter will go straight to the place where the carcass of a single deer was cached many months before on the open beach. The Eskimo are faithful guides, and when confidence is shown to be reposed in them they take a pride in leading the party by the best route. In traveling by night they use the north star for the guide. Experience teaches them to foretell the weather, and some reliance may be placed on their predictions.

Their knowledge of the seasons is also wonderful. The year begins when the sun has reached its lowest point, that is, at the winter solstice, and summer begins with the summer solstice. They recognize the arrival of the solstices by the bearing of the sun with reference to certain fixed landmarks.

The seasons have distinctive names, and these are again subdivided into a great number, of which there are more during the warmer weather than during the winter. The reason for this is obvious: so many changes are going on during the summer and so few during the winter. The principal events are the return of the sun, always a signal of joy to the people; the lengthening of the day; the warm weather in March when the sun has attained sufficient height to make his rays less slanting and thus be more fervent; the melting of the snow; the breaking up of the ice; the open water; the time of birth of various seals; the advent of exotic birds; the nesting of gulls, eiders, and other native birds; the arrival of white whales and the whaling season; salmon fishing; the ripening of salmonberries and other species of edibles; the time of reindeer crossing the river; the trapping of fur-bearing animals and hunting on land and water for food. Each of these periods has a special name applied to it, although several may overlap each other. The appearance of mosquitoes, sandflies, and horseflies are marked by dates anticipated with considerable apprehension of annoyance.

In order to sketch the annual routine of life, I will begin with the breaking up of the ice in spring. The Koksoak river breaks its ice about the last of May. This period, however, may vary as much as ten days earlier and twenty days later than the date specified. The ice in Ungava bay, into which that river flows, must be free from the greater portion of the shore ice before the river ice can push its way out to sea. The winds alone influence the bay ice, and the character of the weather toward the head waters of the river determines its time of breaking.

The Eskimo has naturally a keen perception of the signs in the sky and is often able to predict with certainty the effects of the preceding weather. When the season has sufficiently advanced all the belongings of each family are put together and transported down the river on sleds to where the ice has not yet gone from the mouth of the river. It is very seldom that the river ice extends down so far. To the edge of the ice the tent and dogs, with the umiak, kaiak, and other personal property, are taken and then stored on shore until the outside ice is free.

The men wander along the beach or inland hunting for reindeer, ptarmigan, hares, and other land game. The edge of the water is searched for waterfowl of various kinds which appear earliest. Some venturesome seals appear. In the course of a few days the ice in the river breaks up and the shore ice of the bay is free; and if there is a favorable wind it soon permits the umiak to be put into the water, where, by easy stages, depending on the weather, the quantity of floating ice, and the food supply, the hunters creep alongshore to the objective point, be it either east or west of the Koksoak. Sometimes the party divide, some going in one direction and others in another.

The men seek for seals, hunting in the kaiak, the women and children searching the islets and coves for anything edible. As soon as the season arrives for the various gulls, eiders, and other sea birds to nest the women and children are in high glee. Every spot is carefully examined, and every accessible nest of a bird is robbed of its contents. By the 25th of June the people have exhausted the supply of eggs from the last situations visited and now think of returning, as the birds have again deposited eggs and the seals are becoming scarcer.

The Eskimo arrange to assist the company to drive white whales when the season arrives. This is as soon as they appear in the river at a sufficient distance up to warrant that the measures pursued will not drive them out of the fresh water, for if they left they would not soon return. The date usually fixed upon is about the 12th of July. The natives are summoned, and a large sailboat or the small steam launch is sent along the coast to the place where the people were expected to arrive the 5th of the month. The natives are brought to the whaling station, where they encamp, to await the setting of the nets forming the sides of the inclosure into which the whales are to be driven.

The natives spear the whales in the pound, drag them ashore, skin them, and help take the oil and skins to the post, some eight miles farther up the river.

The same natives who engaged in the whaling are employed to attend the nets for salmon, which arrive at variable dates from the 25th of July to the 1st of September. Two or more adult male Eskimo, with their relatives, occupy a certain locality, generally known by the name of the person in charge of that season's work. The place is occupied until the runs of the fish are over, when it is time for the natives to be up the river to spear reindeer which cross the river.

This hunting lasts until the deer have begun to rut and the males have lost the fat from the small of the back. The season is now so far advanced that the ice is already forming along the shore, and unless the hunter intends to remain in that locality he would better begin to descend the river to a place nearer the sea. The river may freeze in a single night and the umiak be unable to withstand the constant strain of the sharp-edged cakes of floating ice.

The head of the family decides where the winter is to be passed and moves thither with his party at once. Here he has a few weeks of rest from the season's labors, or spends the time constructing a sled for the winter journeys he may have in view. The snow has now fallen so that a snow house may be constructed and winter quarters taken up. A number of steel traps are procured to be set for foxes and other fur-bearing animals. The ptarmigans arrive in large flocks and are eagerly hunted for their flesh and feathers. The birds are either consumed for food or sold to the company; which pays 6¼ cents for four, and purchases the body feathers of the birds at the rate of 4 pounds of the feathers for 25 cents.

The Eskimo soon consume the amount of deer meat they brought with them on their return and subsist on the flesh of the ptarmigan until the ice is firm enough to allow the sleds to be used to transport to the present camp meat of animals slain in the fall.

The traps are visited and the furs are sold to the company in exchange for flour, tea, sugar, molasses, biscuit, clothing, and ammunition. Hunting excursions are made to various localities for stray bands of deer that have become separated from the larger herds.

The white men employés of the company have been engaged in cutting wood for the next year's fuel, and the Eskimo with their dog teams are hired to haul it to the bank, where it may be floated down in rafts when the river opens.

Thus passes the year in the life of the Eskimo of the immediate vicinity of Fort Chimo. Some of the Koksoagmyut do not engage in these occupations. Some go to another locality to live by themselves; others do not work or hunt, because it is not their nature to do so.

In all undertakings for themselves they deliberate long, with much hesitation and apparent reluctance, before they decide upon the line of action. They consult each other and weigh the advantages of this over that locality for game, and speculate on whether they will be afflicted with illness of themselves or family. When the resolution is finally made to journey to a certain place, only the most serious obstacles can thwart their purpose.

At all seasons of the year the women have their allotted duties, which they perform without hesitation. They bring the wood and the water, and the food from the field, if it is not too distant, in which case the men go after it with the dog teams. The women also fashion the skins into clothing and other articles, and do the cooking. After a hunt of several days' duration the husband's appearance is anxiously awaited, as is indicated by the family scanning the direction whence he is expected. The load is taken from the sled or boat and the incidents of the chase recited to the ever ready listeners.

In the early spring the women are busily engaged in making boots for summer wear. The skins of the seals have been prepared the fall before and stored away until wanted. The method of tanning the skins is the same for each species, differing only in its size and weight.

Certain large vessels made of wood or metal, chiefly the latter, as they are easily procured from the traders, are used to hold a liquid, which is from time to time added to. When a sufficient amount is collected it is allowed to ferment. During the interval the skin of the seal is cleansed from fat and flesh. The hair has been removed by shaving it off or by pulling it out. The skin is then dressed with an instrument designed for that purpose, made of ivory, deerhorn, stone, or even a piece of tin set in the end of a stout stick several inches long. The skin is held in the hand and the chisel-shaped implement is repeatedly pushed from the person and against a portion of the skin until that part becomes pliable and soft enough to work. It is further softened by rubbing between the hands with a motion similar to that of the washerwoman rubbing clothing of the wash. Any portion of the skin which will not readily yield to this manipulation is chewed with the front teeth until it is reduced to the required pliability. After this operation has been completed the skin is soaked in the liquid, which has now ripened to a sufficient degree to be effective. In this it is laid for a period lasting from several hours to two or three days. The skin is now taken out and dried. The subsequent operation of softening is similar to that just described, and is final. It is now ready to be cut into the required shape for the various articles for which it is intended. If it is designed for boots for a man, the measure of the height of the leg is taken. The length and width of the sole is measured by the hand, stretching so far and then bending down the long or middle finger until the length is measured. The width of one, two, or more fingers is sometimes used in addition to the span. The length is thus marked and the skin folded over so as to have it doubled. The knife used in cutting is shaped like the round knife used by the harness-maker or shoemaker.

There is in our collection a wooden model of this form of knife (No. 3022), which nowadays always has a blade of metal. Formerly slate, flint, or ivory was used for these blades.

The instrument is always pushed by the person using it. The eye alone guides the knife, except on work for a white man, and then greater care is exercised and marks employed indicating the required size. This round knife is called úlo.

Another important duty of the women is taking care of the family boots. When a pair of boots has been worn for some time, during a few hours in warm weather they absorb moisture and become nearly half an inch thick on the soles. When taken off they must be turned inside out and dried, then chewed and scraped by some old woman, who is only too glad to have the work for the two or three biscuit she may receive as pay. Any leak or hole is stitched, and when the sole has holes worn through it, it is patched by sewing a piece on the under side. The thread used in sewing the boots is selected from the best strips of sinew from the reindeer or seal.

Some women excel in boot-making, and at some seasons do nothing but make boots, while the others in return prepare the other garments. When the time comes in spring for making sealskin clothes, the women must not sew on any piece of deerskin which has not yet been sewed, lest the seals take offense and desert the locality which has been selected for the spring seal hunt, to which all the people look forward with longing, that they may obtain a supply of food different from that which they have had during the long winter months. As there can be no harm in killing a deer at this season, the flesh may be used, but the skin must be cast away.

As before stated, the entire family accompany the expeditions; and as the females are often the more numerous portion of the population, they row the umiak at their leisure, now and then stopping to have a few hours' run on shore and again embarking. While thus journeying they are at times a sleepy crowd, until something ahead attracts attention; then all become animated, pursuing the object, if it be a half-fledged bird, until it is captured. Great amusement is thus afforded for the time, after which they relapse until some excitement again arouses them from their apparent lethargy. At the camp the men go in quest of larger game, leaving the women and children, who search the shore for any living creature they may find, destroying all that comes in their way. Smoking, eating, and sleeping occupy them until they arrive at a locality where food is abundant. There they earnestly strive to slay all that comes within reach, and thus often obtain much more than they require, and the remainder is left to putrefy on the rocks. The women do the skinning of the seals and birds obtained on this trip. The skins of birds are removed in a peculiar manner. The wings are cut off at the body, and through the incision all the flesh and bones are taken out. The skin is then turned inside out. The grease is removed by scraping and chewing. The skin is dried and preserved for wear on the feet or for the purpose of cleansing the hands, which have become soiled with blood or other offal in skinning large game.

When the season arrives for hunting the reindeer for their skins, with which to make clothing for winter, the women help to prepare the flesh and bring the wood and water for the camp, while the men are ever on the alert for the herds of deer on the land or crossing the water. The women hang the skins over poles until the greater portion of the animal matter is dry, when they roll them up and store them away until the party is ready to return to the permanent camp for the winter. Here the skins collected are carefully examined and suitable ones selected for winter garments.

The skins are moistened with water and the adherent fleshy particles are removed with a knife. They are then roughly scraped and again wetted, this time with urine, which is supposed to render them more pliable. The operation is practically the same as that of tanning sealskins. The hair is, of course, left on the skin. When the skins are finally dry and worked to the required pliability, they are cut into shape for the various articles of apparel. The thread used in sewing is simply a strip of sinew of the proper size. The fibers are separated by splitting off a sufficient amount, and with the finger nail the strip is freed from all knots or smaller strands which would prevent drawing through the needle holes. The thread for this purpose is never twisted or plaited. The needle is one procured from the trader. Small bone needles, imitations of these, are sometimes used. In former years the bone needle was the only means of carrying the thread, but this has now, except in the rarest instances, been entirely superseded by one of metal.

The thimble is simply a piece of stiff sealskin sewed into a ring half an inch wide to slip on the first finger, and has the same name as that member. In sewing of all kinds the needle is pointed toward the operator. The knife used in cutting skins is the same as that previously described. Scissors are not adapted to cutting a skin which retains the fur. So far as my observations goes, scissors are used only for cutting textile fabrics procured from the store.

In the use of a knife women acquire a wonderous dexterity, guiding it to the desired curve with much skill, or using the heel of the blade to remove strips which may need trimming off.

TATTOOING.

In former years the women were fancifully tattooed with curved lines and rows of dots on the face, neck, and arms, and on the legs up to mid-thigh. This custom, however, fell into disuse because some

shaman declared that a prevailing misfortune was the result of the tattooing. At present the tattooing is confined to a few single dots on
the body and face. When a girl arrives at puberty she is taken to a
secluded locality by some old woman versed in the art and stripped
of her clothing. A small quantity of half-charred lamp wick of moss is
mixed with oil from the lamp. A needle is used to prick the skin, and
the pasty substance is smeared over the wound. The blood mixes with
it, and in a day or two a dark-bluish spot alone is left. The operation
continues four days. When the girl returns to the tent it is known
that she has begun to menstruate. A menstruating woman must not
wear the lower garments she does at other times. The hind flap of her
coat must be turned up and stitched to the back of the garment. Her
right hand must be half-gloved, or, in other words, the first two joints
of each finger of that hand must be uncovered. The left hand also remains uncovered. She must not touch certain skins and food which
at that particular season are in use.

CLOTHING.

Like most Eskimo, the Koksoagmyut are clothed almost entirely
in the skins of animals, though the men now wear breeches of mole-
skin, duck, jeans, or denim procured from the trading store. Reindeerskin is the favorite material for clothing, though skins of the different seals are also used. The usual garments are a hooded frock,
of different shapes for the sexes, with breeches and boots. The latter
are of various shapes for different weather, and there are many patterns of mittens. Rain frocks of seal entrail are also worn over the
furs in stormy weather. Some of the people are very tidy and keep
their clothing in a respectable condition. Others are careless and
often present a most filthy sight. The aged and orphans, unless the
latter be adopted by some well-to-do person, must often be content
with the cast-off apparel of their more fortunate fellow-beings.

The hair of the skins wears off in those places most liable to be
in contact with other objects. The elbows, wrists, and knees often are
without a vestige of hair on the clothing. The skin wears through
and then is patched with any kind of a piece, which often presents a
ludicrous appearance.

The young boys and girls are dressed alike, and the females do not
wear the garments of the adults until they arrive at puberty. It is a
ludicrous sight to witness some of the little ones scarcely able to walk
dressed in heavy deerskin clothing, which makes them appear as
thick as they are tall. They exhibit about the same amount of pride
of their new suits as the civilized boy does. They are now able to go
out into the severest weather, and seem to delight in rolling around in
the snow.

Infants at the breast, so small as to be carried in the mother's
hood, are often dressed in skins of the reindeer fawns. The garment

for these is a kind of "combination," the trousers and body sewed together and cut down the back to enable the infant to get them on. A cap of calico or other cloth and a pair of skin stockings completes the suit.

Both men and women wear, as an additional protection for their feet in cold weather, a pair or two of short stockings, locally known as "duffles," from the name of the material of which they are made. These "duffles" are cut into the form of a slipper and incase the stockings of the feet. Over these are worn the moccasins, made of tanned and smoked deerskin. The Eskimo women are not adepts in making moccasins; a few only can form a well-fitting pair. They often employ the Indian women to make them, and, in return, give a pair of sealskin boots, which the Indian is unable to make, but highly prizes for summer wear in the swamps.

The Koksoagmyut do not wear caps, the hood of the frocks being the only head covering. There is, however, in my collection a cap obtained from one of the so-called "Northerners," who came to Fort Chimo to trade. This cap (No. 3242, Fig. 29) was evidently copied from some white man's cap. The front and crown of the cap are made of guillemot and sea-pigeon skins, and the sealskin neckpiece also is lined with these skins, so that when it is turned up the whole cap seems to be made of bird skins.

We may now proceed to the description of the different garments in detail.

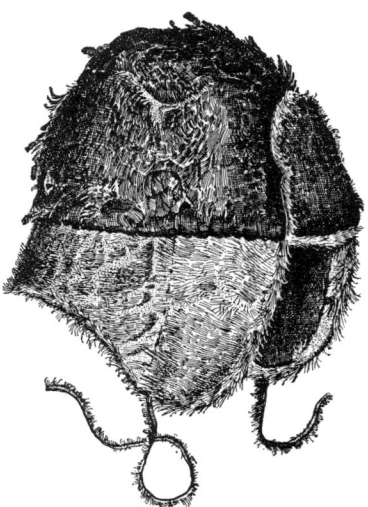

FIG. 29. Eskimo birdskin cap.

The coat worn by the men and boys, and by the girls until they arrive at womanhood, has the form of a loose shirt, seldom reaching more than 2 or 3 inches below the hips, and often barely covering the hips. The neck hole is large enough to admit the head into the hood, which may be thrown back or worn over the head in place of a cap.

The Innuit of the southern shore of the western end of Hudson Strait often cut the coat open in front as far up as the breast (Figs. 30 and 31, No. 3224). The favorite material for these coats is the skin of the reindeer, three good-sized skins being required to make a full-sized coat for a man. Coats made of light summer skins are used as under-clothing in winter and for the only body clothing in summer. The skin of the harp seal (*Phoca grœnlandica*) is also used for coats, but only when the supply of reindeerskin runs short, or when a man can afford to have an extra coat to wear in wet weather. It is not a very good

11 ETH——14

material for clothing, as the skin is roughly tanned, and no amount of working will render it more than moderately pliable. Figs. 32 and 33 represent a sealskin coat. These coats are often trimmed round the edges with fringes of deerskin 2 or 3 inches wide, or little pendants of ivory.

Fig. 30. Eskimo man's deerskin coat (front).

The collection contains eleven of these coats, Nos. 3221, 3498–3500, and 3558 of deerskin, and Nos. 3228, 3533–3537 of sealskin.

The peculiar shape of the woman's coat is best understood by reference to the accompanying figures (Figs. 34, 35, 36, 37 and 38). The enormous hood is used for carrying the infant. When sitting, the female usually disposes the front flap so that it will lie spread upon the thighs, or else pushes it between her legs, while the hind flap is either thrown aside or sat upon.

It is not unusual for the women to display considerable taste in ornamenting their garments, using the steel-gray pelt of the harp seal to contrast with the black of the harbor seal, and so on. The edges of the hood and sleeves are frequently trimmed with skin from a dark colored young dog, or a strip of polar bear skin, whose long white hairs shed the rain better than those of any other mammal.

It is not rare to find loops of sinew or of sealskin attached to the breast or back of a woman's garments. These are for tying small articles, such as a needle case or a snuff-bag, to the clothing for convenience and to prevent loss.

A peculiar style of ornamentation is shown in Fig. 39 and 40, No. 3005, a woman's coat from Fort Chimo. The front of the skirt is fringed

FIG. 31. Eskimo man's deerskin coat (back.)

with little lead drops, bean-shaped in the upper row and pear-shaped in the lower, and pierced so that they can be sewed on. These lead drops are furnished by the trader at the price of about a cent and a half each, in trade. The trimming of this frock cost, therefore, about $4. The four objects dangling from the front of the frock are pewter spoon-bowls. Across the breast is a fringe of short strings of different colored beads, red, black, yellow, white, and blue. Jingling ornaments are much prized.

The tin tags from plug tobacco are eagerly sought for, perforated and attached in pendant strands 3 or 4 inches long to sealskin strips and thus serve the place of beads. I saw one woman who certainly had not less than a thousand of these tags jingling as she walked. I have also seen coins of various countries attached to the arms and dress. One coin was Brazilian, another Spanish, and several were

FIG. 32. Eskimo man's sealskin coat (front).

English. Coins of the provinces were quite numerous. These were all doubtless obtained from the sailors who annually visit the place, in exchange for little trinkets prepared by the men and women.

The collection contains five of these coats, Nos. 3005, 3225–3227 of deerskin, and 3504 of sealskin. The last is a very elaborate garment, made of handsomely contrasted pieces of the skin of two kinds of seals, the harbor seal and the harp seal, arranged in a neat pattern.

It is not common to come across a garment of this kind, as the skins of the proper or desired kinds are sometimes hard to obtain.

The woman may be several years in getting the right kind and may have effected many exchanges before being suited with the quality and color. The darkest skins of the Ka sig yak (harbor seal) are highly prized by both sexes. The women set the higher value upon them. The men wear two styles of leg cov- ering, namely, breeches like a white man's, but not open in front, and reaching but a short distance below the knees, or trousers ending in stocking feet. Sometimes in very cold weather these trousers may be worn under the breeches.   Both breeches and trousers are very short-waisted.   Long stockings of short-haired deerskin with the hair in are also worn.   The women in winter wear breeches made of deer- skin fastened around the hips by means of a drawstring and extend- ing down the legs to where the tops of the boots will cover them a few inches.   Some of the women wear trousers which reach only to the up- per part of the thighs and are con- tinuous with the boot which covers the foot, though in that case a pair of half-boots are added to protect the feet.   The hips are covered with breeches which descend low enough on the thigh to be covered by the leggings.   This style of apparel for the lower portion of the body is

FIG. 33.—Eskimo man's sealskin coat (side).

often extravagantly patched with various colored pieces of white and dark strips of skin from the abdomen and sides of the reindeer. When new and not soiled they are quite attractive and often contrast well with the tastefully ornamented coat.

The long boots or leggings are removed when dirty work is to be done. Thus, skins to be scraped and dressed are held against the bare leg.

The leggings also serve as pockets to hold various kinds of little things, like knives, tobacco, and so on.

A person rarely owns more than a single pair of breeches; con- sequently I was unable to obtain any for the collection.

The boots and shoes are of different materials and somewhat differ- ent patterns for different seasons of the year.   All have moccasin

soles of stout material turned up an inch or two all round the foot, a
tongue covering the top of the foot, joined to a broad heel band which
passes round behind the ankle.   Then the legs are either made long
enough to reach to the knee or else almost to the ankle.   These half-
boots are worn over the fur stockings in warm weather, or outside the

Fig. 34. Eskimo woman's deerskin coat.

long boots in very severe weather.   Indian moccasins are also worn,
sometimes over a pair of inside shoes and sometimes as inside shoes.

For thick waterproof soles the skin of the beaver or the harp seal is
used.   The former wears the better.   White whale skin is also used

for indoor shoes, or for shoes to be worn in cold dry weather; the skins of the smaller seals are used, sometimes with the flesh side out and the hair in, sometimes with the grain side out. These thinner skins are comparatively waterproof if the black epidermis is allowed to remain

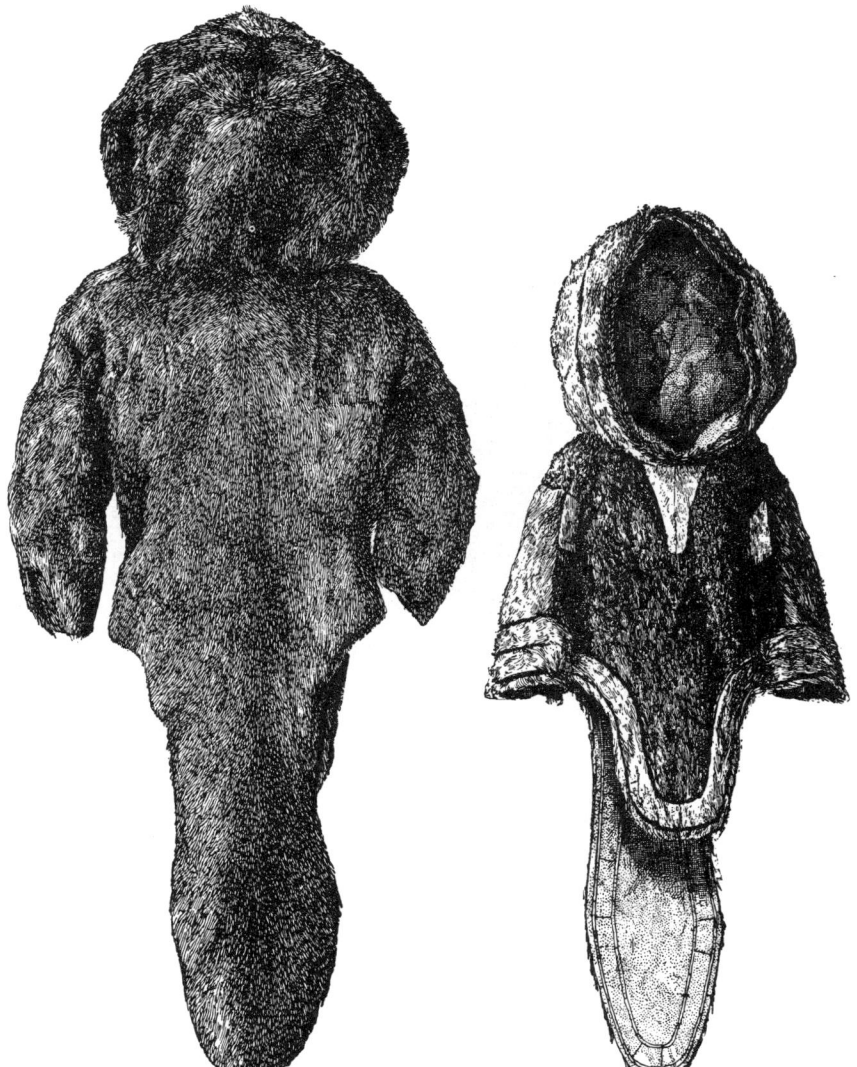

FIG. 35. Eskimo woman's deerskin coat.　　　FIG. 36. Eskimo women's deerskin coat.

on. The beautiful creamy-white leather, made by allowing the skin to ferment until hair and epidermis are scraped off together and then stretching the skin and exposing it to dry cold air, does not resist water at all, and can only be used for soles in perfectly dry weather.

Buckskin soles are also used to enable the wearer to walk better with snowshoes on, as the feet are not so liable to slip or clog with snow as they would be if the footing were of sealskin. This latter has also another serious disadvantage. If it is very cold it does not permit the moisture from the feet to pass out as it freezes, rendering the boot stiff and slippery on the snowshoe, while the buckskin is porous and readily allows the moisture to escape.

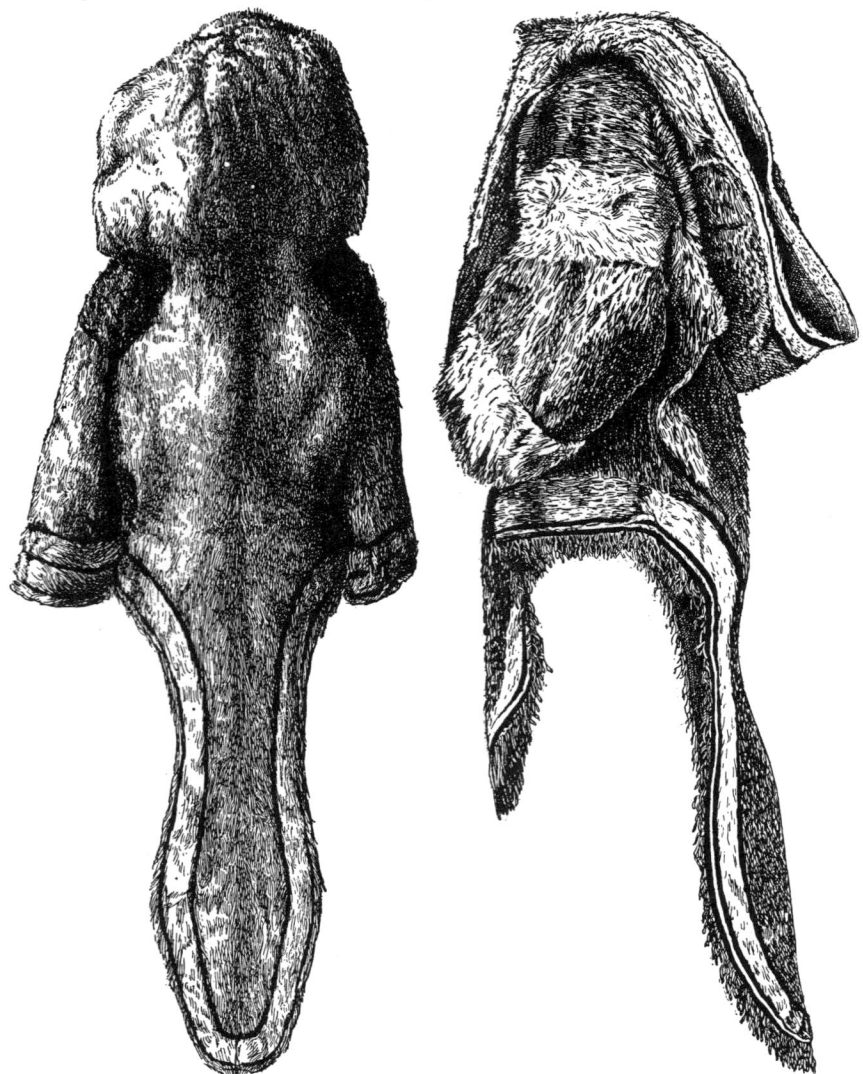

FIG. 37. Eskimo women's deerskin coat (back).   FIG. 38.—Eskimo woman's deerskin coat (side).

The tongue and heel band are generally made of tanned sealskin, contrasting colors being often used. The legs are of sealskin, with the hair on, or of reindeer skin.

The figures represent a pair of sealskin boots with buckskin feet (Fig. 41) and a pair of half boots with white sealskin soles, black sealskin tongue and heelstrap, and buckskin tops (Fig. 42). The tanned and smoked reindeer skin for these tops was purchased from the Nascopie Indians.

A peculiar style of shoe (Fig. 43), of which I collected four pairs, is used by the so-called "Northerners," who derive most of their subsistence from the sea in winter, and who constantly have to travel on the ice, which is often very slippery. To prevent slipping, narrow strips of

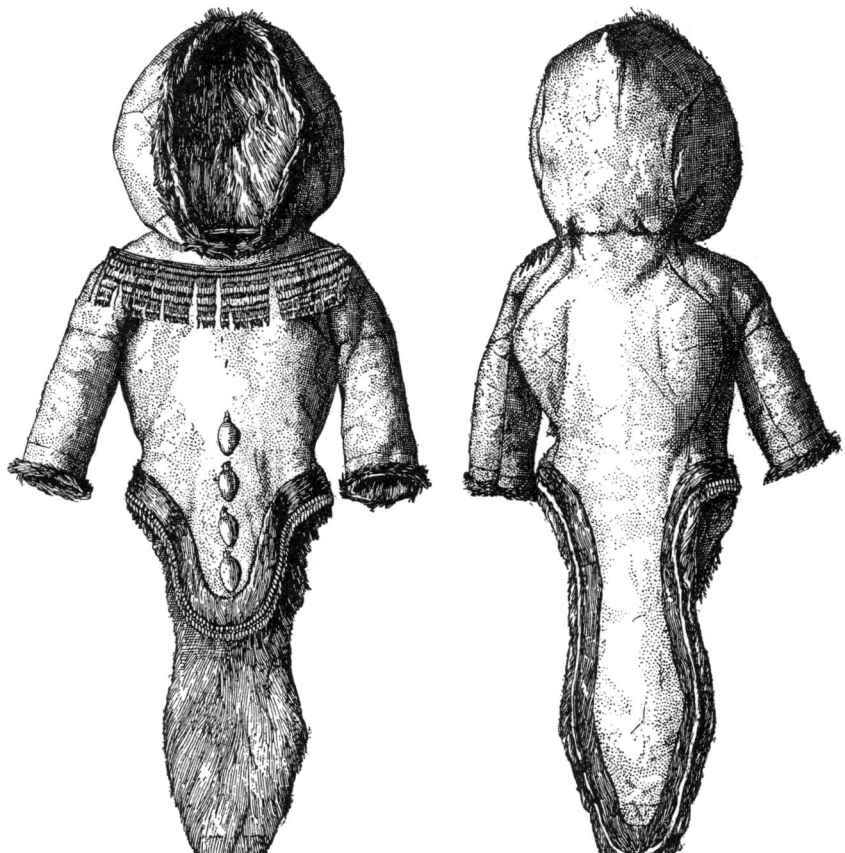

FIG. 39.—Eskimo woman's deerskin coat.　　　　FIG. 40. Backside of same.

sealskin are sewed upon a piece of leather, which makes an undersole for the shoe, in the manner shown in the figure.

One end of the strip is first sewed to the subsole and the strip pushed up into a loop and stitched again, and so on till a piece is made big enough to cover the sole of the shoe, to which it is sewed. These ice shoes are worn over the ordinary waterproof boots.

As I have already said, these boots are all made by the women. The sole is cut out by eye and is broadly elliptical in shape, somewhat pointed at the toe and heel. The leg is formed of a single piece, so that there is but one seam; the tongue or piece to cover the instep may or may not be a separate piece. If it is, the leg seam comes in front; if it forms one piece with the leg piece, the seam is behind. When the leg is sewed up and the tongue properly inserted the sole is sewed on. It is tacked at the heel, toe, and once on opposite sides of the foot, to the upper. The sewing of the sole to the upper is generally begun at the side of the seam and continued around. Perpendicular creases at the heel, and more numerously around the toes, take up the slack of the sole and are carefully worked in. The making of this part of the shoe is most difficult, for unless it is well sewed it is liable to admit water. The creases or "gathers" are stitched through and through with a stout thread, which holds them in place while the operation proceeds, and which besides has a tendency to prevent the gathers from breaking down. The heel, which comes well up the back of the boot, is stiffened by means of several threads sewed perpendicularly, and as they are drawn shorter than the skin, they prevent the heel from falling and thus getting "run down."

The seams of the boots, which are turned inside out during the operation, are so arranged on the edges that one will overlap and be tacked with close stitches over the rest of the seam. This is done not only for comfort when the boot becomes dry and hard while being worn, but also to take the strain from the stitches which hold the edges together. The value of a pair of boots depends much on the care bestowed in tanning and in sewing.

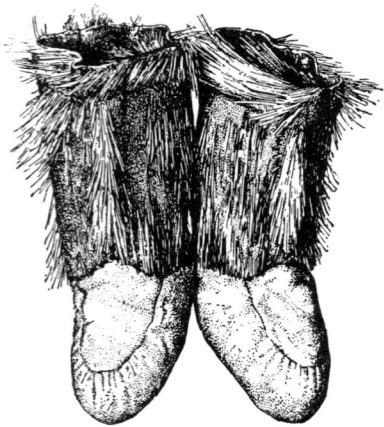

FIG. 41. Eskimo boots.

The hands are protected by mittens of different materials. Fur or hair mittens are worn only in dry weather, as the hair would retain too much moisture.

Among the Innuit the mammals are divided into two classes: the noble and the inferior beasts. The skins of the former are used, though not exclusively, by the men, while the latter may be worn only by the women. No man would debase himself by wearing a particle of the fur of the hare or of the white fox; the skins of these timid creatures are reserved for the women alone. Either sex may wear the skins of all other mammals, except at certain times, under restrictions imposed by superstition.

The women wear mittens of hare or fox skin, with palms of sealskin or Indian-tanned bird's skin. Reindeer skin with the hair on is also used for mittens. The heavy skin from the body is selected for the sake of warmth. When these mittens are to be used when driving dogs the palm is made of sealskin, to enable the wearer to get a firm grasp on the whip handle. The skin of the deer's forelegs, which has hair of a different character from that on the body, also makes excellent mittens, specially suited for handling snow in building the snow huts. Mittens are sometimes fringed round the wrist with a strip of white bearskin to keep out the wind.

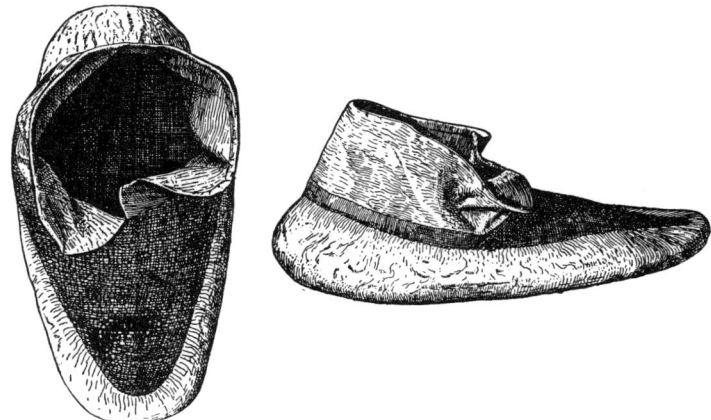

FIG. 42. Eskimo shoes.

All mittens have such short thumbs that they are very inconvenient for a white man, who habitually holds his thumb spread away from the palm, whereas the Innuit usually keep the thumb apposed to the palm. The wrists of the mitten also are so short that considerable of the wrist is often exposed. The sleeves of the jacket are generally fringed with wolf or dog skin to protect this exposed portion of the wrist.

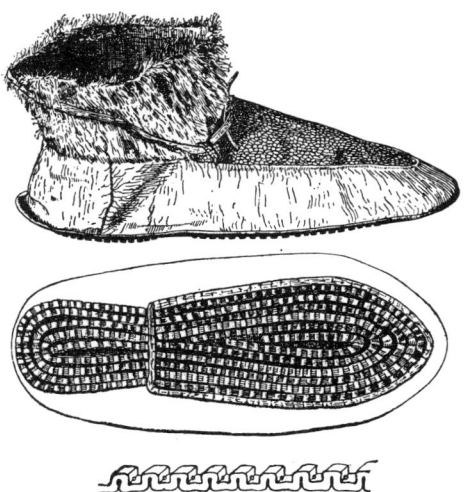

FIG. 43. Ice-shoes, Hudson strait Eskimo.

Similar mittens of black sealskin are also worn by the men during damp weather, or when handling objects which would easily soil a pair of furred mittens. I have never seen a woman wear this kind of covering for the hand. It appears to be exclusively worn by the men.

The men who engage in the late fall seal hunting protect their hands with waterproof gauntlets, which reach well up over the forearm. These keep the hands from being wet by the spray and by the drip from the paddle. Fig. 44, No. 90074, represents one of these long mittens, made of black tanned sealskin, and edged with a strip of hairy sealskin over an inch wide. The back or upper portion of the mitten is made of a single piece of black skin, the edge of which is crimped and turned under to protect the fingers. The palm is a separate piece, joined to the back piece, and on it is a projecting part to form the inner half of the thumb. The outer half of the thumb and the under side of the forearm are made of a single piece, stitched to the palm portion and that which covers the back of the hand and arm, so that, including the edging of hairy skin, there are only four pieces of skin entering into the make of a pair of these mittens. They are worn only by the men, and only when they are engaged in work where the hands would be immersed in water during cold weather. As the skin from which they are made is the same as that used for water-tight boots, it is obvious that no moisture can touch the skin of the hand.

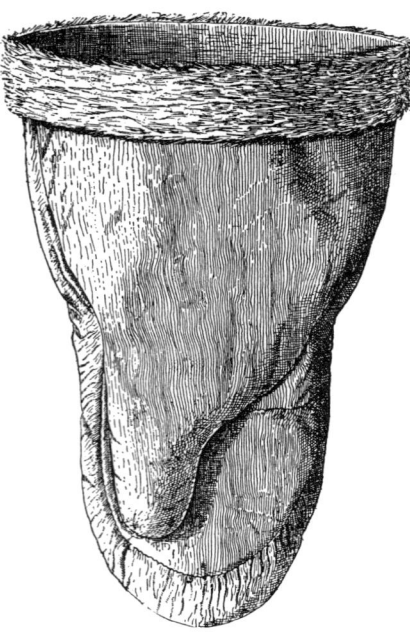

FIG. 44. Long waterproof sealskin mitten.

For protection from rain and wet they wear over their other clothes a waterproof hooded frock (Fig. 45) made of seal entrails, preferably the intestines of the bearded seal (*Erignathus barbatus*). The intestines of animals killed in October are considered the best for this purpose. They then are not so fat and require less dressing to clean them. The contents are removed and they are filled with water and thoroughly washed out. The fat and other fleshy matter adhering are removed by means of a knife used as a scraper. This being done, the intestine is inflated with air and strung along the tops of the rocks to dry. When dry it is carefully flattened and rolled into tight bundles, like a spool of ribbon, and laid away until wanted.

When required for use it is split longitudinally, and when spread open is of variable width from 3 to 5 inches, depending on the size of the animal. The edges of the strips are examined and any uneven portions are cut off, making the strip of uniform width. There are three separate pieces in a garment—the body and hood as one and the sleeves as two. Sometimes the sleeves are made first and sometimes the body is sewed first, and of this latter portion the hood is first formed. Strips are sewed edge to edge with the exterior of the intestine to form the outside of the garment. The edge is turned down, so as to leave a width of a third of an inch, and turned to the right; the other strip is similarly folded, but turned to the left and laid on the other strip. Sinew from the back of a reindeer or from a seal is made into threads a yard or more in length and of the thickness of medium-sized wrapping cord. The needle is usually of a number 3 or 4 in size or of less diameter than the thread in order that the thread shall the more effectually fill up the hole made by the needle. The two strips are then sewed with stitches about nine to the inch, through and through, in a man-

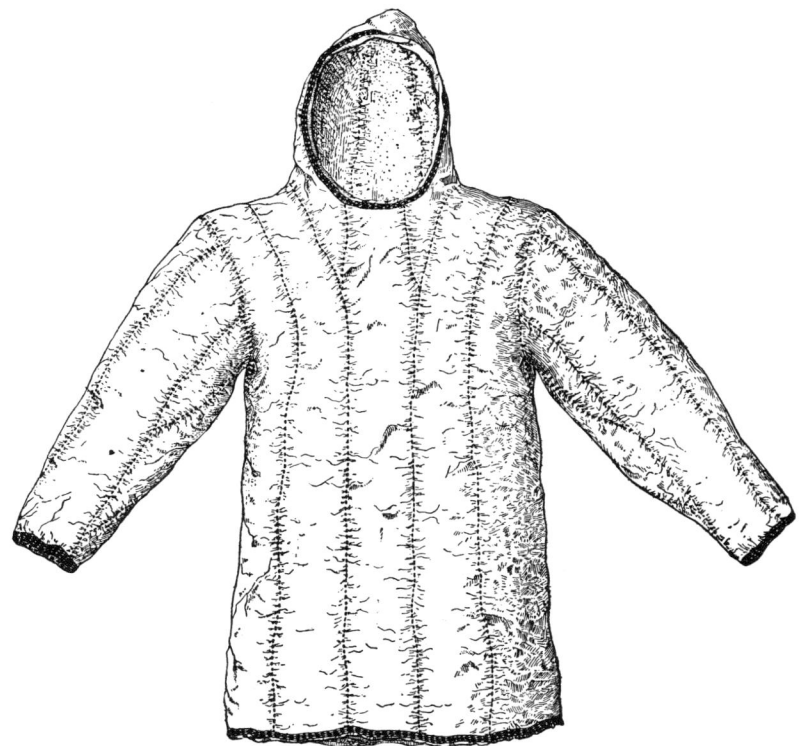

FIG. 45. Waterproof gutfrock.

ner, I believe, termed running stitches. When a sufficient length is obtained a third strip is added, and so on until the required number of perpendicular strips form a sufficient width to surround the body. The outer edges are then joined and the body of the garment is complete. Portions are cut out and the hood assumes the desired shape, resembling a nightcap attached to the body of a nightgown. The sleeves are sewed in a similar manner and affixed to the body of the garment. The seams run perpendicularly and not around the body in a spiral manner as in garments made by the natives of Alaska for similar purposes. The edge of the hood, the wrists, and the bottom of the garment are strengthened by means of thin strips of sealskin sewed on the outside of those parts where they are most liable to be torn. The garment is worn during wet weather or while in the kaiak traveling on a rough sea. The bottom of the garment is tied around the hoop of the kaiak in which the wearer sits and thus effectually sheds the water from the body, except the face, and keeps it from entering the kaiak.

Sometimes a drawstring closes the hood tightly around the face and prevents the spray from entering. The string is usually tied at the top of the hood, in which case it is rather difficult to untie.

When not in use the material must be well oiled and rolled up or it will become so stiff that it can not be worn until it has been relaxed by dipping in water. The sinew with which it is sewed swells when wet and tightens the seams.

There is great difference in the length of the garments worn by the eastern and the western Eskimo as well as in the manner of arranging the strips of which they are made. The one worn by the people of Hudson strait scarcely reaches to the hips of the wearer and is long enough only to tie around the hoop of the kaiak. The ones worn by the Eskimo of Northern sound, Alaska, falls to the knees, and those made by the Aleuts are so long that they interfere with the feet in walking. The material prepared by the eastern natives is not so good, as it is coarser and stiffer than that of the sea lion (*Eumatopias stelleri*), used by the natives of Alaska.

The weight of one of these garments when dry scarcely exceeds 6 or 7 ounces.

To protect the eyes from the glare of the snow, which is especially trying when the sun is still low in early spring, snow goggles are worn made to admit the light only through a narrow slit. (Figs. 46,

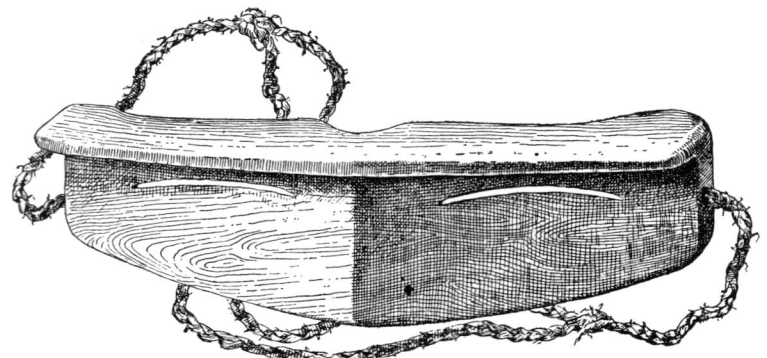

FIG. 46. Snow goggles—front.

and 47.) Nos. 3186, 3187, 3188, 3189, 3190, 3191, 3192, 3193, 3197, 3198, 3199, 3200, and 3201 in the collection show such snow goggles made of wood. A somewhat curved piece of wood is fashioned to fit the face over the eyes; a notch is fitted for the nose to rest in. The lower side is about half an inch thick, forming a flat surface. The front is perpendicular and blackened with soot or gunpowder mixed with oil and applied to darken the front surface to absorb the light of the sun's rays. Above this is a ledge of half an inch projecting over the narrow longitudinal slit through which the wearer may look. This projection is sometimes not blackened on the underside, and where wood is scarce it is left off altogether. Within, on the side next to the eyes, it is usually

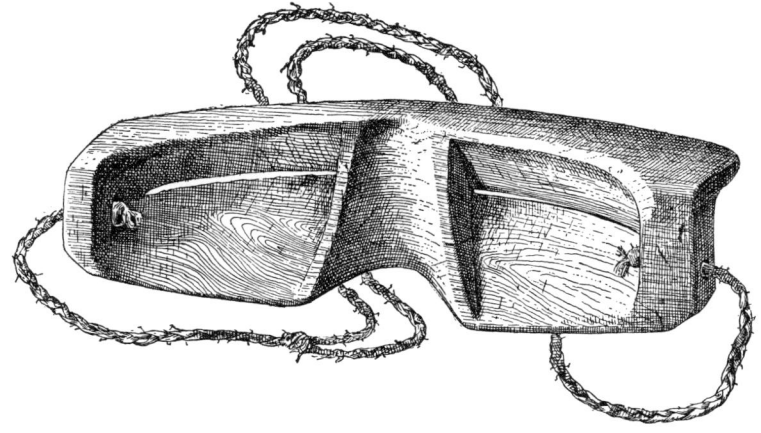

FIG. 47. Snow-goggles—rear.

gouged out to allow the eyelashes free movement. A piece of sealskin is affixed at each end and either tied in a knot over the head to hold the wood in position, or else a wider strip of skin is slit and one portion worn on the top of the head while the other fits the back of the head to prevent the goggles from falling off when the wearer stoops down.

DWELLINGS.

The winter dwellings of the Eskimo of Hudson strait consist of the usual form of snow house. In this connection I may as well state that the popular impression that the snow house described by Arctic travelers is the only thing to be called an iglu is quite erroneous. The word "iglu" is as fully generic in the Eskimo language as the word "house" is in the English language. The correct term, as applied by the Eskimo, to the snow house used as a dwelling is "ig lú ge ak" (Fig. 48.)

The first requisite for a snow house is snow. It must be of sufficient depth and possess certain well-defined qualities. The snow may fall, but until it has acquired sufficient depth for the size of blocks required and firmness enough for strength to withstand the superposed weight of the structure it is useless. An instrument termed snowknife (pŭnŭk), shaped like a short sword, is used for the purpose of cutting the blocks. The Eskimo seeks a place where the insertion of the knife into the bed of snow will prove that the snow is in the proper condition. He must then cut out a block of a size convenient to be lifted. This is usually rejected as it may be irregular or broken. Additional blocks, in size from 8 to 10 inches thick, 2 feet wide, and slightly more in length are cut by a motion much resembling the act of sawing, cutting the depth of the blade. The knife then cuts the bottom off squarely and the block is lifted out, the builder standing where the first blocks were cut from. The blocks are arranged on the bank of snow around the pit in which the man stands. The first block usually is somewhat triangular

Fig. 48. Deserted Eskimo snow houses, near Fort Chimo.

in shape for a purpose hereafter mentioned. The second block is cut out and placed near the first, the end clipped with the knife to allow the first joint to be close together. A third block is cut and placed by the end of the second. It will now be seen that the line of blocks is not straight, but curved concavely within. Additional blocks are cut and placed end to end with each other until the first one laid is reached. Here a longer block is cut to lay upon the inclined side of the triangular-shaped block first used and so placed as to "break" the joints, and thus render the structure more stable. Additional blocks are placed on the first row, and as the operation proceeds it will be seen that the blocks lie in a spiral form, gradually drawing in as the structure rises, forming a dome-shaped wall of snow. The key block at the top is carefully cut to fit the aperture and inserted from the outside by the assistance of another person. All the joints are carefully stopped up with spawls of snow or with snow crushed between the hands and forced within the crevices.

The floor of the snow house is the bed of snow from which the building material was taken. The door is cut by taking blocks of snow from under the bottom row of the foundation blocks. A trench is made, and along the side of it the blocks are placed. An arched covering of the material forms a sheltered passageway to the door.

When the snow house is to be occupied for a considerable time the doorway may have walls of snow blocks piled as high as the shoulders, with the top left open. This shields the entrance from wind and drifting snow. Various forms of entrance are constructed, often very tortuous; and when made a refuge by the numerous dogs they are not pleasant paths along which to creep on hands and knees, for a panic may seize some cowardly canine and all the dogs struggle to get suddenly out into the open air. Vicious animals often wait until a white man gets about half way through the entry and then make a sudden assault on him.

The interior of the house is arranged according to the number of persons inhabiting it.

A raised bed, on which to sit during the day and sleep during the night, is formed either by leaving a part of the snow-bank or else by bringing in blocks and arranging them as a solid mass. On this are spread bows of spruce, or dry grass, if obtainable, otherwise fine twigs of willow or alder, and over these heavy reindeer or bear skins are thrown. On these bed-skins are laid other softer skins of reindeer, with which to cover the person on retiring to sleep. A window is sometimes set in the side of the structure toward the sun. This is simply a piece of thick, clear ice, from a lake, set in the wall of the dome. It admits light, although it is generally light enough during the day within the snow-house unless the walls be built particularly thick, but great thickness in certain situations becomes necessary lest the winds and drifting snow wear away the sides of the structure, causing it to admit the cold or tumble down. Around the outside of the hut is sometimes built a protecting wall of snow blocks, two or three feet high, to prevent the drifting snow from wearing away the side of the dwelling. A storm of a single night's duration is often sufficient to destroy a house.

The interior walls, in severe weather, become coated with frost films from the breath, etc., condensing and crystallizing on the inside of the dome and often presenting by the lamplight a brilliant show of myriads of reflecting surfaces scintillating with greater luster than skillfully set gems.

If the roof is not carefully shaped it is liable to cave in from the heat within softening the snow, especially in moderate weather, and then the entire structure falls.

Where the owner of the house has considerable possessions which must be protected from the dogs and the weather, a similar structure is prepared alongside of the dwelling and often connected with it by

11 ETH——15

means of a communicating passage-way. An exterior opening may be made and closed with a block of snow. The larger articles, such as bags of oil and bundles of skins, are put inside before the walls are up, if intended to be stored for some time.

As I have slept in these snow-houses I can assert that, while very uncomfortable, they afford a protection which can not be dispensed with. When the doorway is open they soon become very cold, and when closed upon several persons the heat becomes intolerable. Odors from the food remain long after the remnants are disposed of, and where one has been occupied for a long period the accumulation of refuse becomes so great that a new structure is indispensable in order to get rid of it. All the work of the different members of the family is performed within the walls. The skins of animals are dressed and tanned there. The offal of game and the hair from dressed skins mingle in one mass, which soon putrefies and creates such a stench that only an Eskimo with most obtuse sense of smell could inhabit the place.

When spring comes the huts begin to melt and in the course of a few warm days fall down. If the weather is too inclement to permit a skin tent to be occupied, the first hole in the wall may be patched with a deerskin, but this will afford very limited protection from the cold of nights, for, however warm the days, the nights will, until late in May, be so cold that only the older individuals withstand the cold.

When the structure falls, melted by sun or rain, the miserable occupants must erect temporary shelter of deerskin or cloth on the bare rocky ridges. Those too poor to own a skin tent have often but a blanket of deerskin, stretched over three or four poles, set to shelter them from the chilly northerly winds usually prevailing at that season.

Here they must sojourn until the ice breaks from the shores of the coves and bays, enabling the hunters to procure seals from the sea. Along the shores one may often find camping sites of these poor wanderers searching through the day for food and at night camping under the lee of a wall of rock with little other covering than that worn during the day and this often soaked with spray or rain.

Improvidence and indolence result in the most cruel privations toward the end of winter. Many who are too weak and emaciated from lack of food to pursue the chase to gain a living starve before reaching the sea and are left to perish.

When the season is more advanced, and the weather warm enough, those who are industrious and provident enough to be the possessors of sealskin tents, move into them for the season.

The skin tent (Pl. XXXVII) is usually made of the skins of the largest square flipper seals, those too heavy for any other purpose or not necessary for other uses.

ESKIMO TENT.

The number of skins necessary to form a tent varies with the size required. Generally as many as ten to fifteen are used, and such a tent will accommodate a good sized family.

The hair is seldom removed from the skin, which is simply stretched as it comes from the animal and freed from fat and fleshy particles. The edges are trimmed and a sufficient number of skins are sewed together to form a length for one side of the tent. The length of the individual skins makes the height of the tent. A similar width is prepared for the opposite side. The two pieces meet at the rear of the structure and are there tied to the poles. A separate piece forms the door and may be thrown one side when a person enters or goes out. The poles of the tent are arranged as follows: Two pairs of poles are joined near the ends with stout thongs and erected with the lower ends spread to the proper width, forming the ends of the tent, on which the ridgepole is laid. A single pole is now placed near each end of the ridgepole, resting on the upright pairs, to prevent lateral motion. Two more such braces are placed on each side and spread so as to give a somewhat rounded end to the tent. Near the middle of the ridgepole is a pair of shorter poles leaning against it to prevent the weight of the sides from bending the ridgepole. It will be seen that eleven poles are necessary to support a long tent, as the skins are very heavy. The skins and poles can be transported when the umiak is able to carry them.

In case of continued rains the skins are placed so as nearly to meet over the ridge and additional skins cover the space left between the edges. When the tent is to be taken down the two widths are folded over, each by itself, and then rolled into a compact bundle by beginning at each end and folding toward the center, leaving sufficient space between the rolls for a person to get his head and shoulders in. Two persons, one for each roll, now assist the carrier, who kneels, bows his head, and places the load on his head and shoulders. The two assist him to rise and the heavy load is taken to the umiak and placed in the bottom for ballast. The shorter poles are first laid in on the ribs of the boat to keep the skins from the water should any seep through the seams. The second bundle of tenting is laid on the first.

The tent of skins is the usual shelter during the season from the first rain until a sufficient fall of snow occurs in the early winter from which to construct an iglu gheak.

The interior of the skin tent is necessarily quite roomy on account of the number of occupants. The farther end often has a stick of timber laid across the floor, and behind this is the bedding for the owner, his wives, and children. A man who is able to own a tent of this character is also wealthy enough to have two or more wives. Along the remainder of the sides within lie the other occupants, either in groups or singly, depending on the degree of relationship existing between them. Guests and others temporarily abiding with the host are assigned any portion of the tent that the host may choose to select, usually, if great honor is to be shown, the place lately occupied by himself. The central portion is reserved for a fireplace for cooking and heating purposes. In this structure is carried on all manner of work incidental to the season. The tent is taken from place to place by means of the umiak when the food supply of a locality is exhausted or another region promises greater abundance.

All these summer occupations require a number of persons to successfully prosecute them, hence the number dwelling in one tent is not often detrimental, as the adults walk along the shore to drag the boat or relieve it from their weight.

The owner of a tent is considered an important individual, and his favor is retained by every means. A period of illness may cause him to lose all his belongings and then on recovery he has to start life anew. Several seasons may elapse before a sufficient number of skins will be procured for him to make a tent, and this is immovable without a boat to transport it, for when a sled might be used for that purpose there is always enough snow from which to erect a shelter.

During the winter the skins are stored away on posts erected for the purpose, or on piles of rocks where the various species of small animals will not destroy them by eating holes in the oily skin. Mice and ermines are very destructive to these skins, often causing sad havoc in a short time. By the spring the owner may be miles away from the scene of the previous autumnal hunt and be unable to go after the tent, which, with the summer rain and decay, becomes useless, imposing the severe task of collecting skins for a second tent.

In former times these people inhabited permanent winter houses like those used by the Eskimo elsewhere, as is shown by the ruins of sod and stone houses to be seen in various parts of the country. These appear to have had walls of stone built up to support the roof timbers, with the interstices filled up with turf or earth. From the depression remaining in the inside of these ruins, the floor seems to have been excavated to a greater or less depth.

The present inhabitants relate that their ancestors dwelt in these huts, but can not explain why they were deserted, or why such structures are not erected at the present day.

HOUSEHOLD ARTICLES.

There is very little in these dwellings that can be called furniture, besides the bed places already referred to. The other articles requisite for housekeeping consist of a lamp of soapstone, kettles to hang over it, a frame suspended above the lamp for drying various articles, and sundry wooden bowls, buckets, and cups, besides similar vessels made of sealskin.

The lamp (poqíla), which is the only source of heat and light in the snow house, is, roughly speaking, a large shallow bowl of soapstone

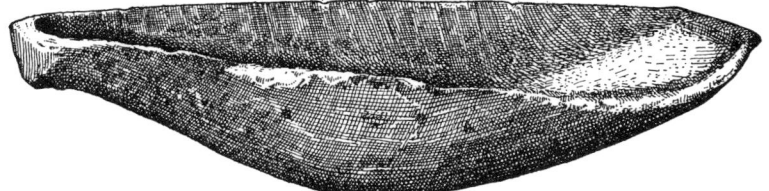

FIG. 49. Soapstone lamp, Koksoagmyut.

filled with oil, which is burned by means of a wick of moss, arranged round one edge of the bowl.

The material from which these lamps are made occurs in isolated

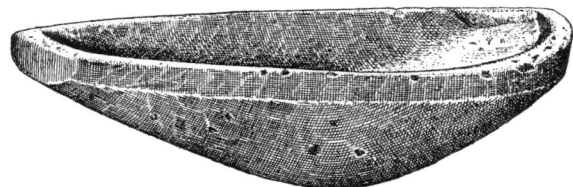

FIG. 50. Soapstone lamp, Koksoagmyut.

bowlders on the surface of the ground at various places in the region. These bowlders are often of great size.

The general form of these lamps, which will be best understood from the figures (Figs. 49, 50, 51), is nearly always the same, the variations being apparently due to the lack of material. The cavity for holding the oil varies in capacity, according to the size of the lamp, from half a pint to nearly three quarts. It is, however, never filled to the brim,

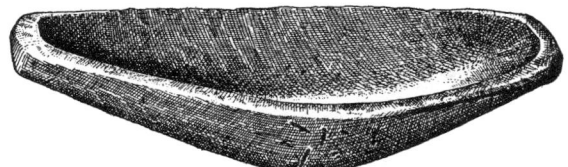

FIG. 51. Soapstone lamp, Koksoagmyut.

for fear it should run over. The consumption of oil depends upon the number of wicks lighted at once, and also on the character of the wick.

The wick in general use is prepared from a kind of moss, which grows in large patches close to the ground, the stalks rising perpendicularly, and the whole so matted together that it may be cut into any desired form. From these patches pieces are cut an inch or two wide, a third of an inch thick and two or three inches in length, and laid

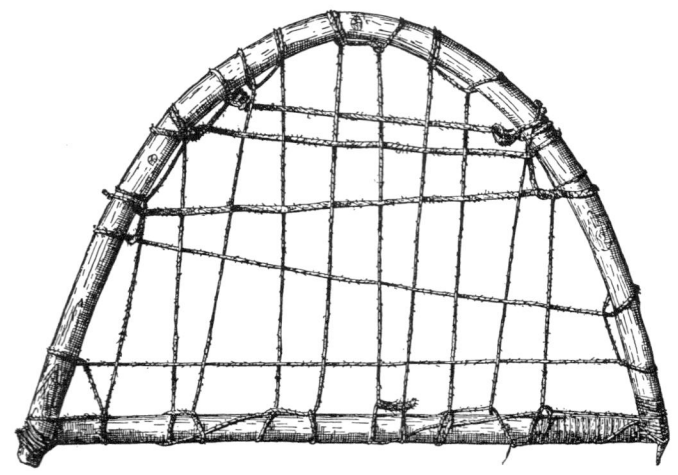

FIG. 52. Frame for drying mittens.

away to dry. When one of these is to be used the woman squeezes the fibers together with her teeth, trims it, and sets it in the oil, and lights it. The light from one of these wicks is nearly equal to that of an inch wick fed with a good quality of kerosene. The heat is very great.

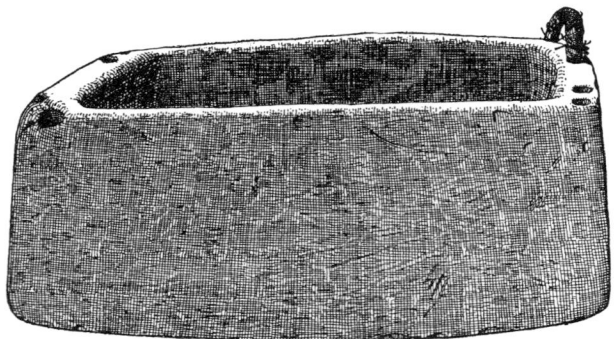

FIG. 53. Soapstone kettle.

For cooking, a larger wick is used, or two of the smaller ones set side by side. Over the lamp is placed a frame for drying wet boots, mittens, and such things. Fig. 52 represents one of these (No. 3048), which is a semicircle or bow of wood with the ends fastened to a straight piece of wood. Across these strands of sinew or sealskin forms a sort of netting having large meshes. On this rests the article to be dried. Under this is a support formed of two sharp-pointed pegs which are stuck into the snow forming the side of the hut. On the outer end of these is fastened, or laid across them, a piece of wood. The shape of the support is that of a long staple with square corners. In some instances the pegs form only a wide V-shape, and the frame for supporting the articles laid directly on this. A block of wood hollowed out to receive the convex bottom of the lamp is sometimes used to support the latter.

In former times cooking over these lamps was universally performed in kettles of soapstone, in which cooking was also done by putting

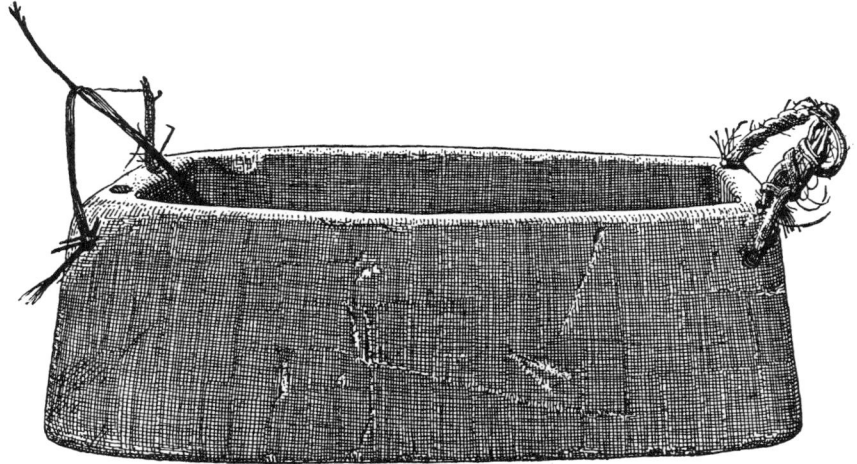

FIG. 54. Soapstone kettle.

heated stones into the water. These soapstone kettles are, however, quite superseded by utensils of civilized manufacture. I, however, succeeded in collecting two full-sized stone kettles, and one little one, made for a child's toy. The figures (Figs. 53, 54) show the shape of these ves-

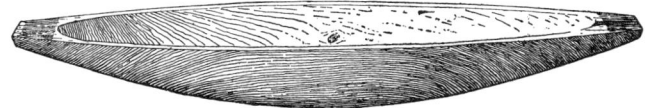

FIG. 55. Wooden dish.

sels sufficiently well. The handles are made of strips of whalebone. The larger kettle (No. 3179) is nearly 13 inches long, and will hold nearly a gallon. They were made of different capacities in former times, varying from about a pint to a full gallon.

Oblong shallow dishes (pu-ghu′-tak) for holding oil or food are carved from larch knots. The figure (Fig. 55) represents a model of one of these. Buckets and cups of various sizes for holding water and other fluids are made of tanned seal skin sewed with sinew. The sides of the

bucket are a strip of seal skin bent into a ring, with a round piece of seal skin sewed on for a bottom. Sometimes a seal-skin bail is added, or a wooden handle sewed to the lips of the cup, making it into a dipper (Figs. 56, 57.) Wooden baskets are made in a simiilar fashion

strip of spruce wood is bent nearly circular. The ends of the strip are fastened with fine iron wire. The bottom is a separate piece and has a rim or edge for the upper part to

FIG. 56. Sealskin bucket.   FIG. 57. Sealskin cup.

set on, and is held in place by means of small wooden pegs driven through and into the bottom.

The capacity of these vessels is seldom more than a couple of quarts, and generally less. They are principally used to ladle water into the cooking kettles. All these vessels of native manufacture are being rapidly displaced by tin cups and small kettles.

FOOD AND ITS PREPARATION

Under certain conditions a great portion of their food is eaten raw, but it is invariably cooked when it conveniently can be. Frozen food is consumed in great quantities. I have seen them strip and devour the back, fat, and flesh from the body of a deer while the fibers were yet quivering. The entrails of many species of birds are taken from the body and, while yet warm, swallowed much after the manner of swallowing an oyster. The eggs which have been incubated to an advanced degree are as eagerly devoured as those quite fresh.

The deer meat, killed the previous fall and frozen for three or four months, is cut into huge chunks and gnawed with as much satisfaction as though it was the finest pastry. On such occasions I have seen the person appointed to chop up the frozen meat scatter the pieces among the expectant crowd with as little ceremony as that of throwing ears of corn to the hogs in a pen. For a change the frozen pieces of meat are sometimes warmed or thawed before the fire.

The blood of the deer is often mixed with the half-digested mass of food in the stomach of the animal, and the stomach, with its contents, with the addition of the blood, eaten raw or boiled. Sometimes it is laid aside to ferment and then frozen and eaten in this condition.

Strips of fat from a seal and the blood of the animal are put into a kettle and heated. The oily liquid is eaten with the greatest relish. Seal oil is used for food in about the same manner as we use syrups. Years of almost daily intercourse with these people have failed to show the ability of any person to drink seal or whale oil without illness resulting. They never drink pure oil under any circumstances, except as a laxative. The statement often made that these people drink oil as food is simply preposterous. Such statements doubtless arose from seeing other preparations of food having an abundance of oil upon them. Lean flesh is often dipped into oil and then eaten. If partaken of without oil in as great quantities as these people require, a torpid condition of the liver and alimentary canal results, and they thus employ the pure oil to relieve themselves.

Vegetable food is little used except in the vicinity of the trading stations. Those accustomed to the use of flour, bread, peas, beans, and rice are very fond of them, and often express regret that they will be deprived of them when on their hunting expeditions.

Native plants afford little help as food. During the season when the various berries are ripe all the people gorge themselves. They have a special fondness for the akpik (*Rubus chæmomorus*). The sun scarcely reddens the side of these berries, locally known as "bake apple," before the children scour the tracts where they grow, and eat of the half-ripened fruit with as much relish as the civilized boy does the fruit purloined from a neighbor's orchard. Other berries contribute their share as food.

When on trips the women often gather a few green herbs and put them in a kettle of water and make an infusion in lieu of tea. They are fond of tea, coffee, and sugar. Molasses is eaten alone or with something dipped in it.

The Eskimo drink often and astonishing quantities of water at a time. If the weather be very cold they often drink the water which has been heated on a fire, asserting that the hot water does not weaken them as much as cold water would do.

When a seal has been killed and is being brought to camp, the hunter signifies his success from a distance, and those in camp raise a joyous shout. The animal is drawn ashore and skinned. The flesh is devoured raw as the process goes on, or may be divided, certain portions being given the different persons. The blood is collected, and when the meat is boiled it is mixed with the hot liquid and forms a nutritious dish, eagerly devoured by both adults and young. The children revel in this dish to a sacrifice of cleanliness.

The feast is continued until the flesh has been devoured and the people gorged to their utmost capacity. Stories are told and general good humor prevails. The different species of fish which frequent the shallow waters of the bays are used as food.

All the adults are addicted to the use of tobacco, both for smoking and chewing and in the form of snuff, although it is not everyone that uses tobacco in all three ways.

The plug tobacco, used for smoking and chewing, is carried in a small pouch of seal skin attached to the belt, which keeps it from being dampened by perspiration or rain. Watches are also carried in the same receptacle. Fig. 58 (No. 74485) is such a bag, made of hairy seal skin. The edges alone are trimmed with lighter colored strips of seal skin. A string holds the mouth of the bag together after it is rolled up. A loop at one corner enables the bearer to affix it to his belt when traveling to avoid the necessity of opening the bag in which he usually carries such small things.

Leaf tobacco is preferred for the preparation of snuff, but as this is not always to be had plug is often used. This is shredded up and

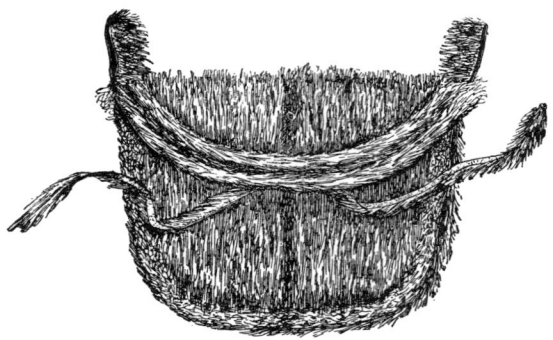

Fig. 58. Tobacco pouch.

dried, and when dry enough is reduced to a powder by inclosing a quantity in a fold of seal skin and pounding it with a stone or stick.

Snuff is kept in a purse-shaped bag, closed at the mouth with a thong. To it is attached a little spoon made of ivory. Various forms of this implement are made. The general appearance is that of a common spoon, of which the ends and sides of the bowl are cut off. At the end of the handle is a slight depression for containing the snuff, which is held firmly against the orifice of the nostril and inhaled by a sudden indrawing of the breath while the thumb of the other hand closes the opposite nostril.

The old women appear more addicted to the use of snuff than any of the men. The effect of inhaling the strong snuff is quickly shown in the face. It seems to affect people more than the use of tobacco in any other way.

MEANS OF TRANSPORTATION.

BY WATER.

The principal means of conveyance by water with the Eskimo of Hudson strait, is the umiak, referred to by most writers as the woman's boat. This appellation is not more applicable than would be the term family boat. The women use the boat alone only on rare occasions, and then in quiet water and for short distances. Men are nearly always in it, and under the guidance of one of these, the boat is used for long journeys.

The form of the umiak, in the region under consideration, differs greatly from that of the Eskimo of Bering sea. (See Fig. 59, from a model.)

The size of the boat is variable according to the means of the builder and the size of the family to be conveyed in it. The length of the keel is from 10 to 25 feet. Over all the length is 1 or 2 feet greater than on the keel. It will be thus seen that the ends are nearly perpendicular. It is difficult to determine at the first glance which is the bow and which the stern, so nearly alike are they. They only differ in the former being somewhat wider at the upper edge or rail.

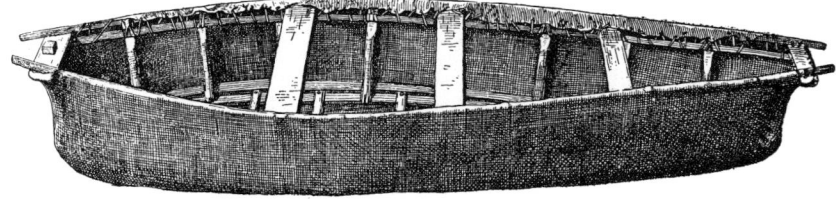

Fig. 59. Eskimo umiak.

The keel is a straight piece of wood hewed from a single stick, nearly 4 inches square. The stem and stern posts are nearly alike, the latter having but little slope, and are cut from curved or crooked stems of trees. A tree may be found, which, when hewed, will form the stern-post and keel in one length. Otherwise the fore and aft posts have places cut out for the insertion of the respective ends of the keel, and are fastened firmly by stout thongs of sealskin thrust through holes bored in the wood and ingeniously lashed. As the bottom of the umiak is flat the sides of the bottom are formed of square rails of sufficient length and given the desired spread. They are held at the ends by being joined to the keel. Crosspieces notched at the ends separate the bottom rails and are steadied in position by being notched so as to sit on the square keel. On the ends of the crosspieces is laid a second rail which prevents them from rising and serves to strengthen the ends of the ribs, which are set alternately with the crosspieces of the keel. The ribs are attached to the lower or bottom rail by means of sealskin lashing. Along the upper ends of the ribs is placed a longer rail of smaller diameter and usually shaved round. This rail is usually set half its diameter into rounded notches of the upper ends of the ribs and fastened by thongs. Within and below the top rail is a shorter rail, generally smaller than the upper, tied by thongs to the ribs and posts fore and aft. A wide board projecting several inches on each side of the stern serves as a seat for the steersman. The ends of the top rails are laid over this board and attached to it. A similar board is placed at the forward end or bow, but is, of course, longer as that end is the wider of the two.

Three to five thwarts, serving as seats for the occupants, are placed at proper intervals, having their ends resting on the inside top rail. One of these thwarts also serves to steady the mast, which is stepped into the keel and lashed to the thwart.

On the side of the boat and resting on the top rail are pieces of wood firmly lashed. A notch, or rowlock, is cut into them to serve as rests for the heavy oars. The oars are held into the notch by means of loops of stout thong, the ends of the loops passing each other, one from forward and the other from aft, and through both of the loop ends the inner end of the oar is thrust. The loops serve to hold the oar when not in use, otherwise it would float away; yet the position of them allows the oars to lie alongside in the water. The oars are heavy and as much as 10 feet long for a large umiak. The women generally run the boat and are assisted by the younger men of the party who may not be walking along the shore. Two or more females sit side by side and if they be insufficient a third person faces them and assists in the labor. It is a favorite place for a young man with his sweetheart. The steersman sits on the after board and attends to the helm and sail when the latter is in use. The sail is a nearly square sheet of cloth spread by a yard across the top. The lower corners have each a rope which the helmsman holds. A fair wind only can be used to advantage as the oomiak, from its flat bottom, is unable to go to windward. With a breeze nearly aft they can be made to sail at a good speed.

The covering of the umiak is made of skins of the largest seals. The skins are freed from hair and all adhering flesh and fat, and stretched to their utmost tension.

They are then cut into the proper shape and sewed together. The edge of one skin overlaps that of the other and the lap is then tacked over the shorter edge and attached to the other skin so as to form two seams at each junction.

Those portions which are to cover the bottom are sewed with special care, as the seams are liable to be strained in shoving the boat over the oars when it is taken from the water at each camp. When skins are sewed side to side in sufficient number to fit the length of the frame they are lifted around it and temporarily placed in position. The superfluous portions are cut out or additional pieces put in until it fits properly on the frame. Holes, 3 or 4 inches apart, are cut in the edges of the skin and stout thongs are passed through these and over the top rail to the inner rail. All the strength of the individual is now applied to draw the skin over the top rail. Being wet it readily stretches, and when the entire covering is drawn sufficiently tight the lashing around the rail is permanently fastened. The boat is then turned keel up to dry. If the skin has been properly cut and stretched it sounds like a drum when struck.

When in use the greatest care must be exercised to prevent contact with rocks, but in shallow water it frequently happens that a hole is cut in the skin of the boat, when the rent must be patched with a piece of skin. During the winter months the umiak is placed on staging of posts to protect it from the ravages of mice and other animals.

Journeys of considerable length are undertaken in these boats. A large family, or two or more families, may remove to a distance to try their fortunes. They always stop at night and during bad weather, and the journey is accomplished by easy stages. All the portable possessions of the family are taken in these boats, which are often loaded to such a degree that the older people have to walk along the shores and only go into the umiak to relieve some one who desires to walk. Where the beach is good a tracking line is attached to the bow and those on shore drag the boat along. The dogs which accompany the party are sometimes harnessed and made to pull. The tracking line is called into requisition whenever a trip is made up a river to the hunting grounds for reindeer.

The kaiak or skin canoe used by the Eskimo of Hudson strait belongs to the Greenland type. It is quite different from that used by the natives of Alaska. These boats vary from 18 to 26 feet in length; the greatest width, one-third of the distance aft the hole where the rower sits, being one-seventh to one-ninth of the entire length of the kaiak. The ends are sharp, the prow much more acute than the stern. The bottom is quite flat and the frame for the keel and sides at the bottom is arranged similarly to that of the umiak. The prow is simply an extension of the keel and slopes above the water to a height nearly double that of the stern. The slope of the stern is gradual and short. The side timbers at the bottom have the upper surface gouged so as to allow the lower ends of the nearly perpendicular ribs to rest in the groove. The ribs extend across the bottom, resting on the side timber and keel. Their upper ends are inserted in the upper rail, which extends the entire length of the kaiak. The upper rails are held apart by crosspieces of different lengths, according to position. On the top of these upper crosspieces is laid a piece which extends to the nose of the kaiak. A similar, but shorter one, is laid from the hole where the rower sits to the stern of the kaiak. The hole for his body is placed between a pair of crossbars where the equilibrium will be best maintained. The hoop of wood which outlines the hole is variable in shape, but resembles half of a short ellipse, the posterior of which is slightly curved to fit the back of the rower. Just forward of the seat the upper surface of the canoe is somewhat elevated by the curvature of the crossbars, and it thus enables the rower to have greater freedom for his limbs than he otherwise would. This particular part, the elevation just forward of him, alone resembles any portion of the kaiaks used by the Alaskan Eskimo, and of these, only the sub-tribes in the vicinity of Bering strait [and thence to Point Barrow.—J. M.] have that part of the kaiak so fashioned. With that exception the top of the Hudson strait kaiak is flat on the top. Just forward of the hatch, two or three stout thongs are sewed to the outer edge of each side of the boat and extend across the top. A similar thong is placed behind. Under these thongs are placed the paddle, also the spears, and other hunting gear. Small game is sometimes tied to these.

The outfit, consisting of spears and their appurtenances, properly belongs with the kaiak. Of these implements, there are different kinds, depending on the game and the season of the year. As the kaiak is used only during the seasons of open water it is laid aside during the winter.

I remember an instance occurring opposite Fort Chimo. A kaiak had been left until the ice in the river was firm enough to enable the vessel to be brought over on it to the station. One day a woman declared that she could see a wolf tearing the skin from the frame. It was scarcely credited, but in the course of half an hour the wolf started across towards the post. It was met and showed some disposition to attack, but was shot. I watched to see where the men went to look at the kaiak, and when they reached the place I was astounded that the woman could discern even the kaiak at such a distance.

The spear used for white whales and large seals consists of a wooden shaft of 6 or 8 feet in length, having a projection on the side, made of ivory and shaped like the fin of a fish. This fin shaped piece rests against the forefinger, while the remainder of the hand grasps the shaft. The lower end of the shaft terminates in a piece of bone or ivory of 1 to 1⅓ inches in diameter. (Fig. 67.) A socket is made in the end of the bone portion, and the wooden shaft is nicely fitted into it and fastened either by thongs or rivets. At the farther end of the bone head is a thimble-shaped hole gouged out, and into this a short piece of straight bone or ivory is fitted, having the ends so shaped that they will work smoothly into the hole at the end of the bone head of the spear. The farther end of this bone shaft is so shaped that it will work into the bone or ivory portion of the piece into which the spear point is fastened. The point is shown in the accompanying figure (Fig. 68) and is not much varied in general shape. There are two joints between the spear point and the bone shaft head. This enables the spear-point to become easily detached when the game is pierced. If this were not so, the bone or ivory would soon break with the violent motions of the animal, and the implement would be rendered useless until repaired. Thongs connect the various parts together, also connecting them with the main shaft of the spear. A long line, usually left lying in a coil just in front of the hunter, gives ample scope for play until the animal is exhausted. If the sea is rough or the hunter unable to cope with the quarry, the float, to be described below, is thrown over and the seal or whale allowed to take its course, the hunter following and endeavoring to harass the animal as much as possible, giving it a stab with the hand spear whenever occasion offers.

In addition to the whale or seal spear, the hand spear, float, and paddle, the kaiaker may have a wooden shaft, on the end of which are three prongs of barbed iron, each prong 8 to 10 inches long, and set in the form of a divergent trident. With this implement, small seals and the white-coated young are killed. Birds, too, are sometimes speared with this trident.

The hand board, or implement with which certain spears are hurled, is a piece of wood of such shape that a description will give but little idea of its form. It is about 14 inches long, flat, and has a groove on one side into which the rear end of the spear shaft rests, and is supported by the three fingers of the hand while the index finger fits into a hole cut through the board, of the shape to accommodate that digit. The tip of the finger rests against the shaft of the spear. Other notches are cut along the side of the board to enable the three fingers to lie in position to give a firm grasp on the end or handle of the board. The thumb turns over so as to lie directly on the spear, to steady it, while the other fingers give the spear the necessary straight motion when the arm is drawn back and raised nearly perpendicularly. When it reaches that position the motion is arrested and the fingers release the implement held along the groove. The hand board or thrower is retained and the spear recovered if the object has not been struck. If the aim was good the spear remains attached to the struggling animal, and the hand board is quickly placed under one of the thongs stretched across the top of the kaiak. The paddle is held in the left hand and ready for instant use.

The paddle is quite heavy and of variable length, having long, narrow blades, which are alternately dipped into the water. The use of the paddle requires some practice before one becomes accustomed to it. When in use the paddle rests on the edge of the hoop, forming the rim of the hatch, and moves along it in the motion of propulsion.

As the paddle dips into the water the dripping often causes the clothing to become wet. To obviate this, these people use a piece of plaited rope or skin to slip nearly to the beginning of the blade. This causes the dripping to fall outside of the kaiak; and in cold weather is very necessary, unless heavy mittens of tanned sealskin be worn.

An implement used for hooking into the body of a sunken seal or whale is made in the following manner: A piece of wood is prepared about 8 feet long and three-fourths of an inch thick, having a width of an inch and a half. The lower end of this has a strong hook made of stout iron set into it. Along the inner edge of the wooden shaft two or three notches are cut. The end near the person has a V-shaped notch cut into it. This is used for all the purposes of a boat hook, and also to retrieve a sunken animal. A weight is attached to near the hook end to keep the shaft perpendicular in the water. A line of sufficient length is attached to it. The hunter has marked the locality, and with the hook "feels" the bottom for the game. When found the hook is jerked into the skin and the object brought to the surface. The staff is very necessary while the kaiak is being moved through narrow channels among the ice fields. It is, in fact, available in many instances where the paddle would, from its length, be useless. The kaiak outfit would be incomplete without the hook.

A young man starts out in life with a gun and ammunition with which to procure game. If he has the energy to become a successful hunter he will soon be able to make a kaiak, and thus procure the marine mammals whose skins will afford a covering for an umiak and in the course of time additional skins for a tent. These possessions usually come in the order laid down, and when they are all procured he is generally able to have others under his direction assist in transporting them from place to place; and thus he becomes the head of a gens or family, including his brothers and sisters with their husbands, wives, and children. These usually move in a body wherever the head may dictate, and all their possessions accompany them on the journey. Brothers often live together and own the tent and umiak, the remainder of the household affairs being considered as individual property and not to be used by all without permission.

Some of the men are too improvident to prepare these skins when they have the opportunity, and thus they are unable to own a kaiak, which prevents them from providing themselves with the umiak and tent. These persons must live with others or dwell by themselves and pass a miserable existence, scarcely noticed by their fellows even during a season of abundance.

The collection contains one full-sized kaiak, with all its fittings, and their models, including a toy kaiak cut from a walrus tusk. The model is just 9 inches long and quite perfect in form. The double-bladed paddle accompanying is made from the same material, and is six inches long.

ON LAND.

The universal means of transportation on land is the sled, drawn by dogs. The number of dogs used to draw a sled varies according to the distance to be traveled, the character of the country, the condition of the animals, and the weight of the load to be drawn. From one to twenty dogs may be used. The common team for general purposes is seven or nine animals.

The method of constructing sleds differs slightly in different parts of the region, and then only where the material may be difficult to obtain or a heavy sled may not be needed. A tree of a suitable size is selected, generally larch, because of its greater strength, although somewhat heavier than the spruce.

It is necessary, for greater strength, that each runner be of a single piece of timber. The length of the runner is from 12 to 16 feet; the height varies from 10 to 12 inches. The piece must be as nearly free from knots and crossgrain as possible, for these defects render the wood very brittle during cold weather. The runners are roughly hewn at the place where originally cut, and, when needed, they are brought to the temporary camping place of the Eskimo, and there dressed with plane and saw to the required form. The bottom of the runner is usually $2\frac{1}{2}$ to 3 inches thick, gradually becoming thinner by one-half an inch to an inch toward the top. This enables the sled to make a wider track at the bottom and encounter less friction of the runner sides against the snow crust. The curve at the forward end is long and very gradual. There may be as much as 3 feet of the curved part, which rises above the level of the lower edge of the runner. This enables the sled to creep easily over any obstruction. The runners are now placed parallel, separated by a distance of 14 to 16 inches, and on these are fastened crossbars 3 inches wide, of sufficient length to allow about an inch to project over the outer edge of each runner. Near the ends of these slats is cut a notch on each edge. Sometimes a hole is also bored through the slat between the notches. These are for the purpose of fastening the slats to the runners. A sufficient number having been prepared, and placed 1 or 2 inches apart, they are now laid on the flat top of the runner. Holes are bored through the top of the runner to correspond with the holes and notches of the slats. Through these and over the slats a stout piece of heavy sealskin line is threaded, and so on through and over the slats and runner until it is firmly fastened. The line must be well soaked in water to render it flexible and allow it to stretch, otherwise the joints where it was tied would soon work loose. The line shrinks while drying, and draws as tight as though made of the best iron. No metal is used, for the reason that it would snap as easily as chalk during cold weather. The use of the thongs in binding the slats to the runners allows free-dom to the motion of the sled when passing over inequalities of sur-face, where a rigidity of the sled would soon cause it to break. The bottom of the runner is shod with iron brought by the traders for that purpose. It is simply extra-wide hoop-iron and of a width to fit. It is fastened on with screws, the heads of which are countersunk.

Another kind of shoe is put on when traveling in very cold weather. A swampy track is searched for soil of half-decomposed vegetation and pure humus, as nearly free from sand and gravel as possible. It must possess certain qualities or it may not have the requisite strength— much, I presume, as mortar often requires to be tempered with more or less lime or sand when it is too rich or too poor. The Eskimo tempers his mortar with the almost impalpable soil found under the larger spreading trees of the forest. It is the slowly decomposed vegetation fallen from branches and trunks. The manner of preparing it is as follows: A large kettle is partially filled with the material and heated to the boiling point, being constantly stirred, and while yet cool enough all coarse sticks, grass blades, pebbles, etc., are carefully re- moved as the fingers discover them in working the mortar. The sled is turned over with the bottom of the runner up. The mud is now applied by the hands, a couple of pounds being taken and pressed on the runner, which has previously been wetted. This process of adding to the runner is continued until it attains an additional depth of 3 or 4 inches and a width of 3 to 5 inches. It now resembles the rail of a stairway. When it has been thoroughly gone over to fill up any in- equalities the sled is set aside in order that the mud may freeze solid. The sled must be handled with care, as the least jar or jolt will break the "setting" mud. After it is frozen the owner takes a plane and planes it down to the proper shape and smoothness. It is somewhat difficult to describe the shape in words, unless it be compared to the upper part of the T rail of a railroad inverted—neither rounded nor flat, but so fashioned as to give the best bearing surface with the least friction. When the plane has finished its work the color of the mud is a rich chestnut brown. The builder now takes water in his mouth and spirts it in a spray along the mud. As soon as the water touches the runner it must be spread evenly with a hand incased in a mitten of reindeer skin, rubbing back and forth until the runner looks like a bar of black glass. The sled is then ready for use. Great care is necessary to avoid rocks or stones, as these cut the polished mud and roughen it. If a sudden lurch causes a portion of the mud to drop out the piece is frozen on again by means of water, or if crumbled a piece of ice is cut to the shape and caused to adhere by water freezing it to the runner.

It is not often that one may find a sled shod with bone, as is the custom with the Eskimo farther north, and especially farther west. The only instance where I have seen bone used was by some of the people from the western extremity of Hudson strait. These had only a portion of the curve and a part of the runner shod with bone and pieces of reindeer horn, secured to the runner by means of pegs.

The greatest objection to the use of mud is that a few hours of warmth may cause it to loosen and render it worthless. The polish suffers when traveling over rough ice, and especially where sand has drifted from some exposed bank to the surface of the snow. This causes very hard pulling, and soon roughens the running surface of the sled. To repair such damage the native stops, at a convenient place, to obtain water, which is spirted on the runner and rubbed evenly until it acquires a thickness of one-eighth of an inch. This coating of ice may last for the entire day of travel where the "roads" are good.

The harness for the dogs consists of two large nooses, placed one above the other. These are joined by two perpendicular straps of 4 or 5 inches in length at a sufficient distance from the end to allow the head of the dog to pass through so that one noose will lie along the back and the other between the forelegs. At the rear ends of the nooses is a long thong of the heaviest sealskin of variable length depending on the position or place the dog is to have in the team. The body harness is made of sealskin, with or without the hair on, stout canvas, or other material which may be convenient. Thin undressed sealskin makes the best harness, and is not so liable to chafe the neck of the animal. The trace attached to each dog is generally of stout sealskin thong cut three-eighths of an inch wide, and the corners are carefully pared until the trace in form resembles a hoop for a small keg. The trace varies from 10 to 30 feet in length, and is attached to a longer but much stouter thong of heavier sealskin or walrus hide prepared in the form described for the trace. The thong to which all of the traces of variable lengths are fastened is termed the "bridle." The bridle has, usually, a piece of ivory, called "toggle," at the end farthest from the sled. A few inches back of the toggle is a short piece of stout thong plaited in the bridle end. This thong has a slit cut in the farther end. It is passed through slits cut in the end of each trace and then looped on the toggle. It will now be understood that the traces all start from one place, but their different lengths give different positions to the dogs of the team so that they may move freely among rough pieces of ice without interfering with each other. This has some advantages, but it necessitates watching the traces as they are liable to catch around any projection above the surface.

The bridles are also of varying lengths, from 15 to 40 feet. The rear end has two stout thongs plaited into it, forming a loop for each thong. These are known as the "yoke," and are looped over toggles, one on each inner side of the runner.

Any load to be carried on the sled is usually placed so as not to project much over the side, for in deep snow, with a crust too weak to support the weight, it would simply act as a drag and seriously impede travel if not entirely stop it. The load must also be distributed to the best advantage along the sled so as not to have too great a weight at either the front or rear, although generally a heavier portion is placed behind to allow the sled to steer or follow. The runners are so low that the sled seldom upsets unless the ice is very rough, in which case it often requires two men to attend to it, another to free the traces from obstructions, and a fourth to lead or drive the dogs. A smaller number render traveling under such conditions very tedious.

The driver is always armed with a whip (Fig. 60). There appear to be as many kinds of whips as there are individuals using them. Each whip characterizes, in a manner, the person who makes it. A

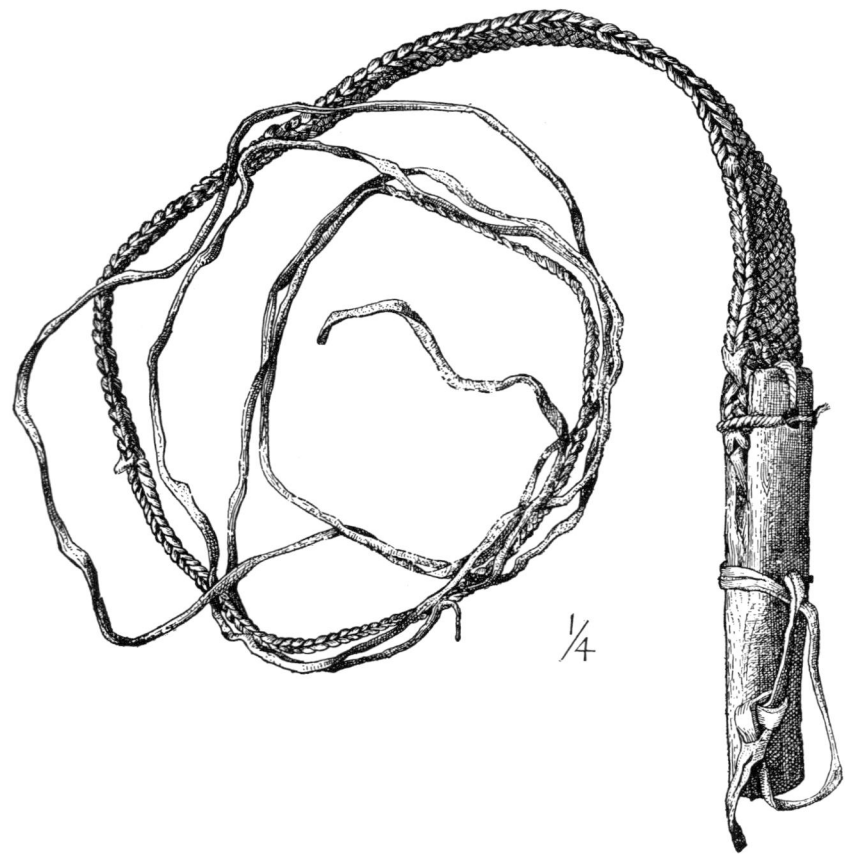

FIG. 60. Dog whip.

great amount of ingenuity is expended in preparing the lash, which is simply indescribable. The handle of the whip is from 9 to 11 inches in length and shaped somewhat like the handle of a sword without the guard. A stout loop of thong is affixed to the stock above where the hand grasps it. This loop is thrown over the wrist to prevent the weight of the whip drawing the stock from the hand and also to retain the whip when it is allowed to trail behind.

At the farther end of the stock a portion of the wood is cut out to allow the insertion of the end of the lash which is fastened by means of finer thongs. The butt end of the lash is five-sixteenths of an inch thick and nearly 2 inches wide. It is composed of eight heavy thongs plaited in a peculiar manner, depending on the number of thongs used and the fancy of the maker. The thongs are plaited by inserting the end of each thong through a succession of slits cut at the proper distance and so matted together that it is difficult to determine the "run" of the thong. The size decreases from the handle by dropping out a strand until at 18 inches from the stock only four thongs are left, and these form a square plait for a foot in length. This square form is succeeded by only two thongs which make a flat plait of 2 feet in length. At the end of this a simple piece of heavy thong completes the lash. The length of a whip may be as much as 35 feet, weighing 3 or 4 pounds. Some of the natives acquire a surprising dexterity with this formidable weapon, often being able to snip the ear of a particular dog at a distance of the length of the whip. I have known them to snap the head from a ptarmigan sitting along the path of the team. Children practice with the whip as soon as they can manage it.

The Eskimo dog fears nothing but the whiplash. They attack each other with savage ferocity, and several dogs may be engaged in terrific battles, yet the swish of a whip or even a stick thrown hurtling through the air is sufficient to cause them to slink off in abject terror, whining piteously in fear of the expected lash.

The weight or load put upon a sled may be as much as 1,200 pounds. The character of the road alone determines the weight, number of dogs, and rate of travel. The latter may average over a smooth surface 5 miles hourly for twelve hours continuously, excluding the few minutes given the dogs to "blow" (rest), etc. I knew an instance where three men with empty sled and seven dogs traveled 94 miles in eighteen hours. I have gone 19 miles in three hours; and again I have known only 3 or 4 miles to be made in ten hours, through rough ice or deep, newly fallen snow.

The disposition and condition of the dogs chiefly determines the number attached to the sled. With these animals there is the same difference as is to be found in horses or other beasts of draft. Some are energetic and well-behaved; others as stubborn or lazy as is possible. Strange dogs in the team are liable to be pitched upon by all the others and with the long traces ensues such an entanglement of lines, dogs, and flying snow as is difficult to conceive. The good qualities of the driver are manifested by his ability in keeping the dogs in order and showing promptness in separating them when quarreling. Fighting among the dogs can always be prevented by the driver keeping the dogs in proper position.

WEAPONS AND OTHER HUNTING IMPLEMENTS.

These people are now provided with firearms, which have entirely superseded the bow and arrow.

The bow formerly used in this region appears to have been similar to the one obtained from a party of East Main Innuit, who made their way to Fort Chimo. This bow has accordingly been figured and described (Figs. 61 and 62—90137).

It is made of larch wood and has a backing of eight double strands of twisted sinew. This sinew is in one piece sixteen times the length of the bow. One end is looped and passed over one "nock" of the bow and carried back and forth from nock to nock eight times. This backing has two turns of twist put in from the middle to increase its elasticity, and is lashed to the middle of the bow with a stout thong of reindeer skin. The bowstring is of twisted sinew with a loop at each end.

With this bow were seven arrows. Three of these are for shooting reindeer and wolves. They have an iron point set in a short foreshaft of reindeer antler, and a wooden shaft about 16 inches long (Fig. 63). Three more are pointed with large nails, one of which has been beaten to a chisel-shaped point (Figs. 64 and 65). They are intended for large game at short range, or for small game, such as hares and ptarmigan. These six arrows are feathered with the tail feathers of the raven. The last arrow is a simple shaft, without feathering or head, and is intended for small game, such as a wood hare crouching under a spruce tree, or the little red squirrel on the top of a low tree.

In drawing the bow, the Innuit invariably hold the arrow between the middle two fingers of the right hand, and the string is drawn with all four fingers, and released by straightening them.

The bow and arrows are carried in bow case and quiver fastened together and slung on the back. Fig. 66 represents a model (No. 3257) of such a bow case.

The bow case is made of buckskin and is of sufficient length to con-

FIG. 61.—Bow. East Main Eskimo (back).

FIG. 62.—Bow. East Main Eskimo (side).

tain the bow, excepting the extreme end, which is left projecting for convenience in handling. The case is tied around the bow at the projecting end. The quiver is attached to the bow case and contains two models of arrows for shooting large game. The arrows are tipped with leaf-shaped pieces of tin. They are feathered with portions of feathers apparently taken from the tail of a raven. The mouth of the quiver is also drawn up with a string to prevent the loss of arrows. I have not seen the Eskimo of Hudson strait use such a cover for their bows and arrows, but the opportunities to observe them are very limited, as few are used. I am led to conclude that only the poorer individuals of either locality have the bow and arrow at the present day.

I have already described the large harpoon used for striking white whales and large seals from the kaiak. A short-head spear (Fig 67, No. 90164) is used for dispatching wounded seals or white whales, or for killing white whales when they have been driven into a shallow arm of the sea when the tide ebbs and leaves them partly uncovered. It has a short wooden shaft with a ferrule of ivory, holding a short ivory loose shaft, kept in place by thongs, on which is mounted a toggle head like that used on the big harpoon. The line is either attached to the kaiak or to a small float made of the inflated intestine or skin of a seal. The toggle heads for these spears are made of ivory, and fitted with iron blades (Fig. 68). I have already referred to the large sealskin float in describing the kaiak.

Fig. 69 (No. 3531) is such a large sealskin float or á va tuk. The skin is removed from the body by skinning around the gums and carefully taking out all the flesh and bones through this orifice. As the operation proceeds the skin is turned back and at the completion of the work is inside out. The flesh side, now the exterior, is carefully scraped to free it from all fleshy matter. The hind flippers are cut off at the ankle and the skin either sewed or stoutly wrapped with thong. The fore flippers are usually left at-

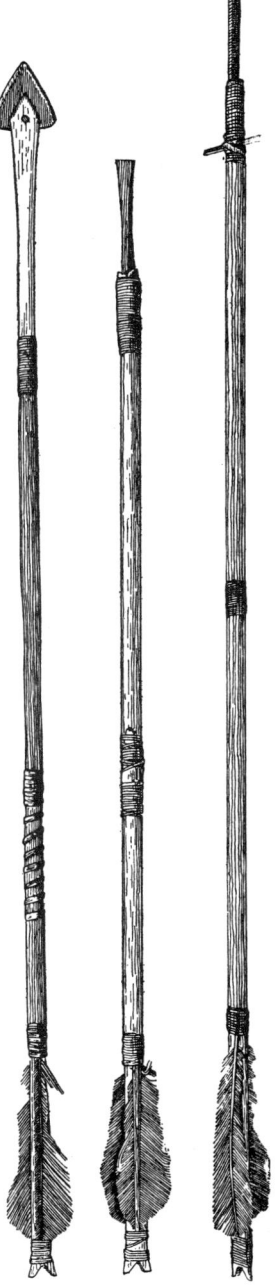

FIGS. 63, 64, and 65.—Arrows. East Main Eskimo.

tached to the skin after the flesh has been scraped from them. The skin is now inflated with air and hung up to dry. In a few hours it is turned with the hairy side out and again inflated for awhile. The mouth and all other openings in the skin are carefully sewed up. A large button of ivory, shaped much like a pulley, nearly 2 inches in diameter, is put where the mouth of the skin is and a portion of the skin carefully wrapped around it, thongs of sealskin tightening the moist skin in the groove of the mouthpiece. This piece has a hole about one-third of an inch in diameter bored through it. The hind flippers and tail have a stick of 2 or 3 inches in length placed within the skin and are then firmly bound around the stick, which serves to stop up any hole and also to furnish a handle by which to drag or hold the float. The hole in the mouth-piece is plugged with a stopper of wood. When the float is wanted for use the skin is inflated. When inflated the float has a diameter about two-thirds the length. If it is to be attached to a tracking line the float is fastened by the stick, which is secured within the skin of the hind flippers and dragged backwards. The function of the float in this instance is to prevent the tracking line from becoming "fouled" among the rocks and stones of the beach along which the line runs in towing a boat (or umiak). In a similar manner it is affixed to the harpoon line used for large marine mammals, such as the white whale and the larger species of seals. This float not only retards the flight of the speared animal, but it serves to mark the spot where it sinks, for at certain seasons the seals sink as soon as they die. A speared animal always sinks more quickly than one shot dead with a ball, probably because its struggles are more prolonged in the first instance and exhaustion of breath is more complete.

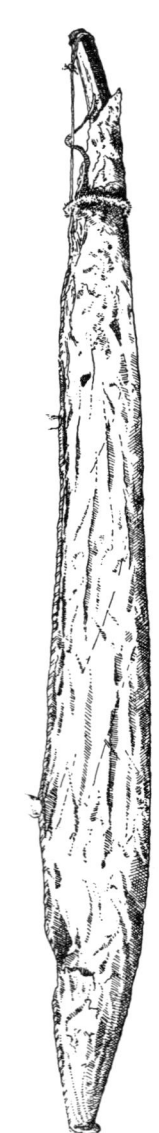

FIG. 66. Bow case. East Main Eskimo.

The hair of the animal whose skin is intended for a float is sometimes scraped off before the skin is removed from the body, otherwise it may be left until the skin is partly dry and then be shaved off. The manner of loosening the hair is similar to that used by butchers of hogs, only that the boiling water is poured on and a small patch of hair pulled off at a time, instead of submerging the entire animal. The hair from the green skin must be carefully pulled out or else the black scurf adhering will be detached and thus render the skin less nearly waterproof.

The skins or bags used for holding oil and fat are prepared in a similar manner, excepting that the hair is left on the skin and the hairy side left within. The oil and fat are put in the skin at the posterior end and it is then tied up like a float. The largest sealskins are used for oilbags, and may contain as much as 300 pounds of fat or oil.

When a sack of oil is sold the bag is usually returned to the seller, who again fills it with oil or converts the skin into bootlegs or soles. The leather having become thoroughly impregnated with the oil makes the best for wear, often resisting moisture for three or four days of continuous wet.

Before leaving the subject of weapons and their accessories, I may mention No. 3069, a small pouch made of thick sealskin. The shape is somewhat like that of a leg of mutton. This is used for carrying gun caps. The neck is only large enough to permit one cap to fall out at a time.

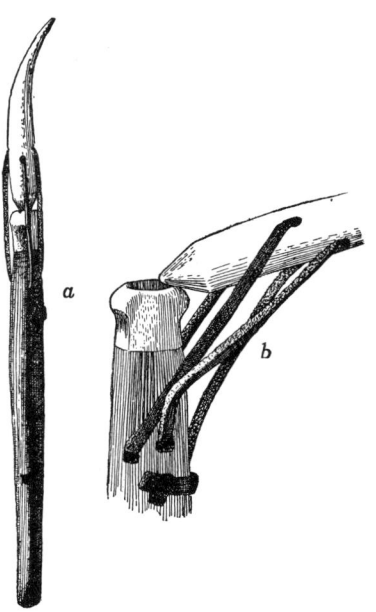

FIG. 67.—Hand spear for killing seals from kaiak; Koksoak.

HUNTING.

I have already referred briefly to the various methods of taking seals, white whales, and other game, while describing the boats, spears, and other apparatus used in their pursuit.

The most important hunt of the year, however, comes in the autumn, when the reindeer are migrating in large herds and crossing the rivers. The deer are wanted now for their flesh for food and their skins for clothing. Everything necessary for the chase is taken in the umiak, or, perhaps, a whaleboat, to a locality convenient to where the animals cross over. Here the tent is pitched, and a camp is made. The hunters scour the neighboring land for herds of reindeer, which are seen running about under the impulse to seek the opposite sex. As they arrive from different directions, those of one sex must cross the river. Since the females furnish the lighter skins for clothing, and the males the greater amount of meat and a heavier skin for various purposes, deer of both sexes are equally useful.

A band of three or four, or as many as a hundred, may be sighted slowly winding their way through the openings of the timbered areas on the opposite side of the river. The native with telescope, or binocular in focus, observes their movements until they pause a moment on the bank and then plunge quickly into the water, where they keep well together until the opposite shore is reached. Here, if undisturbed, they will stand to allow the water to drip from their bodies, and then will walk slowly along to a convenient place to climb the bank and

penetrate the strip of woods or bushes and emerge into the open country beyond. As soon as the native sees the deer everything is put in

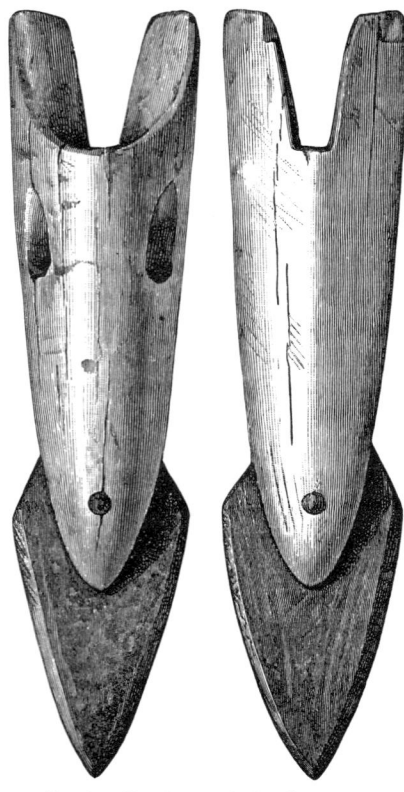

readiness on the kaiak, and with
quick strokes of the double-bladed
paddle he is behind and below the
now terrified animals. They rear
and plunge in frantic confusion,
endeavoring to escape their most
dreaded foe. The hunter calmly
drives the herd through the water
as the shepherd does his flock on
land. Those disposed to break
away are rounded up and driven
back. The greatest care must be
exercised not to let the animals
get below the kaiak, or they will
swim faster with the stream than
the hunter can paddle. As there
are, generally, two or more kaiaks,
it is an easy matter for the men
to drive the animals wherever
they desire. When the camp is
above, the deer are driven diag-
onally across so as to make them
come out near the camp. If the
site is below, the animals are
allowed to drop down to a convenient place. These maneuvers
depend on the wind, as the sense
of smell of the deer is very acute

FIG. 68.—Togglehead for hand spear.

at this season, and the scent of the camp, if detected, would throw the
animals into such terror that the greater number would escape.

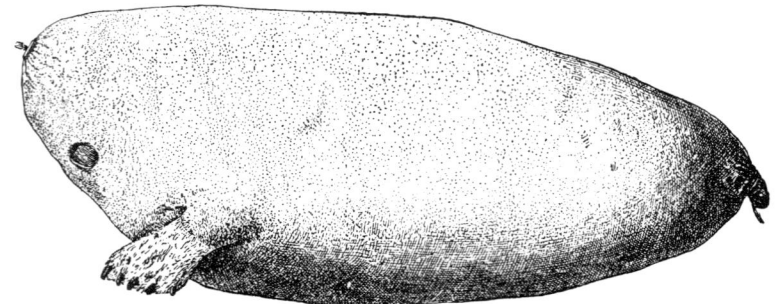

FIG. 69.—Sealskin float.

When near the place the hunter takes his deer spear, which is exactly
like the one used by the Indians, and quietly stabs the animal in a

vital spot, endeavoring so to wound the beast that it will have only enough strength to enable it to attain the shallow water or shore, and not to wander off. Among the hundreds of times I have had the opportunity to witness this, I never knew a deer wounded with the spear to turn back to swim in the direction from which it came. They appear to dread the water, and strive most frantically to regain the land where, if mortally wounded, they stand; the limbs gradually diverging to sustain their trembling body; the eyes gazing piteously at the foe, who often mocks their dying struggles, or pitches a stone at their quivering legs to make them fall. A convulsive struggle as the blood fills the internal cavity, a sudden pitch, and the life is gone without sigh or groan. As many of the herd as can be speared are quickly dispatched and the entire number secured if possible. It is supposed that the ones which return to the shore whence they came give the alarm and frighten other arrivals away from the starting point. The hunters strive to prevent their return, and will often allow two, near the camp, to escape in order to pursue the retreating animal.

Those which have been killed and are lying in the water are dragged on land and skinned. The pelt is taken off as that of a beef is when skinned by a butcher. The ears and the skin of the head are left on. The body is opened and the viscera are removed. The intestines are freed from the fat; the stomach is cleansed of the greater portion of its contents, and the blood which collected within the cavity is scooped up with the hands and ladled into that receptacle; and both are reserved for food. The heart and liver are taken to the camp, where they help to form a variety in the animal food of these people. Other portions of the flesh are also consumed. The sinew, which lies along the lumbar region just below the superficial muscles, is exposed by a cut, and with the point of a knife or tip of the finger loosened from its adherent flesh. One end, usually the forward end, is detached and a stout thong tied to it, and it is jerked from its attachment by a vigorous pull. It requires a strong person to remove this tendon from the body of a lean animal. A stroke of the knife frees the wide layer of sinew from blood and particles of flesh. This is now laid aside for awhile, then washed to free it from the blood, which would stain it dark in color and also tend to diminish the strength of the fibers by rotting them. It is now spread out and allowed to dry. The body is cut across the small of the back and laid aside. The head is severed from the neck and discarded if there be no portion of the horns which is needed to serve some purpose, such as a handle for a knife or other tool. If the head be that of a young deer it is often taken to the camp and put into a pot and boiled in the condition in which it comes from the field. When cooked for a long time it becomes very soft; the muscles of the jaw being reduced to a semigelatinous condition, which makes an excellent article of food.

The tongue is invariably taken out entire, and is considered the greatest delicacy, either frozen, raw or cooked, or dried and smoked. In fact a tongue from the reindeer is good at any time or condition.

The hindquarters are seldom separated, but are placed within the thoracic cavity, and either cached near the scene of slaughter or placed on the kaiak and taken to a spot where others are deposited from which supplies may be taken when the food for the winter is required.

Here and there along the bank will be placed the body of a single deer, sometimes two or three, which have been killed too far from the present camp for the hunter to bring them home. These spots are marked or remembered by some visible surrounding, lest the deep snows of winter obscure the locality, and often the place can not be found when wanted. The cache in which the flesh is deposited is simply a few stones or bowlders laid on the ground and the meat put upon them. A rude sort of wall is made by piling stones upon the meat until it is hidden from the ravages of ravens, gulls, foxes, wolves, and the detested wolverine.

As soon as the hunter considers that the deer of that particular locality have ceased to cross, he will repair to another station and go through the same process. The deer which are first slain, when the hunting season arrives, and the weather is still so warm that the flies and decomposition ruin the meat, are reserved for supplies of dog food.

MISCELLANEOUS IMPLEMENTS.

I have already, in the earlier pages of this paper, referred to various tools and implements.

In addition to these, the Koksoagmyut have comparatively few tools.

In former ages stone and ivory were fashioned into crude implements for the purposes which are now better and more quickly served by instruments of iron or steel.

These people have now been so long in more or less direct contact with traders who have supplied them with these necessaries that it is rare to find one of the knives used in former times. Certain operations, however, are even to this day better performed with a knife made of ivory. The ice from the kaiak bottom or the sides of the boat may best be removed by means of an ivory knife, resembling a snow knife but shorter. The steel knife is always kept sharp and if so used would, on the unyielding, frozen skin-covering of those vessels, quickly cut a hole. The Eskimo living remote from the trading stations use a snow knife made from the tusk of a walrus or the main stem of the reindeer antler.

That steel or iron is deemed an improvement on the former materials from which cutting instruments were made is shown by the crude means now employed. If the person has not a knife an unused spearhead, having an iron point, is often employed instead for skinning animals and dressing the skins.

Stone heads for weapons of all kinds have been discarded. Ivory spears are at times used but these only when the hunter is close to the prey.

Some of the men have acquired considerable skill in fashioning iron into the required shape. They eagerly stand around anyone who may be at work, and evince the greatest curiosity in anything new.

The collection contains two of the snow knives referred to above. No. 3067 is a large snow knife, made from the lower portion of the main stem of the horn of the male reindeer. It is simply half of the split horn with the middle scooped out. The length is 12 inches. This form of instrument is used more especially to smooth down the inequalities of the blocks of snow after being placed in position. No. 3140 (Fig. 70) is a large snow knife made of walrus ivory. It is 13 inches long and nearly 2 inches wide for the greater part of the blade, which terminates in a rounded point. The instrument has two edges, and in general appearances resembles a double-edged Roman sword. The handle is cut to fit to the hand.

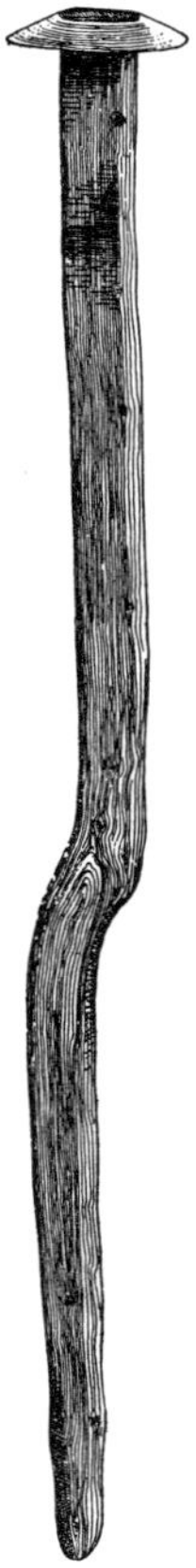

Among other peculiar implements collected is one represented in Fig. 71 (No. 3555), which is a "back-scratcher." This instrument consists of a shaft made from a limb of a larch tree. It is 17 inches long and about three-fourths of an inch through, flattened to less than half an inch and tapering toward the end to be held in the hand. On the lower end is a dish-shaped piece of reinder horn, two and one-eighth inches long and seven-eighths of an inch wide. Through the center of the piece of horn an oblong hole has been cut for the insertion of the shaft or handle. The edges of the horn piece are sharp as can be made. This piece is one-third of an inch thick, and having the sharp edge up is convenient for thrusting down the back to scratch one's self in places where the hand could not reach on account of thick deerskin clothing. The Eskimo name of the instrument is ku-mé-u-tîk, or that which removes lice.

FIG. 70.—Ivory snow knife, Koksoagmyut.

FIG. 71.—Back-scratcher, Koksoagmyut.

The steel needles obtained from the traders are kept in a little ivory receptacle of various shapes, two of which are shown in Figs. 72 and 73.

This is hollow and filled with any sphagnum moss. One end is permanently closed by a wooden or ivory plug, held in by little pegs. The plug in the other end is easily taken out. The needle case is usually pierced to receive a loop by which it may be hung to the belt or the workbag.

Needles are also kept in a kind of small cushion (Fig. 74) made of

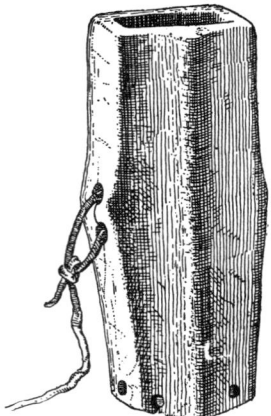 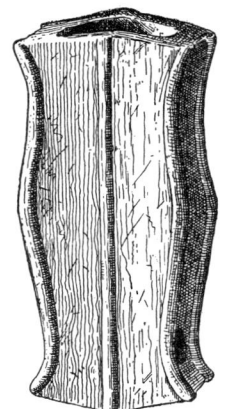

FIG. 72.—Ivory needle case.
Koksoagmyut.

FIG. 73.- Ivory needle case.
Koksoagmyut.

sealskin, elaborately ornamented with beads and stuffed with sphagnum moss. The cushion is perforated around the edge to receive the needles, which would not easily go through the tough skin.

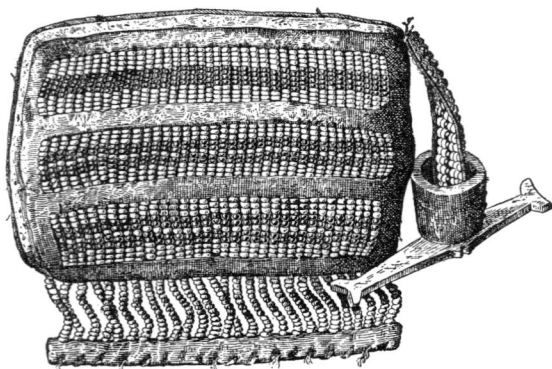

FIG. 74.—Sealskin needle cushion, with thimble.   Koksoagmyut.

Accompanying one of these needle cushions in the collection is one of the old-fashioned thimbles such as are still used, although metal thimbles are preferred. It is simply a strip of sealskin sewed into a ring large enough to fit the forefinger, and is usually attached to the needle cushion by a thong with an ivory toggle on the end, to prevent the thimble from slipping off.

Small articles used in sewing, such as scraps of skin, needle cases, sinew thread, thimbles, etc., are carried in small bags of deerskin, which are often elaborately ornamented with beads of various colors, like the specimen in the collection, No. 3047.

AMUSEMENTS.

Notwithstanding the fact that these people have had their lot cast upon the frozen shores of the sea, they appear happy and contented and loath to leave the land of their birth. Although it is a constant struggle amidst the terrible storms of a region where for eight months in the year the soil is frozen and the few warm days of summer bring forth a scanty vegetation, yet so strong is their love for these inhospitable shores that the absent pine for a return and soon lose their hold on life if they are not able to do so.

During the intervals between the hunts and when food is still plentiful, the Eskimo divert themselves with games of various kinds of their own. They are also quick to adopt other games which require outdoor exercise.

Football calls out everybody, from the aged and bent mother of a numerous family to the toddling youngster scarcely able to do more than waddle under the burden of his heavy deerskin clothes. Wrestling among the men is indulged in for hours at a time. The opponents remove all their superfluous garments, seize each other around the waist and lock hands behind each other's backs. The feet are spread widely apart and each endeavors to draw, by the strength of the arms alone, the back of his opponent into a curve and thus bring him off his feet. Then with a lift he is quickly thrown flat on his back. The fall must be such that the head touches the ground. Where the contestants are nearly matched the struggle may continue so long that one of them gives up from exhaustion. The feet are never used for tripping. Such a procedure would soon cause the witnesses to stop the struggle.

The Eskimo and Indians often engage in comparative tests of their strength in wrestling. The Eskimo prove the better men in these engagements. Throwing stones at a mark is a sport for the younger men, some of whom acquire surprising dexterity.

If a pack of playing-cards can be obtained they engage in games which they have learned from the white people and teach each other. Small stakes are laid on the result of the game. The women appear to exhibit a greater passion for gambling than the men do. They will wager the last article of clothing on their persons till the loser appears in a nude condition before spectators. Then the winner will usually return at least a part of the clothing, with an injunction to play more and lose less.

The young girls often play the game of taking an object and secreting it within the closed hand. Another is called upon to guess the contents. She makes inquiries as to the size, color, etc., of the object. From the answers she gradually guesses what the thing is.

A favorite game, something like cup and ball, is played with the following implements: A piece of ivory is shaped into the form of an elongate cone and has two deep notches or steps cut from one side (Fig. 75). In the one next the base are bored a number of small holes and one or two holes in the upper step. The apex has a single hole. On the opposite side of the base two holes are made obliquely, that they will meet, and through them is threaded a short piece of thong. To the other end of the thong is attached a peg of ivory, about 4 inches long. The game is that the person holding the plaything shall, by a dextrous swing of the ball, catch it upon the ivory peg held in the hand. The person engages to catch it a certain number of times in succession,

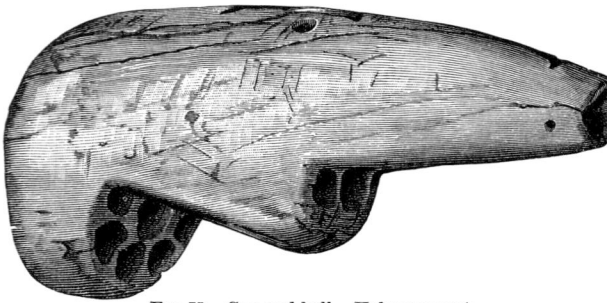

and on failure to do so allows the opponent to try her skill. The skull of a hare is often substituted for the ivory "ball," and a few perforations are made in the walls of the skull to receive the peg.

FIG. 75.—Cup and ball. Koksoagmyut.

It requires a great amount of practice to catch the ball, as the string is so short that one must be quick to thrust the peg in before it describes the part of a small circle.

The children sometimes use a stick or other sharp-pointed instrument to make a series of straight lines in the newly fallen snow and at the same time repeat certain gibberish. This was at first very confusing to me, but a woman repeated the words and I guessed from her description where the idea sprang from.

These people had heard of the teachings of the Labrador missionaries (Moravians), all of whom are Germans, and as the Eskimo of that coast use the German numerals in preference to their own, the natives of that region have at some time repeated the names of those numerals to certain of the Hudson strait people and they have taught each other.

The names of the German numerals as sounded by the Koksoagmyut are as follows. The numbers are one to fifteen, consecutively:

Ái i; chu vái i; ta lái i; pi û′ la; pi li pi; tsék si; tsé pa; ák ta; nái na; tsé na; ái lu pûk; chu vái lu puk; ta lak si na; pi ûk′ si na, and pi lip′ si na.

I have already referred to the game of football as played by these people.

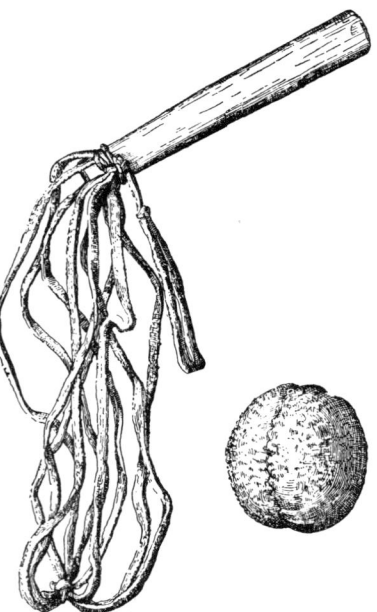

FIG. 76.—Football and driver. Koksoagmyut.

Fig. 76 represents the football (No. 3070) and the whip for driving it. The Eskimo are very fond of this game. All the people of every age, from the toddling infant to the aged female with bended back, love to urge the aí uk toúk, as the ball is termed. The size of the ball varies from 3 to 7 inches in diameter. They have not yet arrived at perfection in making a spherical form for the ball, but it is often an apple shape. It is made by taking a piece of buckskin, or sealskin, and cutting it into a circular form, then gathering the edges and stuffing the cavity with dry moss or feathers. A circular piece of skin is then inserted to fill the space which is left by the incomplete gatherings. This ball is very light and is driven either by a blow from the foot or else by a whip of peculiar construction. This whip consists of a handle of wood 8 to 12 inches in length. To prevent it from slipping out of the hand when the blow is struck, a stout thong of sealskin is made into the form of a long loop which is passed over the hand and tightens around the wrist. To the farther end of the whip handle are attached a number of stout thongs of heavy sealskin. These thongs have their ends tied around the handle and thus form a number of loops of 12 to 20 inches in length. These are then tied together at the bottom in order to give them greater weight

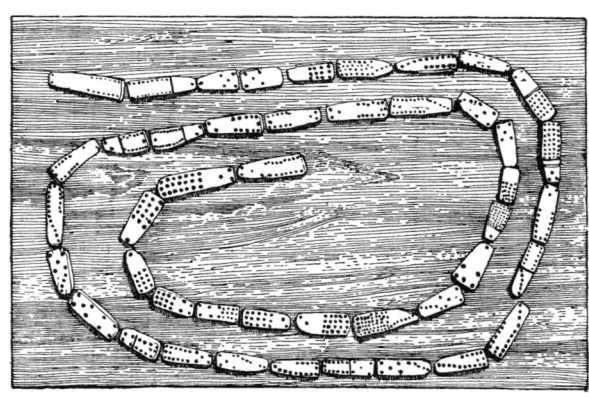

FIG. 77.—Dominoes. Hudson Strait Eskimo.

when the ball is struck by them. A lusty Eskimo will often send the ball over a hundred yards through the air with such force as to knock a person down.

At Fort Chimo the game is played during the late winter afternoons when the temperature is 30° or 40° below zero. It is exciting and vigorous play where a large crowd joins in the game.

Sometimes the ball is in the form of two irregular hemispheres joined together, making a sphere which can be rolled only in a certain direction. It is very awkward and produces much confusion by its erratic course. Nos. 3461, 3287, and 3460 are footballs of the pattern first described.

The Innuit who come from the western end of Hudson strait, the so-called "Northerners," have a game which they play with sets of pieces of ivory cut into irregular shapes, and marked on one face with spots arranged in different patterns (Fig. 77). The number of pieces in a set varies from 60 to 148. The name of the set is Á ma zu′ a lát, and somewhat resembles our game of dominoes.

The game is played in the following manner: Two or more persons, according to the number of pieces in the set, sit down and pile the pieces before them. One of the players mixes the pieces together in plain view of the others. When this is done he calls them to take the pieces. Each person endeavors to obtain a half or third of the number if there be two or three players. The one who mixed up the pieces lays down a piece and calls his opponent to match it with a piece having a similar design. If this can not be done by any of the players the first has to match it and the game continues until one of the persons has exhausted all of the pieces taken by him. The pieces are designed in pairs, having names such as Ka miú tik (sled), Kaiak (canoe), Kalé sak (navel), Á ma zut (many), a taú sïk (1), Má kok (2), Pïng a sut (3), Si tá mût (4), and Tá li mat (5). Each of the names above must be matched with a piece of similar kind, although the other end of the piece may be of a different design. A Kamutik may be matched with an Amazut if the latter has not a line or bar cut across it; if it has the bar it must be matched with an Amazut.

This game is known to the people of the Ungava district, but those only who have learned it from the Northerners are able to play it. The northern Eskimo stake the last article they possess on the issue of the game. Their wives are disposed of temporarily, and often are totally relinquished to the victor. I have heard that the wives so disposed of often sit down and win themselves back to their former owners.

The little girls play with dolls like civilized children, and build little snow huts, where they have all their playthings and play at keeping house. The collection contains eleven dolls, most of them elaborately and accurately dressed, as shown by the illustrations (Figs. 78, 79, 80, 81) and large quantities of doll clothing.

The only musical instrument which I observed among these people

FIG. 78.—Eskimo doll, man.

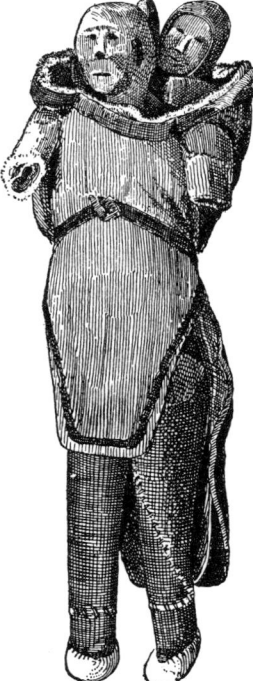

FIG. 79.—Eskimo doll, woman.

was a violin of their own manufacture, made, of course, in imitation of those they had seen used by the whites. Its form is sufficiently well shown by the figure (Fig. 82), and is made of birch or spruce, and the two strings are of coarse, loosely twisted sinew. The bow has a strip of whalebone in place of horsehair, and is resined with spruce gum. This fiddle is held across the lap when played.

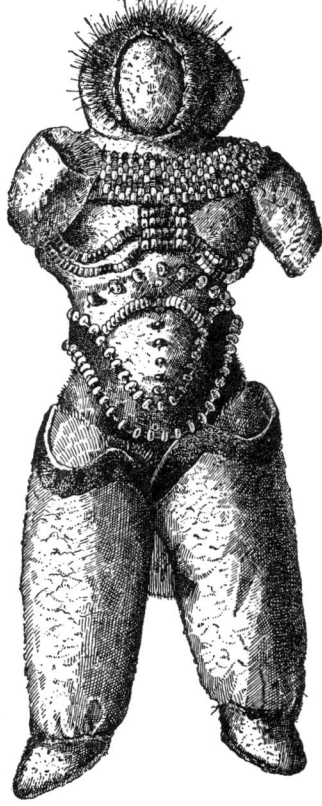

The old woman of whom I procured the instrument was able to play several airs—such as they sing among themselves. I was surprised at the facility with which she made the various notes on such a crude imitation of a violin.

ART.

Art is but slightly developed among these people. Their weapons and other implements are never adorned with carvings of animals and other natural objects or with conventional patterns, as is

FIG. 80.—Eskimo doll, woman.

FIG. 81.—Eskimo doll, woman.

the case in so great a degree among the Eskimo of Alaska. They are, however, not devoid of artistic skill, as is shown by the good taste

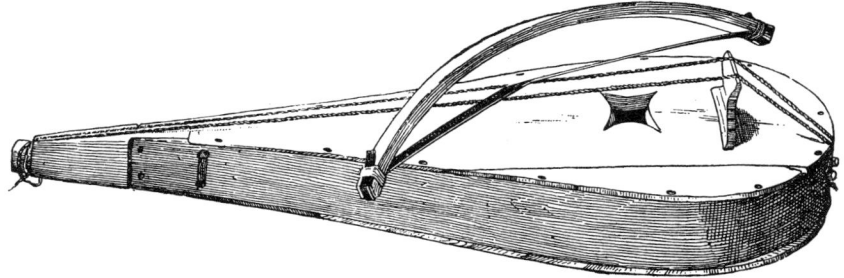

FIG. 82.—Eskimo violin.

often exhibited in the trimming of their garments, and also by the dolls, which I have already referred to and figured.

The collection also contains several small ivory carvings, which possess considerable artistic merit. Among these, the small ob-

jects, (Fig. 83), collected from the so-called Northerners, represent various waterfowl cut from pieces of walrus ivory. The various species thus carved are loons, ducks, geese, sea pigeons, and murres. One represents a female eider with two young mounted upon her back. It is readily discerned, in most instances, what position and action of the bird was intended to be represented. The last shows in the plainest possible manner that the loon is just starting to swim from an object which has given it alarm.

These carvings are fashioned from the tusks of the walrus or the teeth of various large mammals, and are simply tests of the skill of the worker, who prepares them as toys for the children. Notwithstanding the assertions of others, who claim to have knowledge of it, I must state

FIG. 83.—Birds carved in ivory.

that on no occasion have I seen or heard, while among these people, of these objects being used in any game.

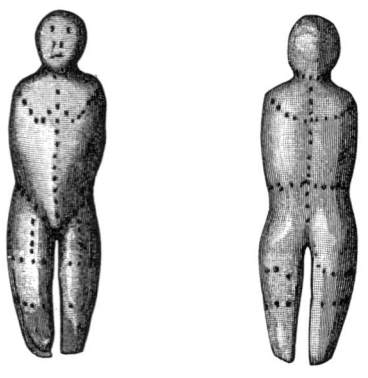

In addition to these we have a very artistic figure of a polar bear, and two human figures, 1¾ inches long (Fig. 84), representing tattooed women, and two carvings representing bags of oil.

STORY-TELLING AND FOLK LORE.

Like all other Eskimo, the Koksoagmyut are exceedingly fond of story-telling. Sitting in the hut, engaged in their evening work, the old men tell what they have seen and

FIG. 84.—Human figure, carved in ivory.   heard. The old women relate the history of the people of former days, depending entirely on memory, often interspersed with recitations apparently foreign to the thread of the legend. The younger members sit with staring eyes and countenances which show their wondering interest in the narration. Far into the night the droning tone of her voice continues reciting the events of the past until one by one the listeners drowsily drop to sleep in the position they last assumed.

I was fortunately able to collect a number of these ancient legendary stories, some of them of considerable length.

Origin of the Innuit.—A man was created from nothing. It was summer and he journeyed until he found a woman in another land. The two became man and wife, and from them sprang all the people dwelling there. [It is extremely difficult to get the native to go beyond the immediate vicinity in which he lives while relating these stories and legends. They invariably maintain that it was "here" that the event took place.]

The Coming of the White People.—The Eskimo were on the verge of starvation and had eaten nearly all their food. They saw that in a few more days death would come. The greatest Tungaksoak or great Tung ak determined to bring relief and prophesied that people having light hair and white skins would come in an immense úmiak. He placed a young puppy on a chip and another on an old sealskin boot, and set them adrift on the water. The puppies drifted in different directions, and in the course of time the one on the chip returned and brought with it the Indians. A long time after that, when the people had nearly forgotten the other puppy, a strange white object like an iceberg came directly toward the shore. In a few moments the puppy, now a man, announced that the people had come with many curious things in their vessel. The man immediately became a dog.

Origin of living things on the earth and in the water.—A long time ago a man who was cutting down a tree observed that the chips continued in motion as they fell from the blows. Those that fell into the water became the inhabitants of the water. Those that fell on the land became the various animals and in time were made the food of mankind. (This was the version given me by a person living at Fort Chimo.) Another person from farther west gave the following account of the origin of the living things of the earth: Previous to a time when water covered the earth the people lived on such food as they could always find prepared for them in abundance. They did not know of any animals at that time on the land or in the water. The water finally went away and the seaweeds became trees, shrubs, bushes, and grass. The long seaweeds were the trees and the smaller kinds became the bushes and grass. The grass, however, was in some manner put in various places by a walrus at a later date than the appearance of the trees.

A woman who had lost her husband lived among strangers. As they desired to change the place of their habitation, they resolved to journey to another point of land at a distance. The woman who was depending on charity had become a burden of which they wished to rid themselves.

So they put all their belongings into the umiak and when they were on the way they seized the woman and cast her overboard. She struggled to regain the side of the boat, and when she seized it, the others cut off her fingers which fell into the water and changed to seals, walrus, whales, and white bears. The woman in her despair, screamed her determination to have revenge for the cruelty perpetrated upon her. The thumb became a walrus, the first finger a seal, and the middle finger a white bear. When the former two animals see a man they try to escape lest they be served as the woman was.

The white bear lives both on the land and in the sea, but when he perceives a man revengeful feelings fill him, and he determines to destroy the person who he thinks mutilated the woman from whose finger he sprang.

Origin of the guillemots.—While some children were playing on the level top of a high cliff overhanging the sea, the older children watched the younger ones lest they should fall down the bluff. Below them the sea was covered with ice, and the strip along the shore had not yet loosened to permit the seals to approach. Soon afterward a wide crack opened and the water was filled with seals, but the children did not observe them. The wind was cold, and the children romped in high glee, encouraging each other to greater exertion in their sports and shouted at the top of their voices. The men saw the seals and hastened to the shore to put their kaiaks into the water to pursue them. At this the children increased their shouts, which frightened the seals till they dived out of sight. One of the men was angry, and exclaimed to the others, "I wish the cliff would topple over and bury those noisy children for scaring the seals." In a moment the cliff tipped over and the poor children fell among the fragments of huge rocks and stones at the bottom. Here they were changed into guillemots or sea-pigeons, with red feet, and even to this day they thus dwell among the débris at the foot of cliffs next to the water of the sea.

Origin of the raven.—The raven was a man, who, while other people were collecting their household property preparatory to removing to another locality, called to them that they had forgotten to bring the lower blanket of deerskin used for a bed. This skin in the Eskimo language is called kak. The man used the word so often that they told him to get it himself. He hurried so much that he was changed into a raven, and now uses that sound for his note. Even to this day when the camp is being removed the raven flies over and shouts "Kak! kak!" or, in other words, "Do not forget the blanket."

Origin of the quadrangular spots on the loon's back.—A man had two children that he wished might resemble each other. He painted the one (loon) with a white breast and square spots on the back. The other (raven) saw how comical the loon appeared, and laughed so much that the loon became ashamed and escaped to the water, where it always presents its white breast in order to hide the spots of the back which caused so much ridicule. The raven eluded the attempt to be painted in like manner, and stoutly refused to come near.

Origin of the gulls.—Some people in a boat desired to go around a point of land which projected far into the water. As the water there was always in a violent commotion under the end of the point which terminated in a high cliff some of the women were requested to walk over the neck of land. One of them got out with her children in order to lighten the boat. She was directed to go over the place, and they promised to wait for her on the other side. The people in the boat had gone so far that their voices, giving the direction, became indistinct. The poor woman became confused and suspected they wanted to desert her. She remained about the cliff, constantly crying the last words she heard. She ultimately changed into a gull, and now shouts only the sound like "*go over, goover, over, ove,*" etc.

Origin of the hawks.—Among the people of a village was a woman who was noted for the shortness of her neck. She was so constantly teased and tormented about it that she often sat for hours on the edge of high places. She changed into a hawk, and now when she sees anyone she immediately exclaims, "Kea! kea! kea! who, who, who was it that cried 'short neck?'"

Origin of the swallow.—Some small children, who were extraordinarily wise, were playing at building toy houses on the edge of a high cliff near the village in which they dwelt. They were envied for their wisdom, and to them was given the name "Zulugagnak," or, like a raven, which was supposed to know all the past and future. While these children were thus amusing themselves they were changed into small birds, which did not forget their last occupation, and even to this day they come to the cliffs, near the camps of the people, and build houses of mud, which they affix to the side of the rock. Even the raven does not molest them, and the Eskimo children love to watch the swallow build his iglugiak of mud.

The hare.—The hare was a child who was so ill treated and abused by the other people, because it had long ears, that it went to dwell by itself. When it sees anyone the ears are laid down on the back, for, if it hears the shout of a person, it thinks they are talking of its long ears. It has no tail, because it did not formerly have one.

The wolf was a poor woman, who had so many children that she could not find enough for them to eat. They became so gaunt and hungry that they were changed into wolves, constantly roaming over the land seeking food. The cry of the mother may be heard as she strives to console her hungry children, saying that food in plenty will soon be found.

Lice are supposed to drop from the body of a huge spirit, dwelling in the regions above, who was punished by having these pests constantly torment him. In his rage to free himself the lice dropped down upon the people who condemned him to this punishment.

Origin of mosquitoes.—A man had a wife who was negligent and failed to scrape his skin clothing properly when he returned from his expeditions. He endeavored to persuade her to mend her ways and do as a wife should do. She was again directed to remove the accumulated layer of dirt from the man's coat. She petulantly took the garment and cleaned it in such a slovenly way that when the husband discovered the condition of the coat he took some of the dirt from it and flung it after her. The particles changed into mosquitoes, and now (in spring), when the warm days come and the women have the labor of cleaning clothes to perform, the insects gather around them, and the women are thus reminded of the slovenly wife and what befel her.

Story of the man and his fox wife.—A hunter who lived by himself found when he returned to the place after an absence that it had been visited and everything put in order as a dutiful wife should do. This happened so often with no visible signs of tracks that the man determined to watch and see who would scrape his skin clothing and boots, hang them out to dry, and cook nice hot food ready to be eaten when he returned. One day he went away as though going off on a hunt, but secreted himself so as to observe the entrance of anything into the house. After a while he saw a fox enter. He suspected that the fox was after food. He quietly slipped up to the house and on entering saw a most beautiful woman dressed in skin clothing of wondrous make. Within the house, on a line, hung the skin of a fox. The man inquired if it was she who had done these things. She replied that she was his wife and it was her duty to do them, hoping that she had performed her labor in a manner satisfactory to him.

After they had lived together a short time the husband detected a musky odor about the house and inquired of her what it was. She replied that she emitted the odor and if he was going to find fault with her for it she would leave. She dashed off her clothing and, resuming the skin of the fox, slipped quietly away and has never been disposed to visit a man since that time.

The following is a story obtained from Labrador:

The rivals.—Between two men there existed keen rivalry. Each asserted himself to be the stronger and endeavored to prove himself superior to the other. One of them declared his ability to form an island where none had hitherto existed. He picked up an immense rock and hurled it into the sea where it became an island. The other, with his foot, pushed it so hard that it landed on the top of another island lying far beyond. The mark of the footprint is visible to this day, and that place is now known as Tu kik′ tok.

The jealous man.—A man fell in love with two women and was so jealous of them that he would not permit them to look upon others, much less speak to them. The women finally wearied of the restrictions placed upon them and resolved to desert the man. They fled along the coast until they were faint from hunger. At length they came upon the body of a whale cast on the shore. Here they determined to dwell for a time. The man sought for the women in every possible place with no success. A conjurer was consulted, and after much deliberation, he told the deserted man to journey to a place where he would find the carcass of a whale and to secrete himself in the vicinity and watch for the women. He started out accordingly and before long had the pleasure of seeing the two women. They detected the man hastening toward them and tried to secrete themselves until he should get by. He seized one of them, however, and bound her with thongs. The other was less disposed to submit, and the man put out her eyes to deprive her of the privilege of looking at any man. They remained about that locality for some time, and various animals of the land came to the carcass to feast upon the remains. The man caught a great number of foxes and other valuable furs and after a time returned to the camp whence he came.

Story of the orphan boy.—A small boy, who had neither father, mother, nor any living relatives, was dwelling with some people who maltreated him in every way their fancy could suggest. He was kept in the entry way to the hut, like a dog, and was permitted to eat only of the skin of walrus when they had it to give him. At other times they would throw to him what they themselves would not eat. They forbade him to have a knife with which to cut his food, and he was compelled to gnaw the bones like a dog. A little girl, the daughter of the head of the family with whom he lived, would secretly take to him a knife with which to divide the tough skin of the walrus. She also carried food of better quality to him when she could do so clandestinely. These kind attentions pleased him very much, and made him long for an opportunity to escape. But how was he to better his condition when the hand of everybody was raised against him on account of his treatment at home? The little girl who had so often befriended him could not assist him to escape from such a life. He endeavored to lay a plan, but it came to naught. There seemed no help for him. One night he abandoned all hope and threw himself on the ground in despair. While there he gazed at the bright moon, and the more intently his gaze was fixed upon it the more he thought he discerned the face of a man in it, and at last he cried to the man to come and help him escape from his miserable life. The man came down from the moon and gave the poor boy a frightful beating, but the more he was beaten the larger he seemed to grow. After awhile he became so strong that he could handle a large rock as easily as he had hitherto handled a little stone. A large, round bowlder from the beach was no more to him than a bullet held in the hand of a strong man.

The moon man then told the boy that he was large enough to take care of himself and do as he pleased with the people who had treated him so badly. With this the two parted, and the moon man went to his hole in the sky, while the boy walked along the beach picking up rocks and tossing them along the shore until the character of the water's edge was entirely changed. When the boy arrived at the hut it was daylight, for he had tarried so long on the beach testing his strength that the night had slipped away.

The people were terrified when they saw to what enormous proportions the abused boy had grown. He became frenzied the instant he saw his former persecutors, and seizing first one and then the other in his hands dashed them against the rocks. The blood and brains ran in streams. One of the men, seeing his doom, begged for his life and promised his kaiak, spears, sled, and wife if he should be spared. The enraged boy continued the slaughter until only the little girl who had so often befriended him was left. She became his wife, and in the course of a few hours the man, whose name was Kou jé yuk, became of a natural size again and passed his life in comfort.

This story was obtained from a man from Labrador. The Eskimo assert that this occurred near Ohak (often pronounced Okak), now a missionary station. They show the rock, which a little imagination gives the appearance of having dried blood and brains still upon it.

The origin of the sun, moon, and stars.—At a time when darkness covered the earth a girl was nightly visited by some one whose identity she could not discover. She determined to find out who it could be. She mixed some soot with oil and painted her breast with it. The next time she discovered, to her horror, that her brother had a black circle of soot around his mouth. She upbraided him and he denied it. The father and mother were very angry and scolded the pair so severely that the son fled from their presence. The daughter seized a brand from the fire and pursued him. He ran to the sky to avoid her but she flew after him. The man changed into the moon and the girl who bore the torch became the sun. The sparks that flew from the brand became the stars. The sun is constantly pursuing the moon, which keeps in the darkness to avoid being discovered. When an eclipse occurs they are supposed to meet.

Auroras.—Auroras are believed to be the torches held in the hands of spirits seeking the souls of those who have just died, to lead them over the abyss terminating the edge of the world. A narrow pathway leads across it to the land of brightness and plenty, where disease and pain are no more, and where food of all kinds is always ready in abundance. To this place none but the dead and the raven can go. When the spirits wish to communicate with the people of the earth they make a whistling noise and the earth people answer only in a whispering tone. The Eskimo say that they are able to call the aurora and converse with it. They send messages to the dead through these spirits.

The sky.—The sky is supposed to be an immense dome, of hard material, reared over the earth, long from east to west and shorter from north to south. The edges of the land and sea are bounded by high, precipitous sides, shelving outward or sloping inward to prevent anything living on the earth from going to the region beyond. There is the source of light and heat. The dome of the sky is very cold, and at times covered with crystals of frost which fall in the form of snow or frost films to the earth, and then the sky becomes clear. The clouds are supposed to be large bags of water, controlled by two old women who run with them across the sky, and as the water escapes from the seams it falls in the form of rain to the earth. The thunder is their voice and the lightning is their torch. If a spark falls from this on anyone he dies and goes to the region above.

The winds.—At each of the corners of the earth there dwells an immense but invincible spirit, whose head is many times larger than all the remainder of his body. When he breathes the wind blows and his breath is felt. Some breathe violent storms and others gentle zephyrs. The male spirits dwell at the north, northeast, northwest, and west. The females dwell at the remaining points, and each principal spirit has innumerable intermediate and less powerful attendants.

THE NENENOT OR "NASKOPIE."

The Indians of the Ungava district are locally known as Naskopie, a term of reproach applied to them by the mountaineers (the Montagnais of the early Jesuit missionaries) during the earlier days when the former acted falsely in one of their concerted struggles with the Eskimo of the eastern coast.

The name given to themselves is Nenenot, a word meaning true, or ideal red men. To the west of these people dwell a branch of the tribe along the east shore of Hudson bay. To the southeast dwell the mountaineers.

The western people differ greatly in customs and many words of their language from the Nenenots. The mountaineers differ but little in their customs, and only in speech as much as would be expected from the different locality in which they dwell.

These three tribes have distinct boundaries, beyond which they seldom wander. Of late years, however, a gradual influx of the western people has poured into the Ungava district, due to the decrease of the food supply along that portion of the eastern coast of Hudson bay.

The Nenenots appear, from the best information I could obtain on the subject, to have been driven to their present location during the wars waged against them by the Iroquois in times long gone by and remembered only in tradition.

They assert that their original home was in a country to the west, north of an immense river, and toward the east lay an enormous body of salt water. The former was supposed to be the St. Lawrence river and the latter to be Hudson bay. When they came to their present place they say that they found Eskimo alone, and these only along the coast. They are a branch of the Cree stock, as their language clearly indicates.

Many years ago war was waged upon them by the people whose name is remembered with terror even to this day. Most cruel atrocities were perpetrated, and in despair they fled from the land of their fathers, where they had lived as a numerous people, and were pursued by their merciless foes until but a remnant reached what is now known as the "Height of Land."

Being now driven to a strange land, where they found numerous Eskimo on all sides, only a few years elapsed before they encroached too greatly upon the land which the Eskimo had always held. Contention and struggles arose, culminating in a disposition to fight, and in the course of time desultory warfare, carried on by single combat or organized raids. This lasted for many years, even after the advent of the white men as traders along the coast. Some of the battles were attended with great slaughter on both sides. The Eskimo seldom ventured far from the coast on their raids, but fought bravely when attacked on their own ground. In most instances they outwitted the Indians by decoying them into ambush, and killing great numbers of them. Within the present century they have been more peaceably disposed toward each other. Since the arrival of the white men at various points along the coast these troubles have ceased, and the Indians and Eskimo are now on intimate terms; not that either party have any special regard for the new comers, but they have a mutual fear of each other, and the white man now engages their entire attention.

In the early struggles the Indian found the Eskimo to be a sturdy opponent, possessed of greater endurance and perseverance than himself. After the conclusion of the troubles they withdrew to their present haunts, and now wander indiscriminately over the land, although the Eskimo seldom ventures far into the interior unless it be along the valley of some large stream. They even camp alongside of each other, and aged Indian men and women, who have been left behind the parties of young people who are in quest of fur-bearing animals during the winter months, are only too glad to have a camp of jolly Eskimo near at hand. With them they can live as parasites until their hosts are exhausted of supplies, or until they move to another locality to relieve themselves of the importunities of their unbidden guests.

The Indian is not the physical superior of the Eskimo. It is true they are more expert on snowshoes, because the snowshoes belong to their mode of life. They are used by the Eskimo only when they can be purchased by barter from the Indian. The Eskimo snowshoe is merely a rude imitation of the form used by the neighboring Indians. In the canoe the Indian is at home; so also is the Eskimo in the kaiak, which braves the severest weather and the roughest water, on which the Indian would only gaze in dread and never venture.

Ability to endure fatigue is less in the Indian than the Eskimo, who accomplishes by patient persistence what the Indian desires to do in a hurry. I have not observed Indians carry such heavy loads as those borne on the shoulders of Eskimo, who, with ease, ascended a hill of such abrupt steepness that an unencumbered person climbed it with difficulty. Several Eskimo men ascended this hill, each with a barrel of flour on his shoulders.

The Indian is able to withstand the effect of cold as well as the Eskimo. The clothing of the latter is certainly better adapted to protect against cold. In times of scarcity of food the Eskimo is able to go without food for a number of days and yet perform a considerable amount of physical labor, while the Indian would require food on the second or third day, and refuse to move until it had been furnished.

In comparison with a white man under the same conditions the natives of either class would soon show signs of inferiority, and under prolonged exertion but few, even of the Eskimo, would endure the strain. The principal strength of these people is shown in their success in the chase.

The children are obedient to their parents, who seldom ever chastise them. Disrespect to parents is unknown, and in their intercourse with each other there are no clashings during youth. Not until the jealousies awakened under the stimulus of their sexual instincts arouse their passions do they begin to show enmity and hatred toward each other.

The males evidently exhibit jealousy to a less degree than the opposite sex. The men, after a protracted absence from each other, often embrace and shed tears of joy at meeting. The women are less demonstrative.

The number of children born exceeds the number of deaths. Mortality appeared to be low for the two years I was near these people. The prevailing diseases are of the lungs and bowels. The lung diseases are induced by constant exposure to extremes of wet and cold and the inhalation of foul air laden with terebinthine odors, arising from the resinous woods used for fuel. Changes of the wind blowing in at the door cause the interior to become filled with smoke, which is endured rather than admit the cold air from without.

Abstinence from fresh food for a long time, with dry meat only to subsist upon, is often broken by the sudden capture of deer. This affords an opportunity for gorging until the digestive organs are weakened and serious complications arise. It is quite probable that gluttony directly produces half of the illnesses that occur among these people. The insufficiency of clothing does not apparently influence health, as they seem utterly regardless of exposure, and long continued dwelling in the tents probably induces nearly, if not quite, all the other ills afflicting them. Indolent ulcers and scrofulous complications are frequent, but only in few instances are of such character as to prevent their following their usual occupations. During illness they are stolid, and appear to suffer intense pain without the twitching of a muscle. When death approaches it has but little terror, and is awaited with indifference.

The remedies employed are only those afforded by the beating of the drum and the mumblings of the shaman, who claims to have control of the spirit which causes all disease and death. They are, however, firm believers in the efficacy of potions compounded by the white trader, who is fully as ignorant of the disease as the subject himself is. Often a harmless mixture of red ink, red pepper, ginger, or other pungent substance is given, with a multiplicity of confusing directions, bewildering the messenger dispatched for relief, who, in repeating them, often makes mistakes and advises that the whole quantity be swallowed. The effect is sometimes magical, and the patient recovers. Powders are rubbed over the seat of pain and liniments swallowed with avidity. Strange as it may seem, they often report good effects, and rarely fail to ask for more of the same kind. Both sexes attain a great age—in some instances certainly living over seventy years. Some assert that they were well advanced in years before the white men came in 1827.

The marriage ceremony is simply a consent to live together, obtained by request if possible, and by force, if necessary. The man takes a wife as soon as he considers himself able to support one. When the ceremony is to be undertaken the consent of the girl's parents or nearest relatives is sought, and by holding out tempting inducements in the form of presents, the suitor wins them to his favor. The consent of the girl, if she has not yet been married is, of course, granted, if she desires to comply with the wishes of her relatives. If not, the prospective husband is informed that they can do nothing to turn her heart. The matter is understood, and in a short time she is taken forcibly to his or his father's tent. The tie binding the couple is very loose, and on the least provocation may be dissolved by either party. Continence on the part of either wife or husband is unusual, and only notorious incontinence is sufficient to cause the offender to be put away. Their sexual relations are very loose among themselves, but their immorality is confined to their own people. To take a second, a third, or even a fourth wife, is not uncommon, but the additional wives are taken principally for the purpose of performing labor imposed by the energy of a successful hunter. It is only the wealthy men who can afford a plurality of wives. The several wives often dwell in the same tent, but as jealousies frequently arise they resort to fighting among themselves to settle their differences. The husband looks on calmly until matters go too far. When he interferes the women are sure of being soundly thrashed. A woman, however, often assails her husband, and in some instances gives him an unmerciful pounding, much to the amusement of the bystanders, who encourage her to do her best. The man is a subject for ridicule for weeks afterwards. Either sex can endure being beaten, but not being laughed at. They rarely forgive a white man who laughs at their discomfiture. An amusing incident occurred within a

stone's throw of Fort Chimo. An Indian had his clothing stripped
from him by his enraged wife. She then tore the tent from the poles,
leaving him naked. She took their property to the canoe, which she
paddled several miles up the stream. He followed along the bank
until she relented, whereupon their former relations were resumed, as
though nothing had disturbed the harmony of their life. The man was
so severely plagued by his comrades that for many days he scarcely
showed his head out of the tent. Rivalry for the favor of a woman or
man is occasionally the source of serious affrays. An instance was related to me where two men sought the hand of a woman, and to settle
which should have her, they determined to go in their canoes to the
lake near by and fight with their deer spears. One of the men was
killed and the other thereupon obtained the woman, who is now living.

The sexes have their special labors. Women perform the drudgery
and bring home the food slain by their husbands, fetching wood and
water, tanning the skins, and making them into clothing. The labor
of erecting the tents and hauling the sleds when on their journey during the winter falls upon them, and, in fact, they perform the greater
part of the manual labor. They are considered inferior to the men, and in
their social life they soon show the effects of the hardships they undergo.

The females arrive at puberty at the age of 14 or 15, and are taken
as wives at even an earlier age. So early are they taken in marriage
that before they are 30 years of age they often appear as though they
were 50. Some of them are hideously ugly, and are so begrimed with
smoke from the resinous wood used for fuel and with filth that it is
purely guesswork to even approximate their age. The women appear
to be exempted from the curse of Eve, and deliver their children with
as little concern as is exhibited among the brutes. The child is not
allowed to receive nourishment until the third day, and no water must
touch its body. The infant is swaddled in wrappings of skins and
cloths. Sphagnum moss is used next the body and changed every other
day. They begin to walk at an early age, and this is, doubtless, the
principal cause of the bowing of the legs so often observed. The girls
are neglected and the boys given every advantage. The latter soon
discover their importance and rarely fail to show their domineering
ways to the other sex.

It is quite rare that twins are born. It is not usual for a mother to
have more than four children, although as many as six or eight may be
born. As the paternal origin is often obscure, the person having that
woman as wife at the time of the child's birth is supposed to be its
father.

The mortuary customs of the Naskopie were but imperfectly learned,
for when a death occurred at the trading station the body was buried
like a white man's. A shallow grave was dug in a sandy soil, as this
offered less trouble in digging, and the body placed in a rudely con-

structed coffin and covered with dirt. A small branch from a tree was placed at the head of the grave, but with what signification I could not satisfactorily determine. I received the reply that the white men put something at the head of their graves, and so do the Indians.

Away from the post the Indians suspend their dead from the branches of trees, if the ground be frozen too hard to excavate, and endeavor to return in the following summer and inter the body. A person who has distinguished himself among the people is often buried where the fire has been long continued within the tent and thawed the ground to a sufficient depth to cover the body. The tent is then removed to another location. The Indians have not that dread of a corpse which is shown so plainly among the Eskimo. The former have been known to strip the clothing from recently deceased Eskimo, and it is not infrequent for them to appropriate the gun or other implement placed by the side of a dead Innuit.

In response to my inquiry how they disposed of their dead in former ages, I obtained evidence that scaffold burial and suspension from trees were formerly practiced and that subterranean burials were introduced by the missionaries.

The dead are mourned for according to the position they occupied in life, a favorite child often causing an alarming grief in the mother who mourns for many days, constantly bemoaning her loss and reminding the listeners of the traits in the child's nature so well remembered. The body is taken to the place of final rest by the friends, the relations seldom accompanying it.

The life of these people is a constant struggle to obtain food and raiment. Nothing, however unimportant, is done without much deliberation and repeated consultation with friends.

They are also guided to a great extent by their dreams, for they imagine that in the night they are in direct communication with the spirits which watch over their daily occupations. Certain persons obtain much renown in divining the dreams and these are consulted with the greatest confidence. The drum is brought into use, and during its tumult the person passes into a state of stupor or trance and in a few moments arouses himself to reveal the meaning of the other's dream.

Superstition holds these people in its terrible sway and everything not understood is attributed to the working of one of the numerous spirits.

Every object, however simple, appears to have its patron spirit, which, in order that it may perform its services for the welfare of the people, must be propitiated with offerings most pleasing and acceptable to it. The rule seems to be that all spirits are by nature bad, and must be propitiated to secure their favor. Each person has a patron spirit, and these must always be placated lest misfortune come. These spirits assume an infinite variety of forms, and to know just what form it assumed when it inflicted its baneful effects, the shamans or medicine men must be consulted. These are supposed to be in direct contact with such spirits. The spirit will appear only in the darkness of the conjuring house, and then permit itself to be appeased by some atonement made by the afflicted, which can be made known only through the shaman. He alone indicates the course to be pursued, and his directions, to be explicitly followed, are often so confusing and impossible that the person fails to perform them. All these minor spirits are under the control of a single great spirit having its dwelling in the sky, a term as illimitable with those people as with ourselves.

Each animal has its protective spirit, which is inferior to those of man. The soul, if such expression may be used, of all animals is indestructible, and is capable of reappearing again and again as often as the material form is destroyed. There are spirits of beasts, birds, fishes, insects, and plants. Each of these has a home to which it returns after death, which is simply a cessation of that period of its material form, and each may be recalled at the will of the shaman. If an animal be killed it does not decrease the number of that species, for it still exists, although in a different form.

The Canada jay is supposed to inform the various animals of the approach of Indians, and these rarely fail to kill the jay wherever found.

A species of mouse is supposed to have such dread of man that it dies the instant it wanders near the track of a person. They often find these tiny creatures near the path, and believe them to be unable to cross it.

As the dusk of eve draws near, the silent flitting of the common short-eared owl (*Asio accipitrinus*), and the hawk owl (*Surnia funeria*), attracted by the sounds of the camp, creates direst confusion. The announcement of its presence causes the entire assemblage of people to be alert and hastily suspend some unworn garment, that the bird may perceive it and thus know that the people are not so poor in their worldly possessions as the spirit Wiq'-ti-qu may think; as it only annoys people who are too poor to have extra garments. As this short-eared owl frequents only the lower lands, the Indians assert that they are compelled to select the higher points of land as their camping sites in order to escape from him.

The shaman, as I have already said, is believed to be able to control all these different spirits by his magic art, and to foretell the future, but he must be concealed from view while carrying on his mysterious performances. Hence a special structure must be erected in which the shaman goes through various contortions of body until in a state of exhaustion and while in that weakened condition he fancies these things which have such wonderful hold on the minds of the people.

The tent (Fig. 85) is high and of small diameter. Every crack and crevice in the tent is carefully closed to exclude even the least ray of light.

When within it, the shaman begins his operations by groaning and

11 ETH——18

gradually increasing the pitch of voice until his screeching can be heard a great distance. The din of the drum adds confusion to the ceremony. This goes on until the shaman announces the appearance of the spirit with whom he desires to commune. He implores the spirit to grant the request, and in the course of time informs the people outside that he has succeeded in securing the services of the spirit. All within becomes quiet and only whisperings are heard.

The spirit promises to fulfill the obligation he has undertaken, and the conjuror throws over the tent and states the result of the interview. This result is always favorable, as his reputation depends upon its happening. Any untoward circumstance, such as a person turning over a stone or breaking a twig from a bush while traveling, is sufficient cause to break the spell, and the blame can be laid on the shoulders of such

FIG. 85.—Indian medicine lodge.

an offender. If the request be not granted within the stipulated time as announced by the shaman at the end of the ceremony, some one is certain to have been the cause of displeasing the spirit, who now withholds the favor until reparation for the offense is made. The conjurer is not slow to make some one do penance while he himself is gaining time, as he takes good care not to attempt anything out of season.

When an Indian kills one of the larger and fiercer wild beasts it is customary to reserve a portion of the skin or other part of the body as a memento of the deed.

These mementos are sacredly kept to show the prowess of the hunter and at the same time they serve as a token of the wealth procured by bartering the pelt of the animal to the trader. The wolf, bear, and wolverine are considered worthy of remembrance, and of the first and last mentioned animals a claw or a tip of an ear may serve as a souvenir.

The under lip of the bear (Fig. 86) is the portion preserved. The skin is cut off and spread flat to dry. The flesh side of the skin is painted with powdered hematite mixed with water or oil.

The outer edges or lips are ornamented with a single row of many-colored beads. At the apex or middle of the lip is attached a pendant in the form of a fish. The fish is 3 or 4 inches long, made of cloth and has a row of beads extending around the entire circumference of the length of the body.

These mementos are procured with great difficulty from the hunter who has risked his life in the struggles attending the capture of the beasts, for the barren-ground bear of that region is not a timid creature like the black bear; and unless the hunter is well prepared for the animal he would do well to let it alone.

Fig. 86.—Indian amulet of bearskin.

The occupations of the sexes are so numerous that a detailed account alone would suffice, as the various seasons have their regular routine labors besides those unexpectedly appearing. In the spring the Indians of both sexes come to the post of Fort Chino to trade their winter's hunt of fur-bearing animals. About the middle of March word is brought that the camp of old men and women with a number of children, left from the parties scattered in all directions during the previous fall, are slowly approaching the post. They come by easy stages, camping here and there for a day or two, but striving to be near about the time that the earlier parties come in to trade. These latter straggle along from the middle of April to the last of May, those who had ascended the streams to the headwaters often not arriving until after the breaking of the ice in the river, which may be as late as the 15th of June. When they collect at the post they have an opportunity to meet after a separation of months and enjoy a period of rest. The trading of their furs and other articles continues slowly until the parties have made their selections of guns, ammunition, tobacco, and cloths, a quantity of flour, biscuit, peas, beans, rice, and sugar. Molasses is purchased in enormous quantities, a hogshead of 90 gallons sufficing for only three or four days' trade. Other articles of varied character, from needles and beads to calico and cloth, are bought by the women.

The parties receive the allowance given in advance for the prosecution of the ensuing winter's hunt, after which they are relied on to raft down the supply of wood cut by the white men for the next winter's supply of fuel. This consumes the season until the middle of July. Stragglers are out even later. The men, meantime, select the locality where they will remain for the summer and fall. The winter is to be occupied in getting furs. Each head of a party announces his intended location and the parties gradually leave the post for their destination. Some of the Indians in former years were employed to assist the salmon fishing, but they proved to be unreliable, either through fear of the turbulent waters of the Koksoak or inattention to their task. They were easily allured from the nets by the appearance of any game, and as the tides in that river do not wait even for an Indian, serious losses resulted from carelessness. Hence their places in later years are filled by Eskimo, who are better adapted to the work.

The various parties disperse in different directions in order that the entire district may afford its products for their benefit. The Indians know the habits of the animals in those regions so well that they are sure, if they go to a particular locality, to find the game they are in quest of.

The reindeer provides them with the greater part of their food and the skins of these animals afford them clothing.

Although their food consists of reindeer, ptarmigan, fish, and other game, the deer is their main reliance, and when without it, however great the abundance of other food, they consider themselves starving.

The deer are procured in several ways, the principal of which is by the use of the lance or spear. In the months of September and Octotober they collect from various directions. During the spring the females had repaired to the treeless hills and mountains of the Cape Chidley region to bring forth their young on those elevations in early June or late May. After the young have become of good size the mothers lead them to certain localities whither the males, having gone in an opposite direction, also return. They meet somewhere along the banks of the Koksoak river, usually near the confluence of that river with the North or Larch. While thousands of these animals are congregated on each bank small herds are continually swimming back and forth, impelled by the sexual instinct. The hair of the young animals is now in excellent condition for making skin garments. The females are thin, not yet having recovered from the exhaustion of furnishing food for their young and material for the new set of antlers, which appear immediately after the birth of the fawns. The skin is, however, in tolerable condition, especially in late October. The back of the male is now covered with a large mass of fat known as "back fat." This deposit is about 1 to 1½ inches thick by 2 feet broad and 20 inches long. The males are full of vigor and in the best possible condition at this season, as the antlers have become dry and cease to draw upon the animal for material to supply their immense growth.

The hunting parties, always on the alert for the herds of deer which are hastening to the assembling place, follow them up, and in the course of time conjecture at what point they will congregate. Here they establish camps and intercept the deer when crossing the streams. The canoes are held in readiness, while the hunters scan the opposite hillsides for deer filing along the narrow paths through the forests and bushes towards the river bank. Arrived there, the deer, after a moment's pause, eagerly take to the water, boldly swimming as they quarter down stream with the current. The animals swim high in the water, scarcely more than a third of the body immersed. They move compactly, in a crowd, their antlers appearing at a distance like the branches of a tree floating with the current. The Indian crouches low and speeds for the canoe. Silently it is pushed into the water, and two or three rowers take their places within. Rapid but noiseless strokes given by sturdy arms soon bring the boat below and to the rear of the body of deer, who are now thrown into the greatest consternation as they perceive their most dreaded foe suddenly by their side. The deer endeavor to retreat, but the men are between them and the shore. The occupants of the canoe now drive the deer quartering up stream and toward the shore where the camp is situated. Should they, by some mistake on the part of the hunters, start downstream, they are certain to be separated, and swim so rapidly that unless there be two canoes they will, for the most part, escape. If the herd is well kept together they may be driven at the will of the pursuer. He strives to direct them to such spot that when the thrust with the spear is given only sufficient vitality will be left to enable the stricken animal to regain the shore. When the spear touches the vital part, the animal plunges forward and the instrument is withdrawn. A hurried thrust pierces another victim, until all the herd, if small, may be slain. The wounded animal now feels the internal cavity filling with blood, and seeks the nearest land whereon its ebbing strength scarcely allows it to stand. A few wistful turns of the head to the right or left, a sudden spreading of its limbs to support the swaying body, a plunge forward—the convulsive struggles that mark the end. If the band is large, some generally escape. Some may be so wounded that they plunge into the bushes perhaps but a few yards and there lie and die, furnishing food for the beasts and birds of prey.

The carcases of the deer are stripped of skins and fat and the viscera are removed. The fat is laid one side, that from the intestines being also reserved for future rendering.

The skins are taken to the camps and piled up. Those which are not to be tanned immediately are hung over poles to dry, the flesh side turned upwards.

The meat is stripped from the bones and taken to the tents, where it is exposed to the smoke and hot air over the fire and quickly dried. Some of the Indians are so expert in stripping the flesh from the skeleton that the exact form or outlines of the animal are preserved in the process of drying. The drying flesh acquires a very dark brown color from the smoke and blood left within the tissues. Certain portions of the dry meat, especially those from the flanks and abdominal walls, are quite palatable; they are crisp, and have a rich nutty flavor. The intercostal muscles are also choice portions, while some of the flesh from the haunches is dry and nearly tasteless. The back fat is often dried and smoked, but acquires a disagreeable rancid taste.

The long bones are cracked and the marrow extracted. This substance is the most highly prized portion of the animal, and in seasons of plenty the deer are often slaughtered for the marrow alone. The fat is placed in pots or kettles and rendered over a fire. It is then poured into another vessel to cool, and forms a valuable article of trade and a necessity for food, and is also required in the process of tanning the skins.

The bones containing the marrow are cracked and placed in a kettle, hung over a slow fire, and the substance melted. The marrow brings a higher price than the tallow, and is esteemed a choice article of food. The heads are thrown to one side until the decomposing brain is wanted to be mixed with the semi-putrid liver for the purpose of tanning the skins. When the flesh has dried sufficiently it is taken down and put into packages of about thirty pounds' weight each. These bundles are enveloped in the parchment like subcutaneous tissue, and stored away until they are needed for food. A species of mold attacks the flesh if it is not frequently inspected and dried, but as it is harmless, it does not injure the meat. Indians for weeks at a time subsist entirely on this dried meat. They also have a season of plenty when the female deer and the bucks of less than two years are on their way to the Cape Chidley region. Here the females bring forth their young unmolested by the old bucks and also less annoyed by the myriads of mosquitoes which throng the lower parts of the country.

The crossing place of the females and young bucks is at or near Fort Chimo at least each alternate year. About the 5th to the 10th of May the assembled Indians anxiously await the coming of the game. In the course of a few days the welcome cry of "Deer!" is heard, and the camp immediately becomes a scene of great excitement—men hurrying to get their guns and ammunition, women shouting the direction of the game, and children running to the higher eminences to watch the herds.

The men endeavor to occupy a narrow defile, where the herd will pass between the hills to the level land beyond. Some station themselves at the top of the ravine, while the swiftest runners hasten to the head of the defile to lie in ambush until the deer, urged from behind, rush past, to be met with a volley of balls from all sides. Panic seizes the animals, and wherever they turn an Indian confronts them. Until the deer recover from their paralysis, and once more obey their instinct to escape, numbers of them stand quietly waiting to be slaughtered;

others walk unconcernedly about, seemingly deprived of the power of flight. The Indians hurriedly close upon them, and in a few minutes the entire herd is destroyed or dispersed in all directions.

The guns used on this occasion are the cheapest kind of muzzle-loading single-barreled shotguns. The balls used are of such size that they will drop to the bottom of the chamber. No patching is used, and a jar on the ground is deemed sufficient to settle the ball upon the powder. The employment of a ramrod would require too much time, as the Indian is actuated by the desire to kill as many as possible in the shortest time. They do not use the necessary care in loading their guns, and often the ball becomes lodged in the chamber and the gun bursts when fired. When shooting downhill the ball often rolls out. It is surprising that so few fatal accidents occur. A quantity of powder is poured directly into the gun from its receptacle, the ball dropped down, and a cap taken from between the fingers, where it was placed for convenience. Hunters often practice the motions of rapid loading and firing. They are remarkably expert, surpassing the Eskimo in this, though the Eskimo is far the better marksman.

A third method pursued is that of snaring the deer.

A plan adopted to capture deer in the winter is as follows: A herd of deer is discovered, and men and women put on their snowshoes. The deer are surrounded and driven into a snowbank many feet deep, in which the affrighted animals plunge until they nearly bury themselves. The hunters, armed with the lance, pursue them and kill them. This means of procuring deer is only adopted when the herd is near a convenient snowbank of proper depth. The snow falling in the winter collects in gullies and ravines, and only in seasons where there has been an abundance of snow will it attain sufficient depth to serve the purpose.

Smaller game, such as ducks, geese, ptarmigan, hares, rabbits, porcupines, beavers, and an occasional lynx, afford variety of food. Ptarmigan are slaughtered by thousands. Hundreds of pounds of their feathers annually purchase small trinkets for the Indian women, and during this season it is unusual to see a woman without some feathers of these birds adhering to her clothing or hair.

The women and men annually destroy thousands of the eggs and young of these birds. Rabbits and hares, too, fall beneath the arrow or shotgun. Porcupines are more common toward the sources of the streams falling into Hudson Strait. They are found in trees, from which they gnaw the bark and terminal portions of the branches for food. The porcupine must be carefully cleaned lest the flesh be unfit for food. The hair and spines are removed by scorching or by pouring hot water over the body.

Of the carnivorous mammals the lynx only is eaten, and this when other food is scarce. Bears are so rare that they form but an unimportant portion of the Indian's diet. Wolverines, wolves, and foxes are never eaten.

Fish of various kinds are plentiful. The lakes and streams abound with salmon in summer, and trout, white fish, suckers, and a few less common species are eagerly sought for food. Fish are caught with the hook or net. Fishing through holes in the ice affords an ample supply of fine trout, and the net set along the shore upon the disappearance of the ice is sure to reap a rich haul of white fish, suckers, and trout.

In the preparation of the food little care is exercised to prevent its coming in contact with objectionable substances. The deer meat is laid upon the stones of the beach and particles of grit imbed themselves in the substance. The flesh for cooking is often dropped into the vessels in which the tallow or marrow is being rendered. Neither children nor adults have any regular periods of eating, but appear to be always hungry. It is thus not unusual to see a filthy child thrust its hand into the cooling fat to obtain a choice portion of meat as it settles to the bottom.

The dry meat is often pounded into a coarse powder by means of stone or metal pestles. The meat is placed upon a smooth, hard stone for this purpose. The ligaments are picked out, and when a sufficient quantity has been prepared it is put into baskets or bags and stored away for future use. The cracked bones from which the marrow was extracted are calcined and reduced to powder and used as an absorbent of the fat from the skins in the process of tanning.

The unborn young of the reindeer, taken from the mother in the spring, are considered a prime delicacy by Indians, as well as Eskimo. The eggs of various species of birds are eagerly sought for, and it matters little whether they are fresh or far advanced in incubation. The embryo bird, with the attached yolk of the egg, is swallowed with infinite gusto. The Indian seldom eats raw flesh unless dried meat be excepted.

Enough has been written concerning the reindeer to show that without it the very existence of the Indian would be imperiled. Both food and clothing, the prime necessities of life, are obtained from the animal, and its numbers do not seem to decrease with the merciless or thoughtless slaughter. Hundreds of carcases are never utilized. I counted 173 carcases on one side of the river in going a distance of about 80 miles, and when I came to their camps I saw incredible piles of meat and skins going to waste. The winter months are occupied by men in hunting the various fur-bearing animals, the principal of which are white, red, cross, and black or silver foxes, martens, minks, wolverines, wolves, muskrats, and beavers: these are abundant. Few lynxes and bear are obtained. A considerable number of others are found in this region and afford fine skins.

Steel traps are generally set, various sizes of traps being used for the different animals. A great number of otter and beaver are shot in the water. Deadfalls consisting of a log of wood set upon figure-4 triggers rarely fail to kill mink and marten. The lynx is usually taken by means of a snare with the loop over a circle of low pegs surrounding the tongue of the figure-4 set of triggers. The spring, usually a lithe sapling, is strong enough to lift the forelegs of the animal from the ground when the noose encircles its neck.

The Indian conceives the wolverine to be an animal embodying all the cunning and mischief that can be contained in the skin of a beast. To its cunning is added great bodily strength, enabling this medium-sized animal to accomplish destruction apparently much beyond its strength.

Every other animal in the forests where it dwells prefers to give it the path rather than engage in struggle with it. When seized in a trap a wolverine offers a sturdy resistance. Even a famished wolf, to my personal knowledge, will stand and look at it, but not attempt to cope with it. In this particular instance, however, the wolf may have considered the predicament of the wolverine another means of strategy employed by that animal to entrap the wolf, and so deemed it wise to remain at a respectful distance.

Every form of torture which the Indian mind is capable of conceiving is inflicted upon this animal when it is captured. All manner of vile names and reproaches are applied to it. The Indian enjoys relating how he singed its fur off, broke its bones, and tormented it in many ways, as it slowly expired under his hand.

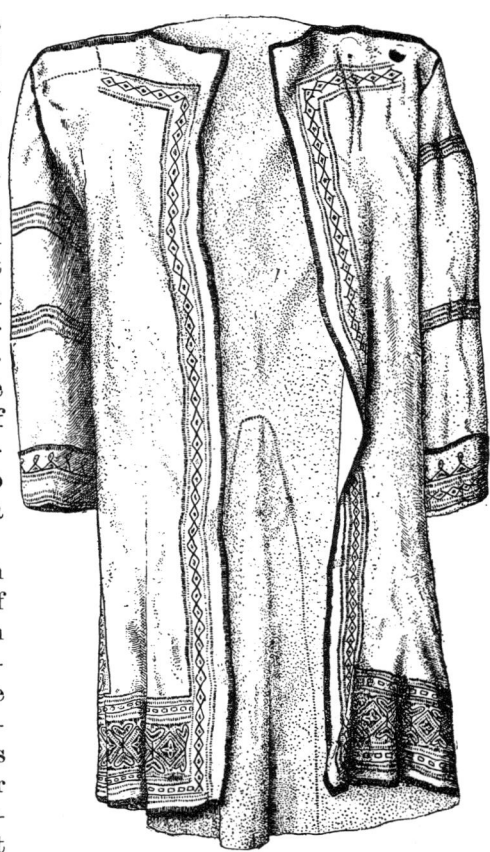

Fig. 87.—Indian buckskin coat, man's (front).

CLOTHING.

The apparel worn by the Ungava Indians is quite distinct for the different sexes. The method of preparing the skins for the manufacture of garments is the same, but the forms of the garments for the sexes are so different as to require special consideration.

The garments worn by the men differ somewhat according to the season of the year, for the extremes of climate are very great. The clothing of the men consists of a coat, breeches, leggings, moccasins, gloves or mittens, and cap or headdress.

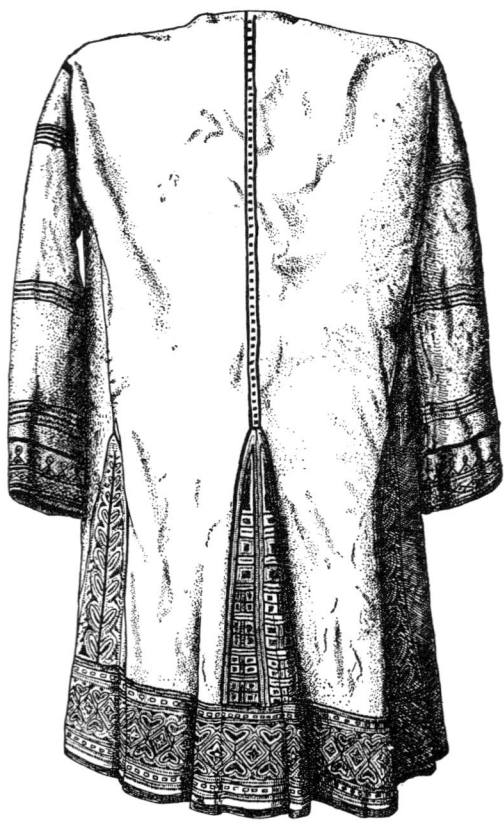

The coat consists of the skins of the reindeer tanned into a thoroughly pliable condition by the process to be described presently.

The shape of the garment worn in summer (Figs. 87 and 88) is somewhat similar to that of a frock coat, but without the tails. The back is cut from a single skin and the skirt cut up from below. Into this is inserted a piece of sufficient width to allow movement of the lower limbs. The sides are from the second skin, split down the middle of the back and sewed to the skin, forming the back of the garment. The back skin forms the covering

FIG. 88.—Indian buckskin coat, man's (back).

for the top of the shoulders and extends to the collar seam. The side skins form the front and neck of the garment. The sleeves are

made of a third skin, and frequently have a roll or cuff to increase the length, if necessary. The collar is merely a strip of skin sewed to the neck. It is usually turned down. The front is usually open, and if made to be closed it is held in position by a belt or gaudily colored scarf of woolen or cotton purchased from the trader.

FIG. 89.—Detail of pattern painted on Indian garments.

The seams of the clothing are always sewed with sinew like that used by the Eskimo. There are but two seams which run the entire length of the coat, and these are the side seams. The seam at the skirt, the armhole, sleeve, and collar are the shorter ones. The coat is always more or less ornamented with extravagant painted designs. The colors and other materials used for painting these designs will be described in another connection, as well as the manner of applying them.

The patterns of these designs will be best understood by reference to the figures, which show some of them in detail (Figs. 89, 90).

The colors used often present startling combinations of red, blue, yellow, and brown. The portions of the garments upon which these colors are placed are the front edges of the opening of the coat, the wrists, and rings around the arms or sleeves, the skirt and pyra-

Fig. 90.—Detail of pattern painted on deerskin robe.

mid-shaped designs over the hips. The piece intended to widen the skirt behind is always entirely covered with a design of some kind.

Over the outside of the seams a line of paint is always applied, nearly always of a red or brown color.

Frequently a series of quadrate blotches or squares produced by variously colored lines runs from the apex of the piece inserted in the skirt to the collar.

The length of the coat is such as to reach to the middle of the thigh. The coverings for the lower limbs and for the hips are quite distinct. For the hips the garment is a sort of breeches of which the legs are so short as only to cover the upper portion of the

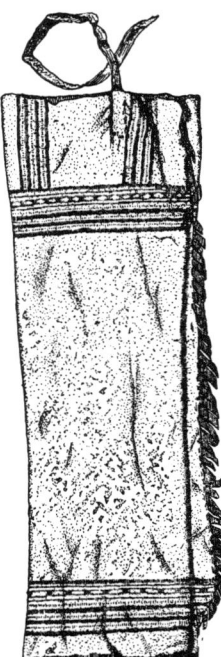

Fig. 91.—Indian buckskin leggings.

thigh. The breeches are held in place by means of a drawstring in front.

A pair of these breeches is never ornamented with paint, as they are usually not exposed to view.

A pair of leggings extends from the upper portion of the thigh to the ankles. The leggings (Fig. 91) are each made of a single piece somewhat in the form of a narrow bag open at each end. They are held in position by means of a string attached in front and fastened to the upper portions of the breeches. The seam is on the outer side of the leggings and along it is sewed a strip of deerskin having the edges cut into fringe. The leggings are painted in much the same fashion as the coat.

The moccasins (Fig. 92) are rarely ornamented, except with beads on the tongue or else with a strip of red, blue, or black cloth.

In the construction of a moccasin the measure of the foot is taken if it is intended for a person of importance or if the maker attempts to do skillful work. The sole is cut out first in the shape of a parallelogram. The edges are turned up and creases made around that portion of the deerskin which surrounds the toes and a part of the side of the foot.

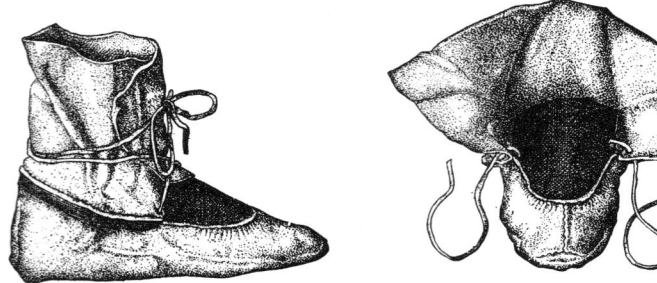

FIG. 92.—Indian moccasins.

The creases are made perpendicular in order to take up a portion of the slack of the skin. They are held in position by a stout sinew thread run through each one and around to the other side to prevent them from separating and thus " bagging " over the toes. This is the most particular part of the work and on these stitches depend the skill of the maker. The sides of the foot and heel are not creased as the heel-seam takes up the slack for the posterior portion of the moccasin.

The tongue of the moccasin is a piece cut into a shape resembling that member with the tip of it over the toes. This is sewed to the edges of the creases, and between it and the creases is often sewed a narrow welt of skin or cloth. The superfluous edges of the slipper-shaped shoe are now trimmed off, and the top, or portion to cover the ankle, is sewed on. This portion is a long narrow strip of inferior skin of sufficient size to overlap in front and to come well above the ankles. It is left open like the tops of laced shoes. Just below, or at the edge of the tops, a long thong of deerskin is inserted through several holes, which allows it to pass around the heel and below the ankles, bringing the ends in front over the tongue. The ends of the tops are laid carefully over one another and wrapped round by the ends of the thongs which hold the moccasins on the feet.

Certain portions of the skin make better footwear than other parts. The neck skin is too thick and stiff to allow the creases around the toes to be properly made; the flanks are too thin; while the neck is useful for the tongues, the sides for the bottoms, and the flanks and portions of the back, scarred by the grubs infesting the animal, for the tops and strings.

Moccasins for young children often have a seam parallel with the toes and the creasing is thus obviated. Those for wearing in the tent or in the dry vicinity of the camp have no tops and are held to the foot by means of a drawstring.

As most of the strain in walking comes upon the tongue, and this portion is usually ornamented, it is necessary that it should be of a good quality of leather. A piece of black, blue, or red cloth is generally laid over the tongue for ornament. There is sometimes bead work on this portion, but as these people are not skillful in the art of disposing the many colored beads they are not much used for that purpose.

A single deerskin will make five to seven pairs of moccasins for an adult, and as they last but two or three weeks as many as fifteen to twenty-five pairs are necessary for each adult.

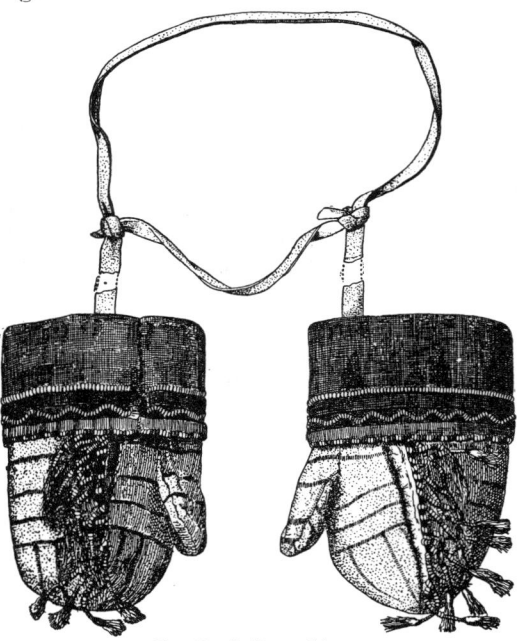

FIG. 93.—Indian mittens.

The hands are protected with mittens (Fig. 93) made of smoked deerskin. The skin is folded, and along the fold the shape of the mitten is cut so as to leave a part by which the two pieces are joined, and the edges formed in the cutting are sewed together. The thumb is made as follows: A tongue-shaped piece is cut out of the palm and the base of that piece is left as the part to form the under or inner covering for the thumb. A piece is now trimmed that will fit the place cut out and the two parts sewed together.

The thumb of the Indian is, as a rule, shorter than that of the white man, and a pair of native-made mittens are quite uncomfortable until the thumb portion has been recut and sewed. The wrists of the mittens are often gaudily ornamented with strips of red or black cloth. Designs of simple character, such as lines and cross lines producing lattice-work figures, are frequently painted on the back of the mitten. Beads in rows and zigzag lines ornament the wrist, and strands of beads are pendant from the outside seams. The strands are often tipped with tassels of variegated woolen threads. The mittens intended for severe weather are often lined with the thin skin of a fœtal reindeer, which has short, soft hair. Great exertion often causes the hands to perspire and moisten the hair, and this freezes the instant the mitten is removed from the hand, and is liable to freeze the fingers within it.

The head-dress of the men for the summer is often a large cotton handkerchief wound turban-fashion around the head to prevent the long hair from blowing over the face. These handkerchiefs are of the most gaudy patterns, and if they are not worn a simple thong of deer-

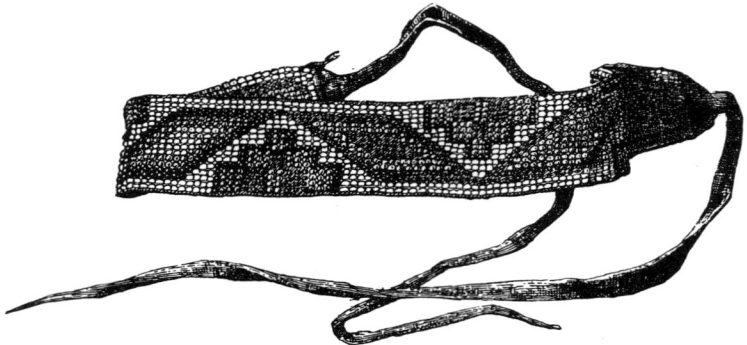

FIG. 94.—Beaded headband. Nenenot.

skin serves the purpose. The girls and newly married wives often make bands of beads, some of which are quite attractively designed, for their lovers or husbands. These bands are about an inch wide and several inches long. The ends are lengthened with strips of skin. The band is placed over the forehead and tied by the strings behind. These headbands are generally the most intricate designs of bead work which these Indians display (Fig. 94).

A cap of deerskin is often worn, but it always seems to be in the way, and is used mostly in wet weather. A piece of stiff deerskin is sometimes made into the shape of a visor of a cap and worn over the eyes during the spring when the glare of the sun on the snow produces such distressing inflammation of the eyes. It is fastened to the head by means of straps tied behind. The greater part of the men prefer to go without head covering. Some who are able and love a display of fancy colors have a cap made of red cloth and ornamented with beads worked into extravagant patterns. The cap is a high conical affair, and from the weight of beads upon it often falls to one side of the head.

The winter coat (Figs. 95, 96) worn by the males is of different pattern from that worn in summer, and is made of skins with the hair inside.

Two skins, one of which forms the back of the coat the other the front, are sewed by side seams running from the armpit to the bottom of the skirt. On the shoulder a seam runs to the neck on each side, the back skin extending high enough to form the neck while the other skin reaches to the neck in front. Here it is slightly cut out or slit for a distance of several inches to allow the insertion of the head through the neck hole.

Sometimes a ᴠ-shaped piece is inserted into the slit at the front of the neck. To widen the skirts a similar shaped piece is let into the middle of the back skin; or it may be put between the side seams for the same purpose. The bottom of the skirt is decorated. (Fig. 97.)

At the back of the neck a piece about 8 inches square is attached to the garment. This sometimes serves as a collar, and sometimes it gives additional protection by a double thickness to the shoulders, very often the first part to feel the effect of the piercing winds.

Fig. 95.—Man's winter coat (front).

A few of the coats for winter have a hood attached to them (Fig. 98, 99) sewed on the back of the neck, which when drawn over the head serves at once as cap and protection.

The collar and hood are invariably made from the skins on the sides of the head of the deer. If two or more head skins are required they are sewed into the form of the deer's head. The collar is ornamented with fringes cut from the edges of the skin. Sometimes the interscapular protection is cut into three or four points, each one of which is the cheek skin of a deer, and sewed only a portion of the length, the remainder being left free and terminating with a series of long strands or fringes. The sleeves of these garments have nothing peculiar about them.

As the Indian is always in the vicinity of the herds of deer it is an easy matter for him to obtain the skins when in best condition, and

from the finer skins superior garments are made. The shape of the Indian's coat is not so well adapted to afford protection as that of the Eskimo; hence, the white men in this region invariably adopt the clothing of the latter in cold weather.

Indians eagerly accept any cast off garment which a white man has worn, and they often procure the clothing offered for trade. Trousers are in much demand. Coats are deemed great prizes, especially in the wet seasons when the moisture would certainly ruin their own clothing by causing the hair to fall off or totally destroy

FIG. 96.—Man's winter coat (back).

the shape of the tanned skin garments. For underclothing the Indian man uses an additional

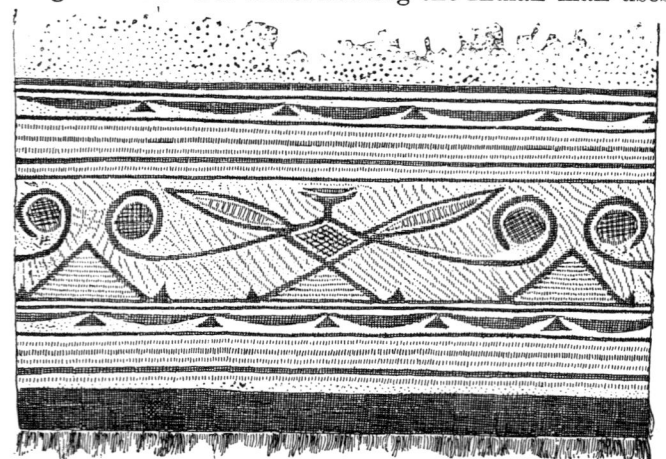

suit of ordinary clothing or else dons a shirt procured from the trader. Drawers are rarely worn.

That these people are little susceptible to the effects of cold may be inferred from the fact that

FIG. 97.—Detail of ornamentation.

I have seen them come to the trading post of Fort Chimo in the mid-

dle of winter when the thermometer had not registered higher than 20°
below zero for weeks, with no protection for their legs except a pair of
old buckskin leggings so short that the bottom did not reach within 3
or 4 inches of the dilapidated moccasins. The feet were, so far as
could be ascertained, chiefly protected by a wrapping of old baling
cloth covered with a pair of moccasins which no white man would have
been seen wearing. I observed also that no additional clothing was
purchased for the return trip.

The garments worn
by the women in the
warmer season consists
of thin dresses of calico
purchased from the
traders. Thin shawls
serve to protect the
head and shoulders.
The feet are incased in
moccasins. Some of
the women are able to
purchase dresses of
cloth, and these are cut
into a semblance of the
dresses worn by the
women of civilized
countries. It is not
rare to see a woman
wearing a skirt made
from the tanned skin
of the deer. The lower
portions of the skirt
are often fancifully or-
namented with lines
and stripes of paint of
various colors, extend-
ing entirely around the
garment. A piece of
baling cloth is often
fashioned into a skirt and worn.

FIG. 98.—Man's winter coat, with hood.

The females appear to be less susceptible to the sudden changes of
the summer weather than the men. At least they exhibit less concern
about the thickness of their apparel. It is not unusual to see a woman
whose only clothing appears to be a thin dress of calico. During the
winter the women dress in the most comfortable skins (Fig. 100), blankets,
shawls, comforts, leggings, and moccasins. During exceptionally severe
weather, they appear as traveling wardrobes, doubtless carrying their
all on their back, and in some instances presenting a most comical ap-

pearance as, loaded with clothing of most miscellaneous character, they waddle over the snow. The winter cap is similar to that worn by the men, but is not so peaked. It is an object on which they expend a great amount of labor. The material is usually a kind of cloth locally known as Hudson bay cloth, either red, dark blue, light blue, or black. The caps of the men and women are usually made from the better grades of this cloth, while the dresses of the women and the leggings of the men are of the inferior grades.

If the cap is to be all one color, in which case it is always red, the cloth is cut in two pieces only, and put together so as to produce a cup-shape. Sometimes five or six pieces are cut from two or three different colors of cloth and the strips sewed together. Over the seams white tape is sewed to set off the colors. In the center of the strip is a rosette, cross, or other design worked with beads, and around the rim rows of beads variously arranged.

FIG. 99.—Man's winter coat, with hood.

The body is covered with a heavy robe made of two deerskins sewed together. This robe is often plain, and when ornamented designs are painted only on the bottom of the skirt. These robes are always of skins with the hair on. The flesh side is often rubbed with red ocher while the extreme edge may be painted with a narrow stripe of the same mixed with the viscid matter obtained from the roe of a species of fish. The edge stripe of paint is always of a darker brown than the other colors from the admixture of that substance with the earth.

This garment is put upon the body in a manner impossible to describe and difficult to understand even when witnessed. It is held together by small loops of sinew or deerskin. A belt around the waist keeps it up.

The women also wear in winter a sleeveless gown-reaching little below the knees and as high as the chin. The sleeves are put on separately, like leggings. They are usually made of red or black cloth.

The gown is often extravagantly decorated with paint. The flesh side of the skin is rubbed with red ocher, on which are painted in describable designs. A strip of deerskin dotted with beads borders the gown, and from the edge of the strip hang strings of these ornaments, terminating in variously colored tassels of thread.

The leggings of the women differ from those of the men. They extend higher and the bottoms cover the tops of the moccasins. They are made of skin or cloth, the latter black or red. To cut out a pair of leggings requires skill. The cloth is doubled and then cut nearly in a circular form. A size sufficient to fit the limb is sewed up leaving the crescent-shaped remainder a flapping ornament. The "wings" are often edged with cloth of a different color and on the outer border rows of beads complete the decoration. The two crescents are left free, and as the wind separates them they flap most fantastically. They are always worn so as to be on the outer side of the legs. The bottoms of the leggings are heavily loaded with numerous rows of fancy beads.

Moccasins are alike for both sexes.

As additional protection from cold the shoulders are covered with a mantle of soft skins from young deer. Blankets purchased from the traders

FIG. 100.—Nenenot woman in full winter dress.

are also sometimes thrown over the shoulders or around the waist.

Children are clad like adults, excepting that their apparel is less carefully made and they often present a disgusting appearance, with their clothing glazed with filth and glistening with vermin.

Infants usually have their garments made in the "combination" form. The cap forms a separate piece and is fitted so closely that it is not removed until the growth of the head bursts the material of which the cap is made.

When traveling men and women smoke or snuff a good deal. Tobacco and a few other necessary articles are carried in a bag known as "fire bag." These are made of cloth and trimmed with beads, and are often quite tastefully ornamented.

The detailed figures which I have presented show much better than any description the designs used in ornamenting their clothing. Some

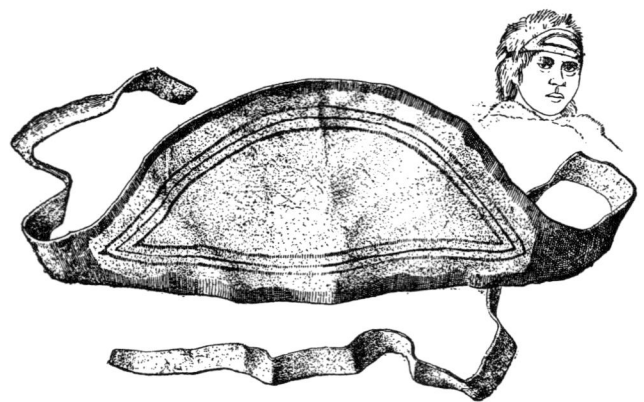

FIG. 101.—Sealskin headband. Nenenot.

of the patterns are rude copies of the designs found upon cheap handkerchiefs, scarfs, and other printed fabrics.

I have already spoken of the headbands worked for the men by their

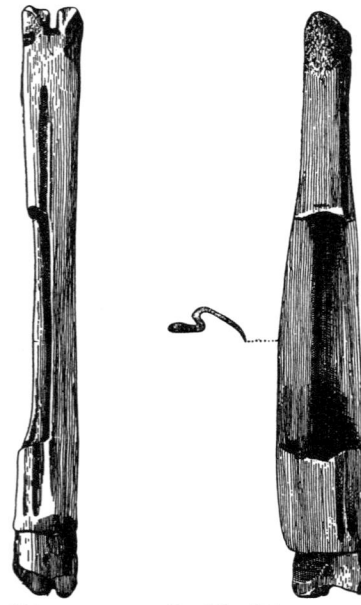

FIG. 102.—Skin scraper (front). Nenenot.

FIG. 103.—Skin scraper (back). Nenenot.

wives and sweethearts. Such a headband, made of sealskin procured from the Eskimo, is shown in Fig. 101 (No. 3449). The headband is used to support the weight of a load carried on the back, relieving the strain on the shoulders and making it easier to breathe. The band passes over the forehead to the back, where it is attached to the load.

Various forms of these headbands or portage straps are made. Sometimes a piece of birch bark is placed under the strap where it touches the forehead. It is said that the bark does not become wet from the moisture induced by the severe exertion and thus burn the head.

PREPARATION OF THE SKINS FOR CLOTHING.

Having now given a general description of the clothing of the Nenenot, I may proceed to describe the process of preparing the skins of which this clothing is made. The skins of the deer, which are to be converted into buckskin and parchment, are laid to one side in a heap, just as they came from the bodies of the animals or after they have gone through a process to be subsequently described.

When the skins have laid in this heap for several days decomposition sets in and loosens the hair so it will readily pull out. When the pelt is ready for scraping it is thrown over a round stick of wood some 3 or 4 inches in diameter and 3 or 4 feet long, one end of which rests on the ground while the other is pressed against the abdomen of the woman who is doing the work. Then she takes a tool like a spoke shave (Figs. 102, 103, No. 3162) made from the radius of the deer, by cutting a slice off the middle part of the back of the bone, so as to make a sharp edge while the untouched ends serve for handles, and with this scrapes off the loosened hair.

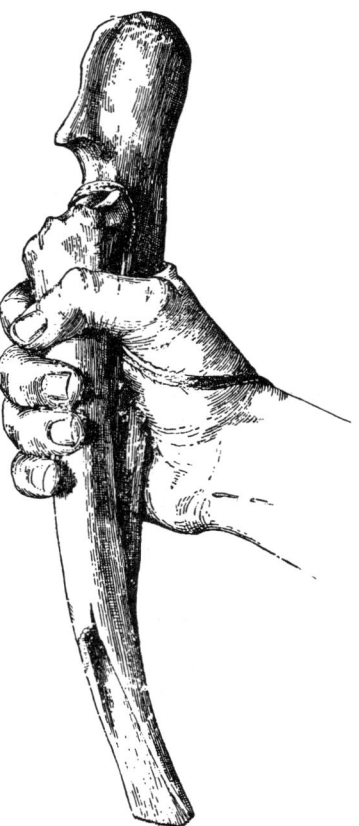

The sharp edge of the bone instrument coming against the hairs pushes or pulls them out but does not cut the skin.

The flesh side of the pelt is now worked to free it from particles of flesh and blood, together with as much of the moisture in the skin as may be hastily done, for if the person has a great number of skins to attend to she must work rapidly lest they decompose too much and putrefy.

Where the hunter has great success in killing deer many of the skins are left untouched because there is no one to attend to them and they are thus wasted.

When the pelts of the deer or other large animals have been taken from the carcass they are allowed to dry with

FIG. 104.—Skin-cleaning tool. Nenenot.

the adherent flesh, fat, and ligaments until a convenient opportunity occurs to remove those portions from the skin, which must be moistened to permit them to be more readily scraped off. If the fresh skins are to be cleaned immediately, they are operated upon in the same manner as those previously dried. All the skins of fur-bearing animals and those furnishing skins for clothing and other purposes must be scraped, otherwise they would soon be soiled by the infiltration of the fat among the hairs.

To remove the adherent particles on the flesh side of the skin a peculiar instrument has been devised. The tibia, or large bone of the hind leg of the reindeer, is used for this purpose (Fig. 104). The peculiar shape of the bone renders it particularly well adapted to form a combination of saw, chisel, and gouge at the same time. The lower

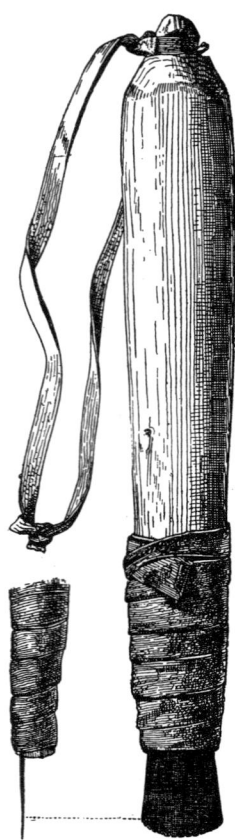

portion of the bone is cut squarely off. A part of one side of the remainder is cut so as to leave one side (the inner side of the bone) in the shape of a chisel, having either a straight edge or else slightly rounded. On this edge are cut a number of fine notches, which give the edge of the instrument a serrated form. Some of the bones have a spatula-shaped piece of iron or steel cut with the serrations upon it and the metal piece set in the cavity of the bone. If the leg of a deer is not convenient a wooden handle shaped like the long handle of a mortising chisel is fashioned, and to it is affixed the metal point by means of stout lashings (Fig. 105). Around the upper portion of the wooden shaft a notch or groove is cut, and in this is tied a stout thong in such manner as to form a loop to prevent the hand from slipping down the smooth bone when the blow is struck.

The manner of using this instrument is peculiar and effective. The skin is thrown, with the flesh side up, over a stake 2 or 3 feet high driven firmly into the ground. The person kneels down before the stake, and when the skin is placed so as to afford a convenient portion to begin upon, an edge is taken between the fingers of the left hand and lifted slightly from the ground. A blow is given with the tool which separates the sub-

FIG. 105.—Skin-cleaning tool, iron-bladed. Nenenot.

cutaneous tissue, and by rightly directed blows this may be separated from the skin entire. The skin is then laid aside for further working. The subcutaneous tissue is washed and dried, after which it is used for a variety of purposes, such as coverings for bundles of dried meat and other articles.

The skin is worked over with this instrument to free it from a portion of its moisture and is now ready to receive the tanning material which consists of a mixture of putrefying brain, liver, and fat. They sometimes soak the skin in wine, which is reputed to add greatly to the lasting qualities of the leather, but the odor of that liquid lasts as long as the skin.

The tanning material is laid on the flesh side of the skin in a thin layer and by rubbing with the hands it is well worked in. Several hours or days elapse and the superfluous matter is scraped off. The skin is then scraped and rubbed between the hands, the harder portions with a scraper resembling a small scoop, until all the skin is worked into a pliable condition. If the skin is yet too oily a quantity of powdered chalk, clay, calcined bone, or even flour, is thoroughly rubbed over it to absorb any fatty matter yet remaining.

The skins having the hair on, for clothing, or those intended for buckskin, are treated in this manner. Those intended for parchment are simply rubbed with a quantity of fat, and then allowed to dry in that condition, being of a yellowish or pale glue color.

Where a great number of skins have to be prepared, and some of the more energetic men have as many as two or three hundred buckskins and parchment skins for the spring trade, a constant application to this labor is necessary in order to prepare them in season. This, in a manner, accounts for the number of wives which an energetic or wealthy man may have in order that the products of the chase falling to his share may be promptly attended to.

When the skins intended for sale are selected they are bundled up and covered with parchment skins or the subcutaneous tissue.

The skins intended for use among themselves are generally inferior grades, such as those cut in the skinning process, or else those obtained in the earlier or the later part of the season.

A species of gad fly infests the deer, puncturing the skin on both sides of the spine, and depositing within the wound an egg which in time is transformed into a grub or larva. These larvæ attain the size of the first joint of the little finger, and at the opening of the spring weather work their way through the skin and fall to the ground, where they undergo metamorphoses to become perfect insects.

A single animal may have hundreds of these grubs encysted beneath the skin, which, on their exit, leave a deep suppurating cavity, which heals slowly. The skin forming the cicatrices does not have the same texture as the untouched portions.

When the skin is dressed it reveals these scars, and of course, the value of the skin is diminished according to their number. The Indian often endeavors to conceal them by rubbing flour or chalk over them.

The season when the skins are in the best condition is from September to the middle of December. The freshly deposited eggs have not yet produced larvæ of sufficient size to injure the skin, and the wounds produced by those dropping out in the month of May have healed and left the skin in condition.

Certain skins intended for special purposes must be smoked. The process of smoking tends to render it less liable to injury from moisture. The pyroligneous vapors act as antiseptics and thus at least retard decomposition of those articles most exposed to wet. The tents and foot wear are always tanned with the smoke and this process is always subsequent to that of bringing the skins into the pliable condition.

The process adopted by these Indians in smoking the deerskins is as follows: The woods are searched for rotten wood of a special character. It must be affected with a kind of dry rot which renders the fibers of a spongy nature. This is procured and thoroughly dried.

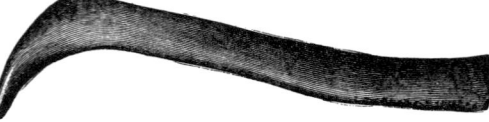

FIG. 106.—Paint stick. Nenenot.

The skins to be smoked are selected and two of nearly the same size and condition are chosen, and sewed into the form of a bag with the hairy side within. The after portions of the skin are suspended from a convenient pole and the head and neck portions left free or open. To the edges of these is sewed a cloth, usually a piece of baling cloth, and this is also left open. The rotten wood is placed in a pan or vessel and as it smolders, never burning into a blaze, the pale, blue, pungent smoke is allowed to ascend within the cavity of the deerskin bag. The cloth is merely to form a conduit for the smoke as the skin should not be too near the fire.

As the process continues the skins are inspected between the stitches of the sewing and when the operation has progressed sufficiently they are taken down. It will now be found that the surface has assumed a pale, clear brown color, the shade of which depends on the length of the exposure to the smoke.

The cloth is removed and the skins are immediately folded, with the smoked side within, and laid away for several days to season. If, however, the skin be left to the influence of the air the coloring matter immediately disappears leaving it of a color only slightly different from what it was before it was smoked.

FIG. 107.

The scars, made by the larvæ of the insects, do not "take" the smoke as well as the healthy portions and so present a pitted or scaly appearance. From the skins having an abundance of the scars are made the tents and inferior grades of moccasins and the

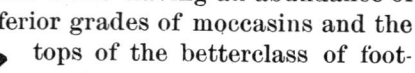

FIG. 108.—Paint stick. Nenenot.

tops of the betterclass of footwear.

The paints used for decorating the buckskin garments are applied by means of bits of bone or horn of a peculiar shape best understood from the figures (Figs. 106–110).

Those with two, three or four tines are used for making the complicated patterns of parallel lines, and are always made of antler, while the simple form is sometimes of wood.

A block of wood with one or more bowl-shaped cavities cut in it (Fig. 111) serves to hold the mixed paints, especially when several colors are to be used in succession.

Small wooden bowls are also employed. (Figs. 112–113.)

FIG. 109.—Paint stick. Nenenot.

The pigments used are procured from different sources. From the traders are obtained indigo in the crude condition or in the form of washing blue, vermilion in small buckskin bags, and a few other colors. An abundance of red earth occurs in several

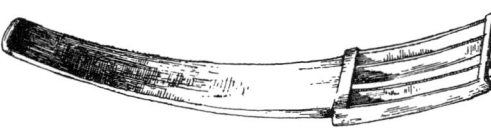

FIG. 110.—Paint stick. Nenenot.

localities. The pigments are reduced to the finest possible condition and kneaded with the fingers until ready for the addition of water often mixed with a slight quantity of oil or tallow. A favorite vehicle for the paint is the prepared roe of a sucker (*Catastomus*) abounding in the waters of the district. The female fish are stripped of the mass of ova which is broken up in a vessel and the liquid strained through a coarse cloth. The color is a faint yellow which becomes deeper with age. The fluid

FIG. 111.—Paint cup. Nenenot.

is allowed to dry and when required for use is dissolved in water. It has then a semiviscid consistence and in this condition is mixed with the various pigments. When a yellowish color is desired the fish-egg preparation is applied alone. The albumen gives sufficient adhesive quality to the paint and produce a rich glaze, giving a good effect to the otherwise dull colors.

FIG. 112 —Paint cup. Nenenot.

The process of preparing the crude mineral colors is quite tedious as the attrition is produced by rubbing the substance between two smooth stones, a little water occasionally being added to hold the particles together. The prepared paints are put in the vessels already described, and when ready for use a quantity is taken with the finger and placed in the palm of the hand while the other fingers hold the instrument by which it is to be applied. The paint stick is carefully drawn through the thin layer of paint spread on the other palm and a quantity, depending on the thickness of the layer, adheres to the edges of the appliance and by a carefully guided motion of the hand the lines desired are produced. The eye alone guides the drawing, however intricate it may be. The artist frequently attempts to imitate some of the delicate designs on a gaudy bandana handkerchief or some similar fabric. The principal source of the hematite is a lake near the headwaters of George's river where it

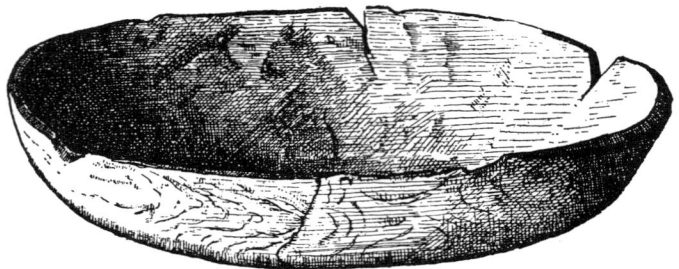

FIG. 113.—Paint cup. Nenenot.

occurs as a mass of disintegrated rock along the margin. The water has by freezing split great quantities from the mass and when there is a strong wind from the opposite direction the water is often lashed into a blood-red foam.

DWELLINGS.

The Nenenot live, both in summer and in winter, in deerskin tent, (see Fig. 114), which are constructed in the following manner: A suffi-

FIG. 114.—Nenenot Indian tent.

cient number of small poles cut from the woods are deprived of their branches and brought to the camp site. A location is selected and the poles are erected in a circle, with tops leaning toward the center so as to form a cone 10 to 14 feet in height, having a diameter at its base of from 10 to 18 feet. The skins forming the cover are those of the reindeer, and those selected for this purpose are usually of an inferior grade. A sufficient number are sewed together to form a strip long enough to reach around the poles when set up. As the tents differ in size according to the number of people who occupy them, the skins sewed together may be from eight to twelve. The first strip is made for the lower part of the poles and is attached to them by means of strings fastened within. A second strip is made to go around the upper part of the poles, and is, of course, correspondingly shorter. It is placed last so as to overlap the lower breadth and thus prevent rain and snow from blowing in. The door is usually made of one large skin or two smaller ones. It is tied to the poles at the upper corners and at the lower has a small log of wood as a weight to prevent it from flapping. The poles at the apex are not covered and through them the smoke from the fire built in the center within ascends and finds exit.

The interior of the tent is arranged to suit the occupants. The floor is usually covered with the branches of young spruce, and when carefully laid these form an admirable protection from the cold ground and a soft carpeting.

The women who lay this flooring display great taste, and certain of them are noted for their skill in disposing the branches. The center of the tent is reserved for the fire which is built there among a few stones.

The occupants arrange themselves according to the importance of the place they occupy in the family. The owner or head man is always to be found on the side opposite the fire. This is considered a place of honor, to which all guests who are to be complimented are invited to a seat.

The other members of the group arrange themselves along the sides of the tent, and those who have been adopted into the family occupy positions next the doorway.

Over the fire may be poles reaching across the tent, and on these will be suspended kettles and pots obtained from the traders. The cooking utensils are few in number, one vessel serving various purposes.

The hunting gear and the skins of animals, together with the articles belonging to the females may be seen suspended from various portions of the interior. Around the edges are the blankets of deerskin, and those bought from the traders, lying in disorder. The outer edge of the interior is slightly raised above the center, and affords a convenient slope for those who desire to sleep. The occupants always sleep with their feet toward the fireplace, around which there is no brush, lest it be set on fire during sleep and destroy the tent.

They have regular hours for sleeping, but as these are only for a period of short duration, it is not unusual to find half the inmates asleep at any time a tent is visited.

The preparation of the food appears to go on at all times, and there are no regular hours for partaking of their meals, as each person eats when convenient. The food is taken directly from the pot or kettle, and each one helps himself. Forks are not used, and the food is divided with a knife or torn with the fingers.

SWEAT HOUSES.

The Nenenot are in the habit of taking steam baths, for which purpose they use a sudatory or sweat house, constructed as follows: A number of flexible poles of small size, usually willow or alder, which grow to sufficient size along the banks of the streams, are bent to form a hemispherical or dome-shaped structure, which is covered with tent skins. A sandy locality is selected or one free from snow in winter, and a fierce fire is built. When it is well under way a number of stones are thrown into the fire to heat. When the heat is sufficient the fire is removed and the structure is quickly erected over the hot stones and some one from the outside fastens down the edges of the tenting with stones to prevent the loss of heat. A kettle of water previously placed within the bath house is used to pour over the stones, when heat rises to a suffocating degree and produces the desired perspiration. Water is not used to bathe in, though sometimes a slight quantity is poured upon the head only. The bather remains within the hut until the heat has nearly exhausted him.

These baths are frequently taken, and often when he has just started on a journey the head of the family will be seized with a desire to have a bath. Everything must await this operation before the journey is resumed.

An amusing incident occurred at Fort Chimo in the spring of 1882. That season the reindeer were extremely numerous at that place, as they were crossing to go to the northeast to drop the fawns. Often when the herds or bands were panic stricken they rushed among the Indian tents, the houses of the station, and, in fact, everywhere, with yelping dogs and screaming women and children at their heels. An old man and wife were in the sweat house at a time when a very large drove of the deer, in their frantic endeavors to escape their pursuers, headed directly for the bath. Some one screamed to the occupants to look out for the deer. The man and wife made their exit just as a score or more of the animals reached the spot. The man tore up the tenting of the bath house and whirled it in the air, while the old woman cut the most astonishing antics. The whole population witnessed the occurrence and did not fail to help increase the tumult. Signs of former sudatories are quite common along the paths where the Indians have traveled for many years.

HOUSEHOLD UTENSILS, ETC.

Each household is supplied with sundry wooden vessels of various sizes (Fig. 115) which serve for buckets for holding water and for drinking cups. They are made of strips of thin boards cut from spruce or from larch trees, the wider strips being as much as six inches wide and one-third of an inch thick. They are steamed and bent into ovoid or circular forms and the ends of the strip overlapping. Then they are sewed with split roots from those trees. A groove is cut near the lower edge and into it is placed a dish-shaped piece of wood for a bottom.

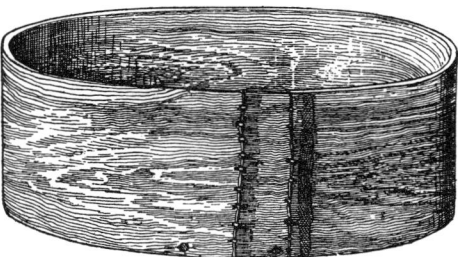

FIG. 115.—Wooden bucket, Nenenot.

These vessels are identical in shape and function with those manufactured by the Yukon river Indians of Alaska.

They also use berry-dishes or baskets like Fig. 116 made from the

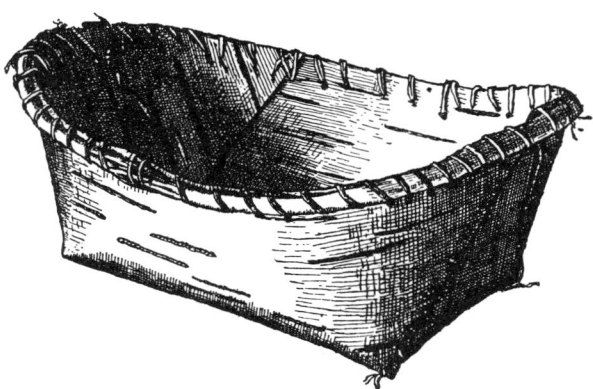

FIG. 116.—Birchbark basket, Nenenot.

bark of the spruce peeled in the spring of the year. At this time the bark is quite flexible and may be bent into the desired shape. The corners are sewed with coarse roots from the same tree and the rim is strengthened by a strip of root sewed over and around it by means of a finer strand. These baskets serve a good purpose when the women are picking berries, of which they are inordinately fond; and during that season it is a rarity to see a woman or man without a mouth stained the peculiar blue color which these berries impart.

Baskets of this shape frequently have a top of buckskin sewed to them, closed with a drawstring, as shown in Fig. 117 (No. 3485). Such things serve to hold trinkets and other small articles.

Large objects are carried in bags, either long or basket-shaped, made of the skins of deer legs. The leg skins are scraped and FIG. 117.—Birchbark basket, Nenenot. worked to a moderate degree of pliability and their edges sewed together until a sufficient number have been joined to make the bag of the required size. This bag is used to hold the clothing, furs, and other valuables. When on a trip they are·invariably carried. If the journey be performed on foot the two ends are tied with a thong and the bag thrown over the shoulder.

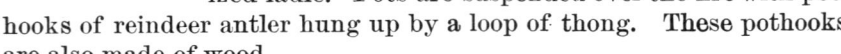

In preparing food stone pestles of various sizes were formerly used of the shape shown in Fig. 118. These pestles are now mostly out of date and superseded by cast-iron ones with steel faces, procured from the traders. The metal pounders, however, are so heavy that they are objectionable to people who have to make their burdens on the portages as light as possible.

Spoons to lift pieces of floating meat from the hot liquor in which it is cooked, are made of reindeer antler and of wood. The pattern of these spoons is shown in the figures (Fig. 119). One shape (No. 3351, Figs. 120, 121, 122), was perhaps copied from a civilized ladle. Pots are suspended over the fire with pothooks of reindeer antler hung up by a loop of· thong. These pothooks are also made of wood.

FIG. 118.—Stone pestle, Nenenot.

TOBACCO AND PIPES.

Like all other Indians, these people are inordinately fond of tobacco for smoking, chewing, and snuff; the latter, however, is used only by aged individuals, especially the females, whose countenances show the

FIG. 119.—Wooden spoon or ladle, Nenenot.

effect in a manner quite disgusting. The men consider a supply of tobacco of as much importance as the supply of ammunition for the prosecution of the chase. The first request upon meeting an Indian is that you furnish him with a chew or a pipe full. Little satisfactory intercourse can be had with him until he is mollified by a gift of tobacco. The first thing that an Indian receives when arriving at the trading post is a

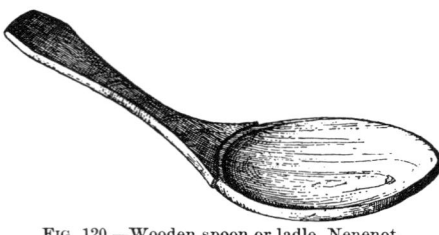

FIG. 120.—Wooden spoon or ladle, Nenenot.

clay pipe and a plug of tobacco. The pint of molasses and the three or four hard biscuit (which have received the local name of 'Canadian padlock," doubtless because they are so difficult to open), are of secondary consideration. When the spring arrivals are camped

STONE TOBACCO PIPES.

at the station it is not unusual for several to contribute a number of plugs of tobacco and a gallon of molasses. These are boiled together and then water is added to the mixture. This villainous compound is drunk until a state of stupefaction ensues. The muddled creature under the influence of that liquor seems like an idiot. The effect is terrible and does not wear away for several days. The pipes used for smoking are made of stone obtained from river pebbles, usually a fine-grained compact sandstone. The color of this stone varies from a dark

reddish brown nearly the color of clotted blood to a lighter shade of that color. The red stones often have spots of every size and shape of a yellowish drab which form a strange contrast with the darker colors. The darker the stone the less spotting it will have. The best

FIG. 121.—Wooden spoon or ladle, Nenenot.

of all the pipes and those most valued are of greenish sandstone having strata of darker colors which appear as beautiful graining when the pipe is cut into form and polished.

Other pipes are of hard slate and very dark without markings. All the material is hard and the effect of the fire within renders them harder and liable to crack if used in very cold weather. These pipes vary but little in shape (I have figured three—Pl. xxxviii and Fig. 123—to show the pattern), but there is considerable difference in size. The largest ones are made of the green stone, while the smaller ones are

made of other stones. The stem is of spruce wood and is prepared by boring a small hole through the stick lengthwise and whittling it down to the required size. It is from 4 to 8 inches long and is often ornamented with a band of many colored beads.

The rough stone for a pipe

FIG. 122.—Wooden spoon or ladle, Nenenot.

is selected and chipped into crude form. The successive operations of wearing it down to the desired size are accomplished by means of a coarse file or a harder stone. The amount of labor bestowed upon a pipe consumes several days' time before the final polish is given.

The value set upon these pipes is according to the color of the stone, as much as the amount of labor expended in making them. They are always filthy, partly on account of the bad quality of tobacco used. The ashes and other accumulations within are removed by means of a bodkin-shaped instrument of bone or horn. The back of a broken horn comb is a favorite material for making a decorated pipe-cleaner (Fig.

124).   The ornamentations consist of cruciform and quadrate figures on the handle.   The tobacco used for smoking is the commonest black plug of very inferior quality, soaked with molasses and licorice.   This moist tobacco is cut into pieces and a coal of fire placed upon it.   They prefer this quality, and purchase the lighter and drier kinds only to serve as kindling for the darker sort.

They do not know how to brew or ferment liquors of any kind, and as the importation of intoxicants is wisely prohibited, the native has no opportunity to indulge in his craving for liquors, the supply of which was plentiful in former years.   A spruce beer is made by the servants of the company for the holidays, and a taste is sometimes given to a

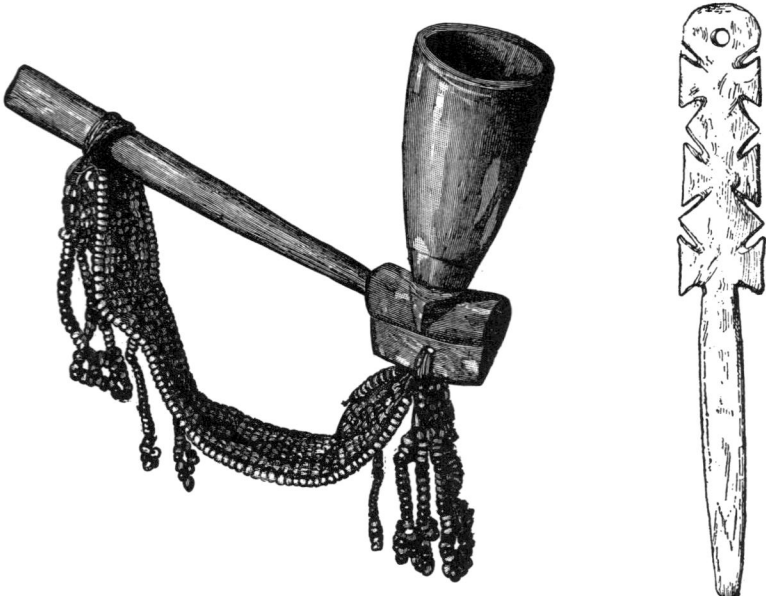

FIG. 123.—Stone tobacco pipe.   FIG. 124.—Pipe cleaner, Nenenot,

favorite Indian, who is so easily affected that a pint of this mild beer will send him reeling and happy to his tent, where it soon becomes known that beer is to be had.   The importunities for drink are now so frequent, that the barrel must be emptied of its contents in order to avoid the constant beggings for it.

MEANS OF TRANSPORTATION.

BY WATER.

All the Indians of this region use birch-bark canoes, of the pattern shown in the figure (Pl. XXXIX, from a photograph; the collection also contains six wooden models of these canoes).   The style of canoe used by the Little Whale river Indians of the eastern side of Hudson bay has very much more sheer at the bow and stern than those used in the

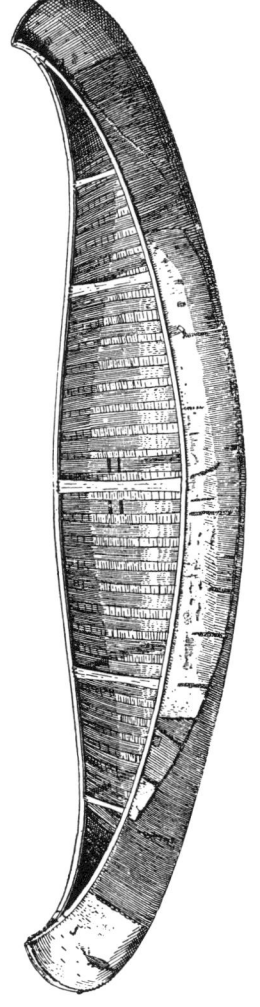
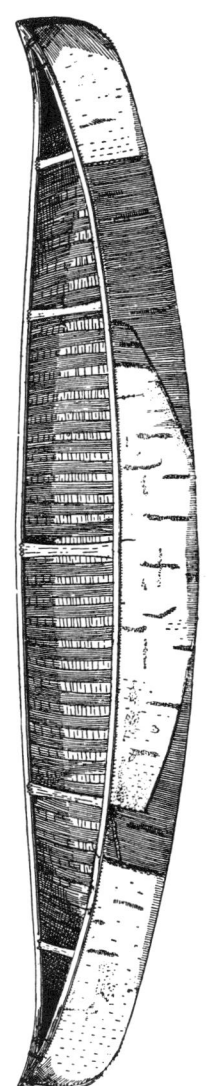

BIRCH-BARK CANOE, NENENOT, KOKSOAK RIVER PATTERN.

valley of the Koksoak. The canoe of each individual differs from others according to the personal taste or need of the maker. The requirements are that the canoe shall be able to transport himself and family, together with the household property, whenever it is desired to change camps. Some of the canoes are small, others large, often possessed by two or more individuals in common.

These canoes are constructed in the following manner: Trees are selected which when split will afford a number of straight-grained slats free from knots. These slats are shaved to the required thickness and laid aside to season. They are 3 or 4 inches wide and less than one-third of an inch in thickness. The exterior or longitudinal strips are placed so that their edges will touch each other. The inside strips or ribs are placed about their own width apart, and of course are placed at right angles to the longitudinal slats. They are thinner than the side strips and become almost like shavings at the bow and stern. The two layers of slats form a kind of shell upon which the skin of bark fits tightly. The first process with the bark is to free it from the outside scaling layers; the next is to soak it for several days in fresh water to soften it; otherwise, when dry it would crack like an eggshell. When it has macerated a sufficient time it is taken out and laid over a form of clay or other earth, which has previously been roughly molded to the shape of the interior of the canoe. The bark is now sewed along the edges of the strips with roots of the spruce tree. These are long and tough, and resemble splits of rattan when properly prepared for the purpose by splitting and shaving with a knife. Various sizes of these roots are used for the different portions. The threads are also soaked in water until they become so flexible that they may be tied into a knot without breaking.

When the bark skin rudely conforms to the shape of the mold of earth, the rails or round strips of wood along the inner edge of the canoe are placed in position and the ends of the bark strips laid over it and sewed. A second rail is now laid upon the first and drawn down to it by means of the root thongs. A piece of wood is shaped for the bow and one for the stern and inserted in position, and the end seams of the canoe are sewed over these pieces.

The interior is then ready for the longitudinal strips, which are placed at the bottom first and gradually built up on each side until the rails are reached. The ribs or transverse strips are next placed in position. Five or more crosspieces, or thwarts, are fastened to the side rails to give stiffness to the sides and to prevent collapsing, and they may be set either below or above the rail. The greatest care must be exercised to give to both sides of the canoe the same shape and to have the keel evenly balanced. This is rudely regulated by the eye during the process of construction. After all the strips are put in, the boat is allowed to season and dry. This causes the bark to shrink, and while drying the whole is frequently inspected to discover any splits or cracks in the bark. The Indian often wets the canoe, lest it dry too rapidly and split under the tension. When the form and make are satisfactory the seams are smeared with a mixture of spruce gum (or resin bought from the traders'), mixed with seal oil to render it less easily broken. This mixture is while hot laid upon the dry surface with a small paddle.

After the gum has seasoned for a day or so the canoe is put upon the water and tested for its speed and seaworthiness. All leaks and needed repairs are immediately attended to, and it is at length ready for use.

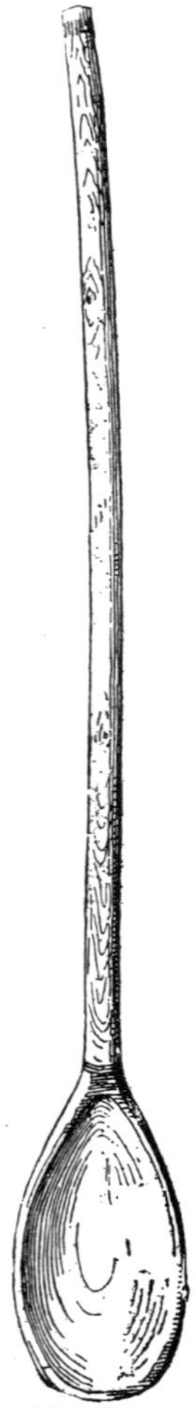

Many persons have not the skill needed to construct a canoe, and they employ those who have had experience and are known to build an excellent boat.

There are two kinds of canoes in use among those Indians, differing only in the shape of the stern and prow. The original form was nearly flat along the rails and had the bow and stern but little turned up. Of later years intercourse with some of their neighbors has induced them to modify the nearly straight edge canoe into an intermediate shape between their own and that of the East Main Indians, whose canoes are very much turned up, and are acknowledged to be far superior vessels to those of the Ungava Indians.

As the forests in the vicinity of Fort Chimo do not contain birch trees, and none are found until the headwaters of the Koksoak are reached, where they are too small to afford bark of sufficient size and thickness, the Indians are compelled to procure the bark from the traders, who import it from the St. Lawrence river and gulf stations to Fort Chimo. It comes in bundles large enough to cover a single canoe of moderate size. If a canoe is to be very large two bundles are required. The value of a black fox skin purchases a bundle of bark.

During the spring months, while the weather is somewhat warm, the men are engaged in preparing the strips and bark for the canoe which is to convey them up the river when the ice breaks and the river is open for navigation.

The paddle has a single blade with a handle scarcely more than half the length of the paddle. It is used with both hands, the strokes being given on alternate sides as it glides through the water.

FIG. 125.—Spoon for applying grease to canoe.

When it is necessary that a portage be made the voyager takes the canoe upon his shoulders by letting one of the center thwarts rest on the back of the neck. The hands are thrown backward to hold up the end of the canoe from the ground. A headband, such as I have already described, of birch bark or cloth, often fancifully ornamented with

beads, fits over the forehead and is attached to the sides of the canoe
by means of thongs, which prevent the canoe from slipping off the
shoulders as the porter quickly trav-
erses the narrow pathway through
the trees and bushes. The ground
is often so uneven and rough that
long detours have to be made by the
porter, while the rest of the party
may go a shorter path to the place
where the canoe will again be placed
in the water. A part of the necessary equipments for a trip in a canoe
are pieces of bark, root threads, and
gum to repair any damage resulting
from an accidental contact with a
stone or snag.

Without the birch-bark canoe the
Indian would have difficulty in obtaining his living, as it is even more
necessary than the sled, and nearly
as useful as the snowshoe.

The paddles used with these canoes are about 5 feet long, having a
blade about 30 inches long and 4½
wide. The handle terminates in a
sort of knob. The paddle referred
to, for applying the gum and grease
to the seams of the canoe, has the
shape of a flattened spoon with
rounded bowl (Fig. 125). The gum
is heated, and while hot is poured
along the seams and pressed into
the interstices of the stitches with
the paddle. When a patch is to be
applied over a fracture or broken
place in the bark, it may be made
to adhere by the sticky properties
of the gum alone, if the distance to
be traveled is not great. A fire is
then made and the wax heated; the
piece of bark is edged with the gum
and pressed firmly over the rent.
A second coat is applied over the
edges of the bark, after the first has
become cold. A few minutes suffice
to repair an apparently alarming hole.

FIG. 126.—Toboggan, Nenenot, side view.

FIG. 127.—Tobog-gan, Nenenot, from above.

BY LAND.

For carrying loads over the snow all the Indians of this region use large sleds (Figs. 126, 127) called tá-bas-kán, which is a word equivalent to the well known name "toboggan." These sleds, as used among the Indians under consideration, differ very greatly in size according to the use for which they are designed.

The method of construction is as follows: A tree is selected as free from knots as possible and two boards of less than an inch in thickness are hewed or split from it. These boards are further dressed to the required thickness and width. The final operation consists in shaving them down with a "crooked knife" to little more than half an inch in thickness. One edge of each board is then straightened and the two edges placed together. The length is rarely more than 13 feet. The front end is steamed or heated in a kettle of hot water until the boards become flexible. The ends are turned up to the desired curve and then bent over at the end, where they are held in position by a transverse bar of wood. This bar is slightly concave on the side next the sled and gives the nose a curved shape. The curved portion of the front may rise as much as 18 inches above the surface over which the sled travels. At the

FIG. 128.—Nenenot snowshoe, single bar.

place where the curve begins a second transverse bar is placed, and at a distance behind it a third, fourth, and fifth bars are fastened. Sometimes an additional bar is to be found on the upper side of the bottom. These bars are all fastened to the two bottom boards by means of thongs of parchment deerskin, and run through holes on the bottom boards. On the under side the thongs are let into places cut out between the two holes, so that the thongs will not be worn when passing over the snow. They are usually fastened in four places, one at each end of the bar and one on each side of the crevice between the edges of the two boards. From the nose of the first bar run a pair of very stout thongs or else twisted sinew, which are drawn tight enough to prevent the nose and curve from straightening out. From the end of the first

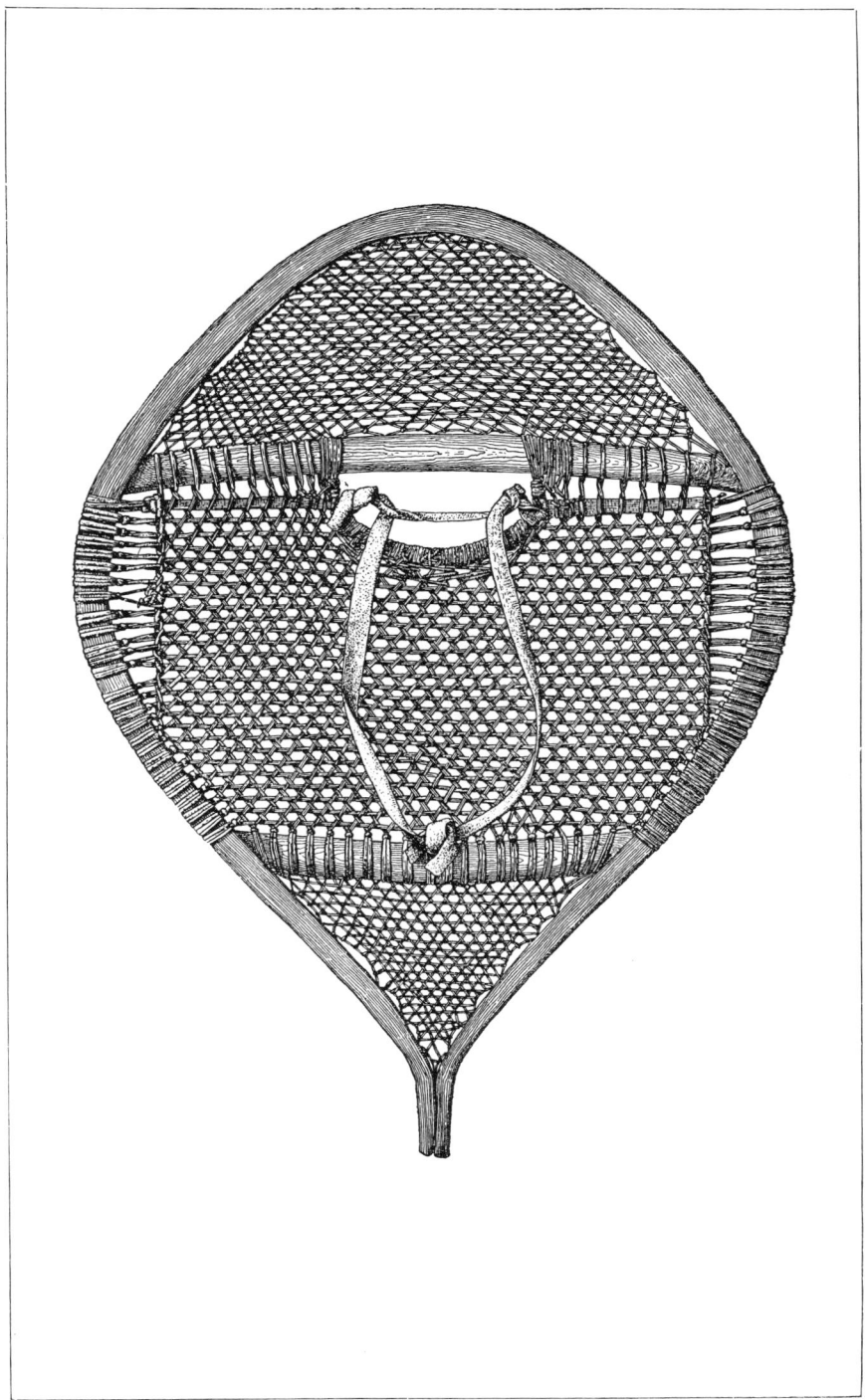

NENENOT SNOWSHOE—"SWALLOW-TAIL."

bar to the last one on the heel of the sled is run a stout twisted thong under the end of each bar, which there has a notch cut on the under side for the line to pass through. This line serves to strengthen the sides and prevent the two boards from slipping past each other when passing over inequalities of the ground. At the ends of the first bar and connected with the side lines are two long stout thongs of twisted skin, often 25 feet long. These are used as traces, by which the sled is dragged. The shape of the bottom is often fashioned after all the remainder of the work has been done. The width of the nose is rarely more than 9 inches; at the first bar it is about 14 inches and as much as 18 inches between the first and second bars. From the widest part to the heel it gradually narrows to a width of 5 to 7 inches.

Two boards are used, as one of sufficient width could not be obtained from the forests of that region. Besides, a single board would certainly split, while two obviate this danger and render the sled less stiff. In passing over rough places the sled must bend to conform to inequalities or else it would break. In the construction of this vehicle the Indian displays much skill and a perfect knowledge of the requirements of the case. The load is placed so as to dispose the weight on that portion which will bear chiefly on the ground. The great length of the sled enables the person to guide it more readily.

When on a journey the younger women and the men drag it along. When the men return to the station to trade they alone drag it. A small dog is

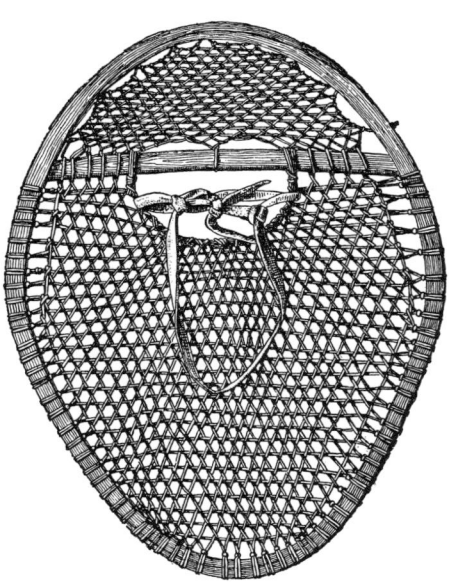

FIG. 129—Nenenot snowshoe, single bar.

sometimes hitched to it by a thong, but as the animal is so small and light, it affords but little assistance. The animal, however, would certainly wander off in search of game along the track, and by being hitched to the sled is kept within bounds.

All the household effects, consisting of tent, cooking utensils, clothing, and other articles are placed on the sled when the people are changing camp.

The Nenenot are skilled in the manufacture and use of snowshoes, of which four styles are used, viz: The "swallow-tail," "beaver-tail," "round-end," and "single-bar" (Figs. 128, 129). The frame is of wood, nearly an inch wide and half an inch thick, usually in two pieces, joined by long lap splices wrapped with deerskin thongs, either at the sides or ends of the shoe. In the single-bar shoe the frame is on one slip, spliced at the toe. Birch is the favorite material for snowshoes, but is rarely to be had except by those Indians who ascend the Koksoak to its headwaters, so that spruce and larch are generally used.

The arrangement of the toe and heel bars of the snow-shoes will be best understood from the figures. They are usually placed within the frame, and set in mortises in the inner side of the frame, before the wrapping of the ends of the frames has been drawn together; otherwise the bars could not be placed in the holes to receive them.

The netting is made of deerskin, with the hair removed, and allowed to dry into a condition usually known as parch-ment. This is cut into strips of variable width, depending on the particular use for which it is wanted.

A needle of bone, horn, or iron (Fig. 130) is used for net-ting the snowshoes. The shape of the implement is flat and rounded at each point, to enable the needle to be used either backward or forward. The eye which carries the line is in the middle. Various sizes of needles are used for the dif-erent kinds of netting, of which the meshes differ greatly in size.

The line is generally 10 to 20 feet in length, and when the netting is completed it somewhat resembles the seating of a cane-bottomed chair. Each individual varies his work according to fancy, but as the netting between the bars is made of coarser line, more compactly woven, there is less difference there than at the toe or heel.

The netting of the toe is of finer line and meshes than the middle or between the bars; while that between the heel bar and heel of the snowshoe is finest of all.

The netting between the bars holds the joints of the frames where they lap over each other.

The toe and heel spaces of netting are held in place by the line passing under the threads which are wrapped around the bars from the netting between them, and again are fastened or slipped through loops of thread or line which are let through the frame of the snowshoe.

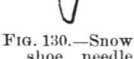

FIG. 130.—Snow-shoe needle, Nenenot.

Near the center of the toe-bar is a space left in the netting between the bars to admit the toes of the wearer and allow them free action while walking. This space is semicircular and is in-closed by several strands of line passing over the toe-bar and forming loops, which have the diagonal lines of the netting passed around them and drawn tight.

The snowshoe is held to the foot by a wide buckskin thong attached at the semicircular space back of the toe-bar. The ends must be far

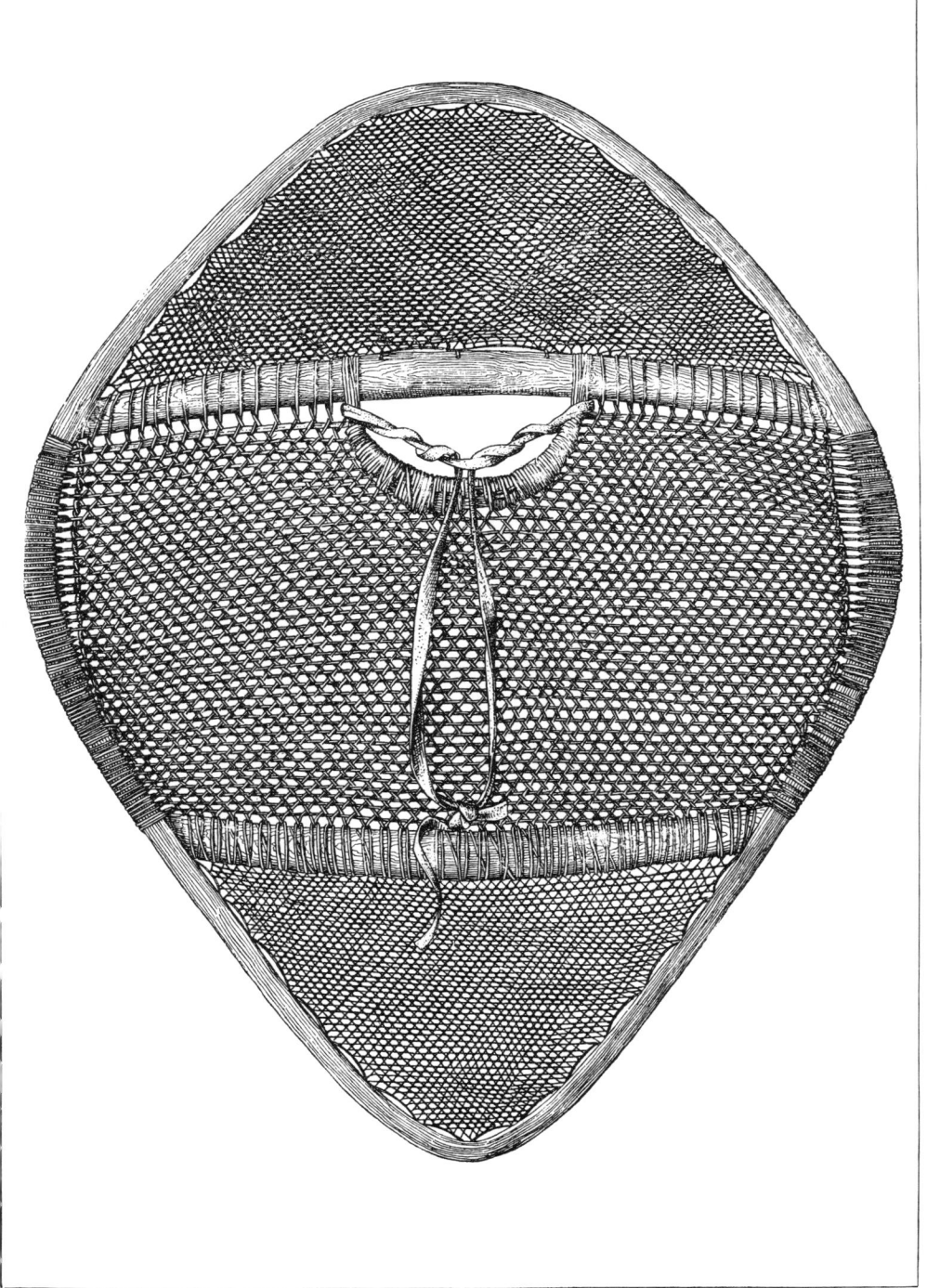

NENENOT SNOWSHOE—"BEAVER-TAIL."

enough apart to admit the width of the foot as far as the toes, and must be then drawn down to prevent the foot from pushing too far forward and striking against the toe-bar. The loop passing over the toes must be slack enough to allow free movement of the foot. When the strap suits the foot it is passed around the heel of the wearer and tied sufficiently tight to give ease and comfort. If too tight, the weight soon presses the tendon of the heel. If too loose, it drops down and the toe slips from under the toe band.

The single-bar snowshoes are not much used, because they are some-what difficult to make. They are of two styles. One has the bar directly under the center of the foot. It is wide, and should be strong enough to sustain the weight of any wearer. The other style is where the single bar is at the front of the toes, which pattern differs from

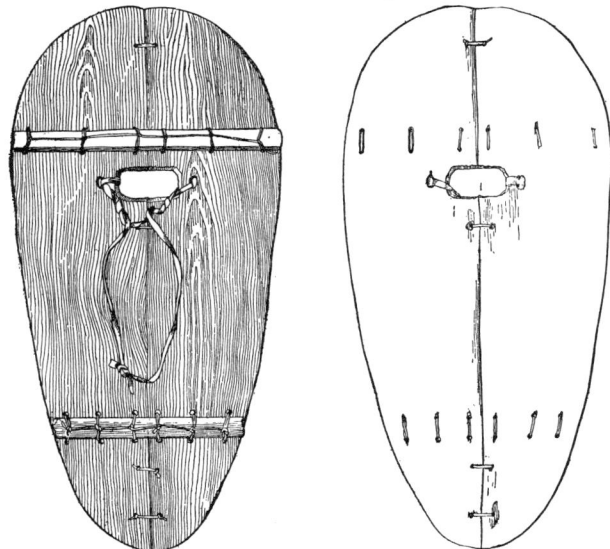

Fig. 131.—Wooden snowshoe, Little Whale river.

the "beaver-tail" style only in the absence of the heel bar. This pattern is considered the easiest of all to wear and walk in when once learned. The foot straps are exactly like those of the common kinds.

The single bar in the middle of the snowshoe renders it a matter of great discomfort until one is accustomed to it, as the straps are simply loops for the toe and heel. This pattern has been already figured. The largest snowshoes measure as much as 28 inches across and 3 feet in length.

Some of the Indians acquire great expertness in the use of these snow-shoes, and are able to run quite rapidly with them. The width of the shoes causes one to straddle widely to allow one snowshoe to pass above and over the other. Care must be exercised that while bringing the rear foot forward the frame does not strike the ankle and produce a serious bruise. In ascending a hill the toe must elevate the snowshoe to avoid a stumble.   In descending the body must be thrown well back or a pitch heels over head ensues, and sometimes the frames strike the back of the head.

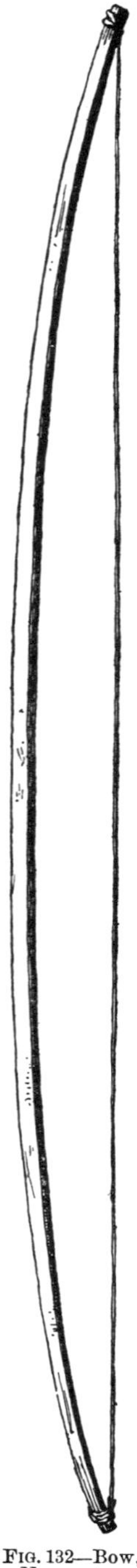

To put them on the feet the foot must enter the loop from forward toward the rear, and when the loop is on the foot the latter must be turned within the loop and then passed under the toe band.

Everybody wears snowshoes—men, women, and children. Without them travel in winter would be an impossibility, and as the capture of furs is made in winter and the ground to be hunted over must of necessity be of great area, the snowshoe becomes a necessity as much as the canoe in summer.

I collected two peculiar pairs of snowshoes, made of flat spruce boards (Fig. 131).   They are shaped exactly like netted snowshoes of the "beaver tail" pattern, and the arrangement of the foot strap is the same as usual.

They came from the Little Whale river Indians, who informed me that they were worn on soft snow.

In the spring of the year, when the snow is rapidly melted by sun, the netted snowshoes become clogged with slush, rendering the weight very fatiguing.   Wooden snowshoes are admirably adapted for that season of the year, and may be made in a few hours, while the netted ones require several days' assiduous labor.   The Indians of the Koksoak valley do not use the wooden snowshoes.

WEAPONS.

In former times these Indians used the bow and arrow exclusively, but they have now nearly discarded these weapons for the guns which they procure from the traders.

The bow and arrow is, however, still used to kill ptarmigan, hares, and rabbits.   The bow (Fig. 132) consists of a piece of larch or spruce wood of 4 to 6 feet in length.   It is only slightly narrower and thinner at the ends, and nearly an inch thick and an inch and a half wide at the central portions.   But little ingenuity is displayed in the construction of these weapons.   They have considerable elasticity, and if broken it is easy to obtain a piece of wood from the forest and fashion another.   The string is a strand of deerskin, twisted or rolled.   It is rare to find a bow that has a single string.

The arrows are usually 2 feet or 30 inches long, and feathered with three ptarmigan feathers.   (Figs. 133–136.)   The head is usually an egg-shaped knob, terminating in a slender point which soon breaks off.

This weapon is used for small game, as the cost of ammunition is too great to spend it upon game as readily procured

FIG. 132—Bow, Nenenot.

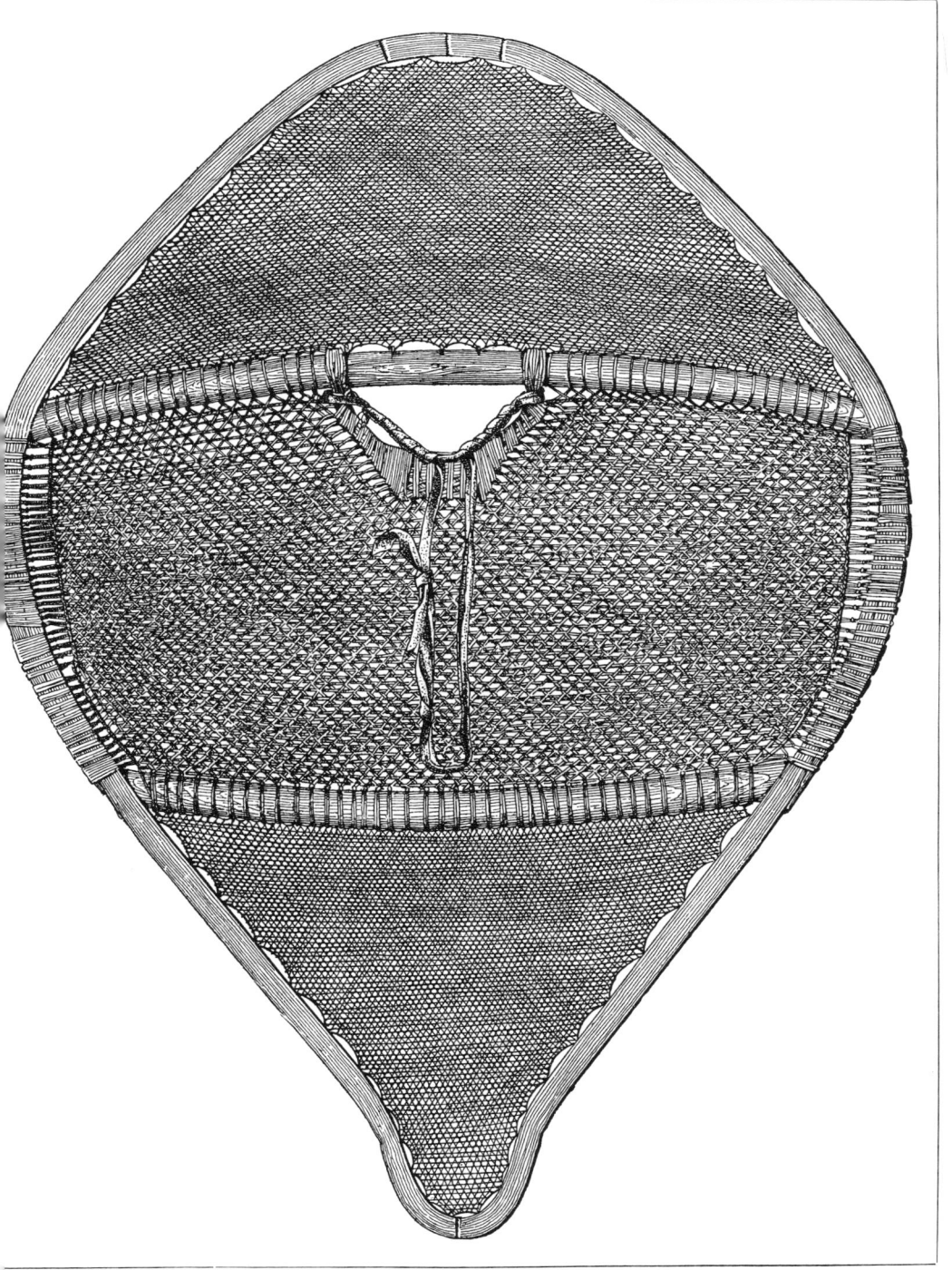

NENENOT SNOWSHOE—"ROUND-END."

by this cheaper method. The Indian is very expert in the use of the bow and arrow, and is able to knock over a ptarmigan or crouching hare every time at 25 yards. The force with which the arrow is projected is astonishing. I have seen a ptarmigan rolled for many yards amid a perfect cloud of feathers when struck by the arrow. It often tears the entire side out of the bird.

In former years the arrow did great execution among the deer in the water or deep snow banks among which they floundered when driven into them by the Indian who, on snowshoes, was able to travel where the deer sank nearly out of sight.

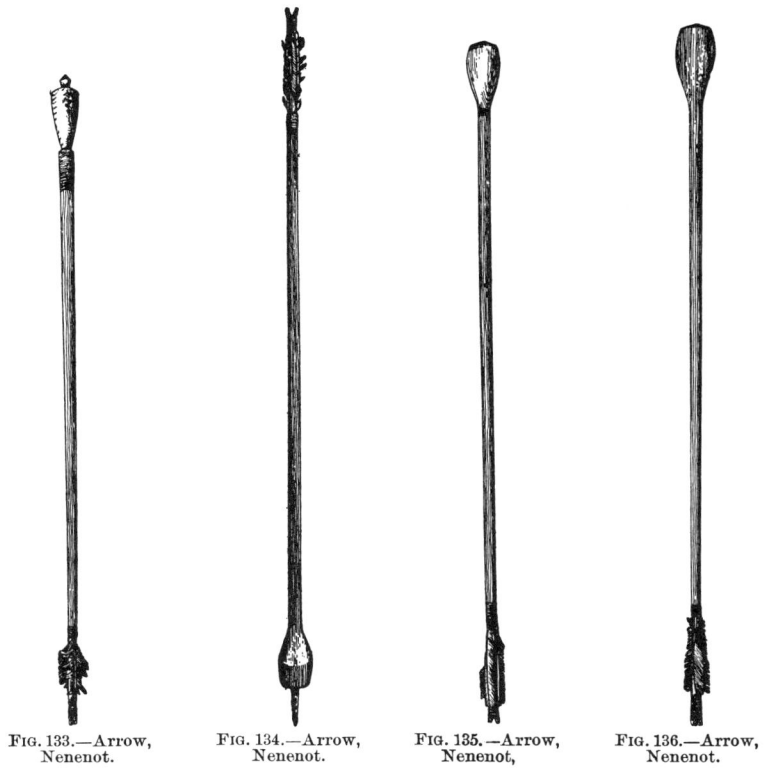

FIG. 133.—Arrow, Nenenot.   FIG. 134.—Arrow, Nenenot.   FIG. 135.—Arrow, Nenenot,   FIG. 136.—Arrow, Nenenot.

Among the Indian boys it is yet a favorite amusement to shoot small birds with the bow and arrow Small crossbows also are used by children. They have doubtless been made after those brought by some white man. The children have great sport with these bows.

The spear, already referred to, for killing the swimming reindeer, is shown in Fig. 137. The wooden shaft is 6 feet long, and the steel point, which is made of a flat file beaten down to a quarter of an inch square, is 11 inches long. It is set into the end of the shaft and fastended by a whipping of sinew.

The weapon is held by the hand in a manner peculiar as well as uncomfortable. The closed hand over the butt end of the weapon is so placed as to have the fingers upward and the outside of the hand toward the point, this rather awkward grasp enables the person to let go of the weapon in case of threatened disaster resulting from a misdirected thrust. The collection also contains three models of deer spears, Nos. 3205–3207. These are often also used as arrows to shoot at larger game when the Indian is out hunting ptarmigan, hares, and rabbits. A hungry wolverene or a famished wolf would prove troublesome to kill with the blunt arrows. These models differ from the larger spear only in size.

The Little Whale river Indians use a peculiar spear for killing white whales. (Figs. 138, 139). It is modeled after the Eskimo harpoon, but has no "loose shaft," or

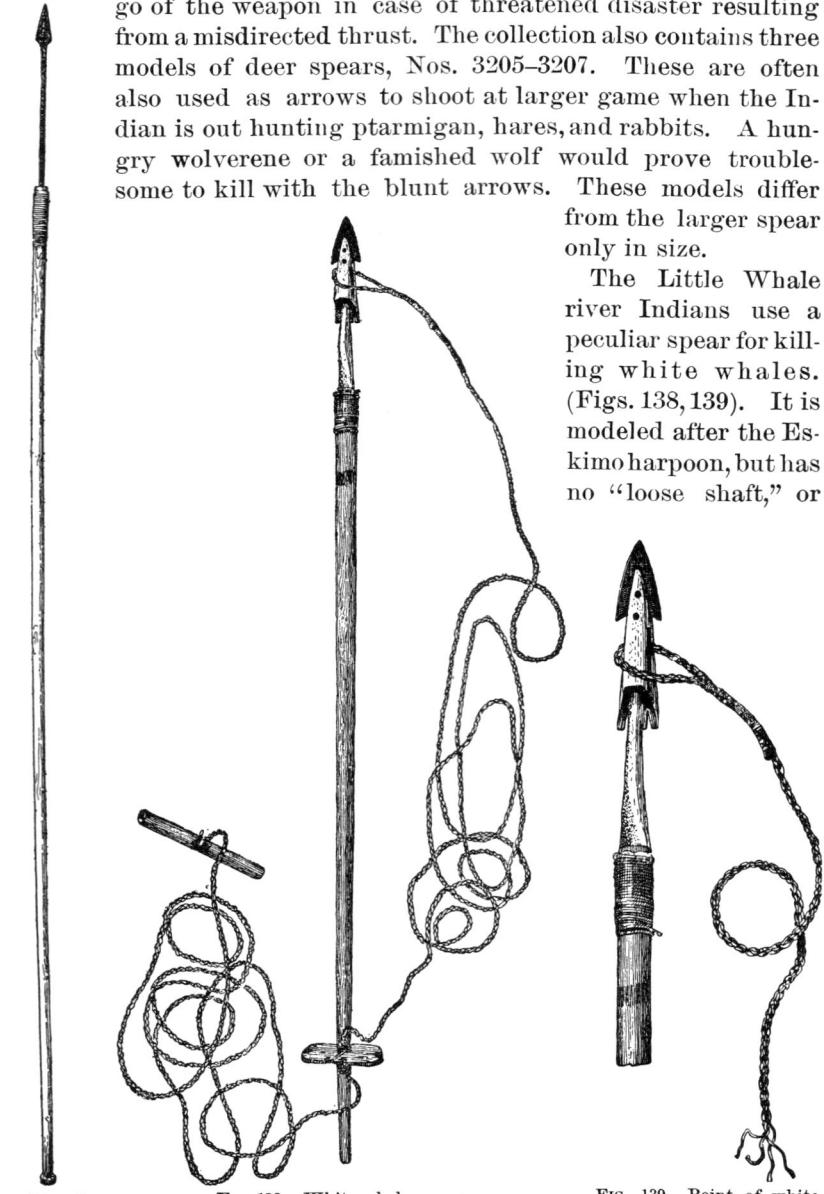

FIG. 137.— Deer lance, Nenenot.

FIG. 138.—White whale spear, Little Whale river.

FIG. 139.—Point of white whale spear enlarged.

rather, the fore shaft and loose shaft are in one piece, and has a circular wooden disk fitted to the butt of the shaft, which takes the place of the bladder float, and serves to impede the motions of the animal when struck. Reindeer antler is substituted for the ivory of the Eskimo weapon. The blades are of copper or iron and riveted in. These spears are 8 or 10 feet long.

The snare (Fig. 140) forms one of the less important methods of procuring these animals. It is of parchment made from the skin of the reindeer cut into thin narrow thongs. Several of these strands, usually three, are plaited together to form a layer; and of these layers three are plaited together to form the snare line. It often is made, however, of three single strands cut somewhat wider and creased so that they will lie well when the three are plaited. The more strands the greater the

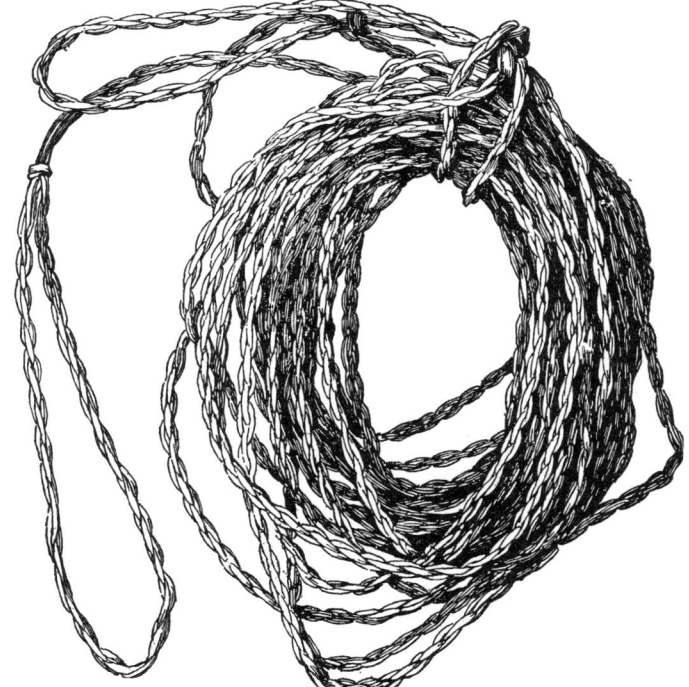

Fig. 140.—Reindeer snare, Nenenot.

flexibility of the line, but as there must be a certain amount of stiffness to hold it in position the many strands must be woven more tightly together. The length varies from 10 to 20 feet, and at the end is a loop formed by turning the strands back and splicing them. Through the loop the other end is passed, and the noose is made.

When a herd of deer is discovered in a favorable locality the people of the vicinity are informed and hasty preparations are made.

The effort is to cause the deer to pass through a narrow defile containing bushes. The snares are then placed in position by tying the free end of the line to a suitable tree and suspending the noose where the heads or antlers will become entangled. Some are placed so that when the foot is lifted the noose is carried along and tightens on it.

The people surround the animals, and at a given signal shout and create the greatest din, to confuse the creatures, which plunge toward the place where the snares are set. One or two hunters concealed in that locality appear suddenly and further confuse the now panic-stricken animals, which rush in every direction before their foes. They become immeshed in the nooses and are held until their throats are cut or they are choked by the cord.

It frequently happens that two deer will be caught in a single snare. The Indians assert that it is a most ludicrous sight to witness two sturdy bucks caught by the antlers in a single snare. They appear to accuse each other of the misfortune, and struggle terribly to free them-selves. In the animals which are strangled by the noose the congested blood distends the veins and renders the flesh very dark.

Previous to the general use of guns the snaring method was of greater importance than at the present day. Even now the Indian does not lose any opportunity of employing the snare.

Some of the snares are made of tanned skin, which is softer and is often ornamented with strands of beads attached to the end of the line. Some of them are colored red, with a mixture of vermilion and hematite earths, thinned with water.

HUNTING.

I have already described the methods of hunting the reindeer and of capturing small game.

The beaver is not plentiful in the Ungava district, and not until the headwaters of the Koksoak and the lakes near the source of George's river are reached are they to be found at all, excepting occasional stragglers.

The Indians have few of the skins of this animal to sell at the trading post of Fort Chimo.

The methods of capture differ in some respects from those elsewhere employed.

The habits of the beaver are so well known that a statement of their manner of life is unnecessary.

The food supply north of latitude 55° is so limited in quality and quantity that the scarcity of the animals is due entirely to the absence of the food necessary for their existence.

When the dams and structures made by the beaver are discovered the people devise means to capture it.

If it is convenient to get at the holes leading to the structure, which are always under water so deep that it will not freeze to the bottom, they are closed with a stick of wood and an opening made in the top of the hut. The animal is then caught by the hind legs or tail and lifted out. It seldom attempts to defend itself at first. As soon as the hunter can do so he jerks the animal out, and with a blow on its head kills it. If he should pause for an instant from the time the hand is put on the animal until the death blow is given, that very instant he certainly will be bitten with teeth so sharp and powerful that the fingers may be snipped from the hand as though with a pair of shears. The wound thus inflicted is often very severe and difficult to heal, as the bite is not only cutting but crushing.

Where the water can be drained from the pond or lake in which the beavers' hut is built, the Indians often leave it high and dry by damming off the supply and allowing the water to drain away. As soon as the house is out of water the occupant emerges and is killed. Beavers are sometimes shot while sporting on the water during moonlight nights.

Some of the animals are captured by means of a net of peculiar construction. This net is of fine deerskin thongs netted into a circle nearly 2 feet in diameter, with meshes about an inch square. The meshes in the outer row are threaded upon a stout thong of deerskin, in length about four times the diameter of the net. This thong is now tied at the ends, and over one end thus tied is slipped a ring made of spruce root and wound with sinew to strengthen it. This ring is about an inch in diameter, only sufficient to allow freedom of the ends of the line. It is fastened to one of the meshes of the net in order to keep its place.

Where the water is too deep and only a single beaver is in the lodge the net is carefully spread over the mouth of the exit so placed as to form a purse into which the head and neck of the animal will be thrust as it leaves the hut. The mouth of the purse now tightens from the ring slipping along the string, and thus strangles the animal or else causes it to drown as it struggles to escape from the tightening cord.

The net is said to be a very effective means of capturing the beaver and will succeed when it has become too wary to be shot on the surface of the water.

The flesh of the beaver is considered valuable food by these people. They prize it highly and prefer the flesh of the female to that of the male.

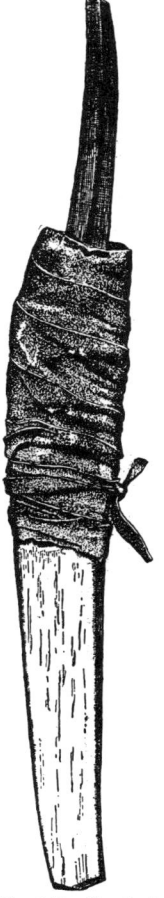

Fig. 141.—Crooked knife, Nenenot.

MISCELLANEOUS IMPLEMENTS, TOOLS, ETC.

One of the most important tools used by the Nenenot is the "crooked" knife (Fig. 141). These instruments are made from steel files or knife blades. They are of various sizes depending on the amount of material at hand. The Indian takes a piece of metal and grinds one side of it flat and smooth; the other is edged like a drawing knife. The blade is now heated and bent to the desired curve. Some are more bent than others and some have only the point bent to one side. The few left-handed persons have the blade formed to suit themselves. It is set in a handle curved from the user and bent upward like the blade. At the end of the handle is generally to be found a thong on which a wooden button is placed for attachment to the belt, as no man ever goes off on a journey without this knife, however short may be the distance.

The handle is held in the hand at right angles or across the body and invariable drawn toward the user. It is employed for all purposes of whittling or shaving wood and one would be surprised to observe what large strips will separate when started with this apparently frail blade.

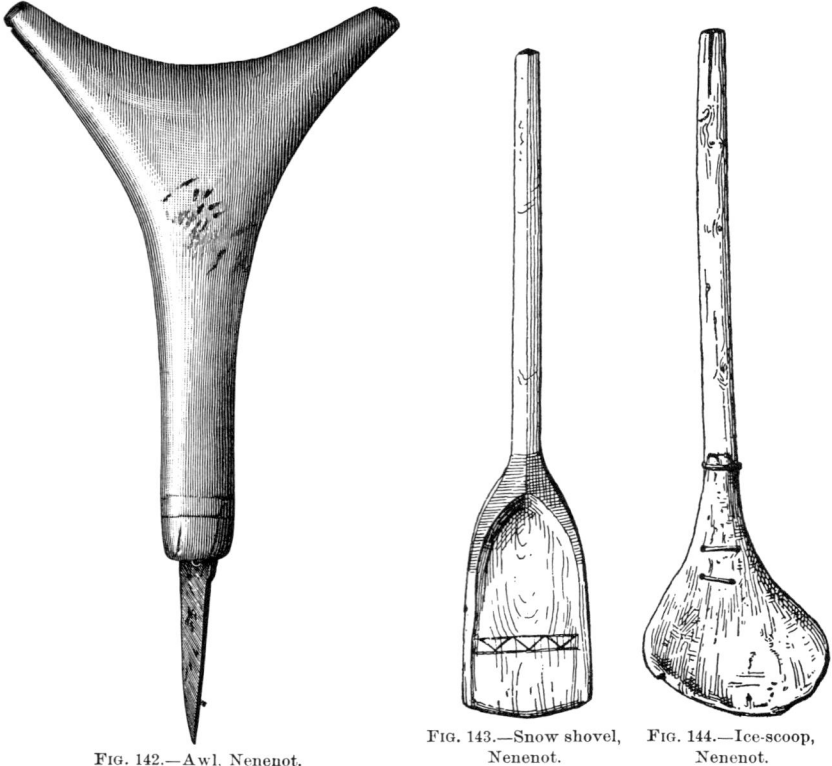

FIG. 142.—Awl, Nenenot.

FIG. 143.—Snow shovel, Nenenot.

FIG. 144.—Ice-scoop, Nenenot.

The strips and slats of canoes, paddles, snowshoes, and in fact everything that can be cut from wood, are made with this knife. It requires much skill to guide the blade so as to cut the wood evenly; and to this end the thumb, which is placed upon the outer extremity of the handle, must steady the blade. The strain of the blade upon the handle is very great, and it must be securely held by means of stout thongs wrapped around it.

The crooked knife is a form of instrument in use among the Indians and Eskimo alike, and one of the few implements which those widely differing people have in common.

Awls (Fig. 142) are made of steel or iron. The back or spring of a pocketknife or a portion of a small file appears to be the favorite material for forming them. They are usually chisel-shaped and have rectangular corners. The handle into which the metal is fastened is generally of deer horn. The shape of the handle varies from a Y shape to that of a crescent.

These tools are constantly required for piercing holes in the various woods used in manufacture. Articles of simple construction the Indian prefers to make for himself, rather than pay an extortionate price to the trader. He is able to accomplish remarkable results with rude tools of his own make.

Snow shovels are made of wood and are much used, for during the winter, when the snows are constantly accumulating around the camps, the occupants necessarily remove some to form a pathway from the door of their tent, and as snow forms an admirable protection, it is thrown or banked up around their tents to prevent the wind from blowing under. In the spring nearly all the aged people carry one of the wooden shovels to clear away a path or as a help to walk while the slushy snow is so treacherous. Fig. 143 represents a common form of wooden snow shovel. These are often painted with vermillion or indigo.

Fig. 144 shows a special form of snow shovel designed for cleaning the ice from the holes through which the people fish. It usually has a blade made from the brow antler or one of the broad palms from the horns of the reindeer. The horn portion is attached to the wooden shaft or handle by means of thongs running through holes bored for that purpose.

The ice-picks (Fig. 145) used in times gone by were pieces of reindeer horn or bone, shaped like a narrow mortising chisel and attached to staffs of wood. The chisel or pick was fastened to the staff by means of stout thongs to prevent a side movement from the groove into which it was set. The upper end of the staff was at times shod with bone or horn so as to be available for a walking staff.

The ice-pick of the present day has a piece of iron or steel substituted for the horn or bone; but, being heavy, it is not so often carried from place to place. An Indian will in an incredibly short time pierce a hole through 3 feet thickness of ice with it. A white man can not equal them in this work.

FIG. 145.

Combs for the hair are purchased from the traders. They are highly prized and are kept in little birchbark bags. For cleaning out the dirt which collects on the comb the tail of a porcupine is used. The needles or spines are picked out of the tail, leaving the stiff, coarse hairs, which serve the purpose of cleaning the comb quite well. This tail is usually appended to the comb-case.

The natives sometimes make wooden combs like the one shown in Fig. 146, in imitation of those purchased.

After a woman's hair has been combed half of it is collected on each side of the head and rolled or wound up on small pieces of board (Fig. 147) similar in shape to the "winders" on which darning or knitting cord is wrapped. Strands of beads are now placed upon these to hold the hair in place.

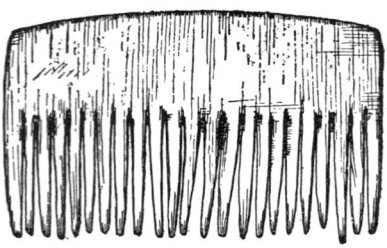

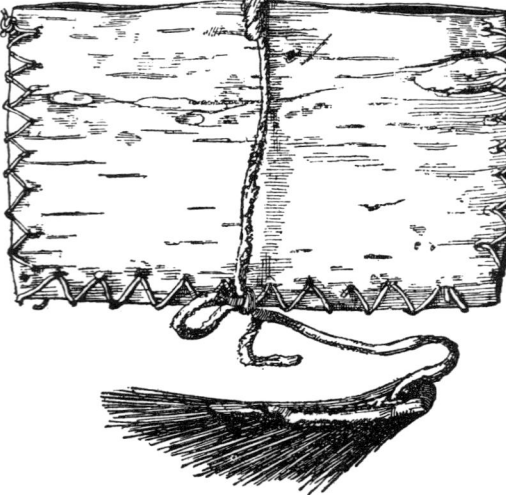

FIG. 146.—Comb, with birckbark case and cleaner.

A remarkable object is shown in Fig. 148. It is one of a pair of boards procured from one of the Little Whale river Indians, by whom they are used to assist in swimming. One board is held in each hand and used as a paddle to push the swimmer along. Indians able to swim are scarce. I have not seen these boards in use, and am not able personally to speak concerning their alleged function.

The fish-hook shown in Fig. 149 has a barb of steel or iron. It is on the smaller hooks made of one of the ribs of the larger trout.

AMUSEMENTS.

The boys have no consideration for the females of their own age, but treat them as inferiors and fit for nothing but to be subjects of almost constant annoyance and persecution. When a number of boys collect they are sure to maltreat the women, even those advanced in years, and appear to delight in any opportunity to subject them to the rudest mis-

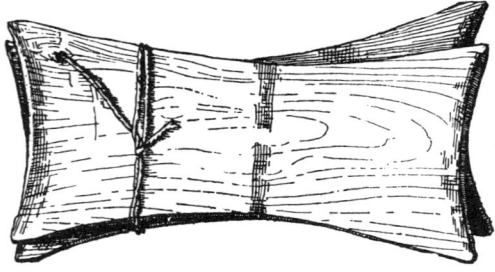

FIG. 147.—Boards for woman's hair.

chief. If a woman ventures to peep from the tent in summer a shower of water is sure to be flung on her by some boy. In winter snow-balling is equally annoying, and when parties of women go to the woods to get fuel the pack of boys is sure to waylay them as they return. If the boys can separate the women their fun is complete; their dresses are torn and their bundles of fuel scattered. They often retaliate, however, and strip the clothing from some unfortunate boy who is compelled to return to camp in a nude condition, much to the

FIG. 148.—Swimming board.

amusement of the people. This form of disgrace appears to be the most severe which can be inflicted upon a male; and the jokes to which he is afterward subjected keep him the object of ridicule for many days.

Besides practical jokes upon women, running, jumping, wrestling, and practicing with the bow and other weapons suited to their age, appear to be the principal amusements of the boys. The girls have never been observed to play at games of any kind. Their chief occupation is to keep away from the boys. While walking out the girls generally toss stones or chips in the air and strive to keep at least two of them up at once. The Eskimo often practice this also, and, as it appears to be a general source of amusement among the Innuit, I suspect that the Indian borrowed it from them. Wrestling appears to be the principal test for physical strength and severe contests often engage the stronger individuals. They wrestle in the Eskimo fashion, and frequently indulge in trials of strength with these people. As would be expected, the stronger

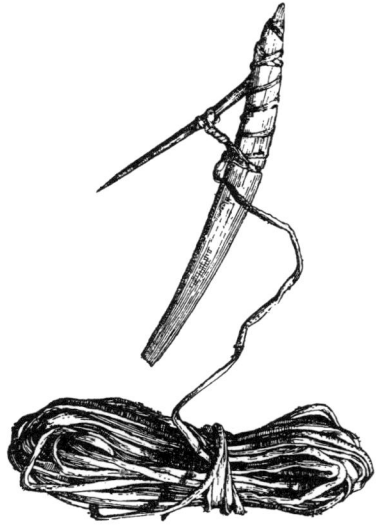

FIG. 149.—Fishhook and line.

Eskimo are always the victors. All these contests, whether among themselves or with the Eskimo, are carried on with the best of good humor.

Feasts are given now and then to celebrate success in hunting and similar achievements.

In 1883 I was invited to attend a feast of furs to be given by one of the most energetic of the Indians. We repaired to the tents spread on the top of a high wall of rock a few rods from my house. As I approached the scene I observed a tent of different construction. It was nearly oval at its base and had a diameter of about 18 feet and a length of about 25 feet. The top was drawn to an apex resembling the common roof of a house. The entrance to the structure faced southeast. On a pole, supported with one end on the apex of the tent and the other resting on a post, were numbers of skins of various animals—wolves, wolverine, beaver, otter, foxes, and muskrat, together with a number of the finest reindeer skins. The sound of the drum was heard within the structure and as I approached the door the noise ceased. I paused and was invited to enter. Immediately two old men next the drummer moved to one side and motioned me to sit down on the pile of deerskins reserved for me. It was evident that the feast had been in progress for some time. Around the interior of the structure groups of men were idly disposed, some reclining and others standing. Not a word was spoken for some time, and this gave me opportunity to look around. The floor was covered with boughs from the neighboring spruce trees, arranged with unusual care, forming a soft carpeting for those seated within. I saw a number of piles of deerskins and several small heaps covered with cloth. To break the silence I inquired if the drum was tired. A smile greeted the inquiry. Immediately an old man came forward, tightened the snare of the drum, and arranged the string, suspending it from one of the tent poles at the proper height for use. He then dipped his fingers into a vessel of water and sprinkled a few drops on the membrane of the drum-head to prevent it from breaking under the blows to be delivered. The performer then seized the drumstick with the right hand and gave the membrane a few taps; the transverse cord of twisted sinew, holding the small cylinders of wood attached to it, repeated the vibration with increased emphasis. A song was begun and the drum beaten in rythm to the monotonous chant of o-ho, o-ho, etc. Three songs with tympanic accompaniment followed. The songs appeared alike and were easily learned. In the meanwhile the guests were treated to a strange-looking compound which had lain hidden beneath one of the cloths and is known as "pemmican." I was solicited to accept a piece. The previously assembled guests had either brought their own bowls and saucers to eat from or else appropriated those available. Not to be at a loss, one of the young men remarked that he would find one. From among the accumulated filth around one of the center poles supporting the structure a bowl was produced. The man coolly took the handkerchief which was tied around his forehead to keep his matted hair from his face and wiped out the interior of the bowl, and placing a piece of the pemmican within it, handed it to the attendant whose duty it was to offer it to me.

I, however, found it quite inedible. Other guests constantly arrived and some departed, made happy by their share of this compound of rancid tallow and marrow with a due admixture of pounded dry meat of the reindeer. I soon departed, and attempted to take the remnant of the pemmican with me. This was instantly forbidden, and information given me that by so doing I should cause all the deer to desert the vicinity, and thus make the people starve. I explained that such was not my desire, and after wishing continued prosperity and enjoyment, I made my way out. I was then informed that the feast would continue for a time, and wind up with an invitation to the women, who had hitherto been excluded, to come and eat the remnants left by the men. At the end of two days thereafter the feast concluded and a dance took place. In this performance there was nothing remarkable. The men sang songs and kicked up their heels, while the women shrugged their shoulders as they swayed their bodies from right to left, and assumed various other postures, although their limbs were apparently kept in a rigid position, occasionally uttering their plaudits as the men made humorous compliments to their generous host.

This feast was given by one who had been unusually successful in the capture of fur-bearing animals, and, to prove his wealth, displayed it before the assemblage and gave a feast in consideration of his ability. Other feasts of a similar character occur, and differ from this in no special feature.

The principal source of amusement with the men is the game of draughts or checkers. While the men are in the tent or on the hillsides awaiting the approach of bands of deer their idle moments are employed over this game. Neither hunger nor the sight of game is sufficient to distract them, so intently are they absorbed.

The game is played as in civilization, with only slight differences. I am not aware that wages are laid upon its issue. Some of the men are so expert that they would rank as skillful players in any part of the world.

Small boards that may be carried in the hunting bag are used on trips to while away the tedium of the long winter evenings with only the light of the flickering fire of the dry limbs of spruce. Far into the night the players engage, and are only disturbed when one of their tired companions starts from his sleep to relate a wondrous dream and have it expounded by the listeners, who sit aghast at the revelations.

They also have a game corresponding to "cup and ball," but it is played with different implements from what the Eskimo use, as may be seen by referring to Fig. 150. The hollow cones are made from the terminal phalanges of the reindeer's foot. The tail tied to the end of the thong is that of a marten or a mink. The player holds the peg in one hand, and tossing up the bones tries to catch the nearest bone on the point of the peg. The object of the game is to catch the bone the greatest possible number of times. It is in no sense a gambling game.

The only musical instrument used by these people is the drum or tambourine, which is of the form shown in Fig. 151. These drums vary

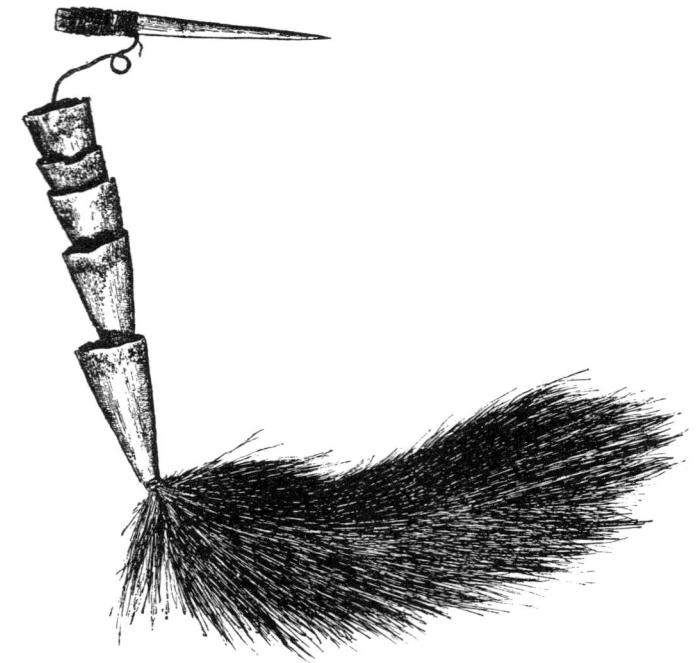

FIG. 150.—Cup-and-ball, Nenenot.

in diameter from 22 to 26 inches, and are constructed as follows: The barrel is made of a thin slat of spruce, bent into a hoop, with the ends

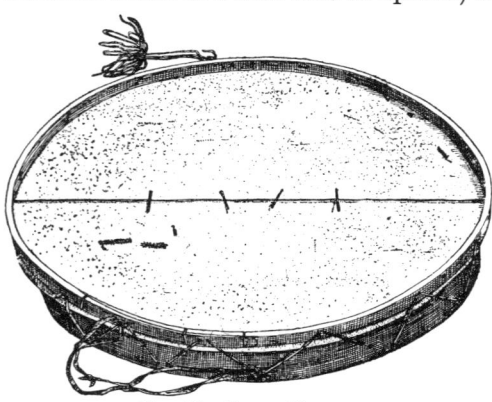

FIG. 151.—Drum, Nenenot.

joined in a lap, spliced nearly a foot long, which length is sewed by four perpendicular seams. The stitches are made with deerskin thread put through perforations, near together, made with an awl. The next operation is to prepare for a head a thin reindeer skin, which has been tanned. The skin is moistened and sewed so that all holes in it are closed. A narrow hoop of a size to fit tightly over the barrel of the drum is made and the moist skin stretched over it. The edges of the skin are turned inward, and within this hoop is placed the barrel of the drum.

A second hoop, two or three times as wide as the first, is prepared and fitted over the barrel and head. It is pushed down as far as the elasticity of the membrane will allow, or about half the width of the top hoop. Through the outer hoop have been made a number of holes and corresponding but alternate holes made in the farther edge of the barrel of the drum.

Through these holes a stout thong is threaded and passing from the edge of the barrel to the outer hoop is drawn so tightly as to push the inner hoop along the outer circumference of the barrel and thus tighten the membrane to the required degree. The outer hoop now projects an inch or more beyond the membrane and thus protects it from injury by careless handling.

Across the membrane is stretched a sinew cord on which are strung, at right angles to the cord, a number of barrels made from the quills of the wing feathers of the willow ptarmigan. Across the underside of the membrane is stretched a similar cord with quills. These serve the purpose of a snare on the drum. The stick used for beating the drum consists of a piece of reindeer horn cut so as to have a thin and narrow handle a foot in length and terminating in a knob more than an inch long and as thick as the portion of horn permits. The drum is suspended from the poles of the tent by means of thongs.

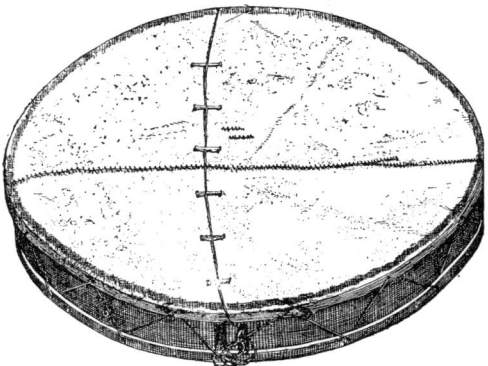

Fig. 152.—Drum, Little Whale river.

The performer tightens the snares, and sprinkles a few drops of water on the drumhead lest the blows, cause it to split under the strain. Nothing is done, nothing contemplated without sounding the drum. It is silent only when the people are asleep or on a tramp from one locality to another.

If a person is ill the drum is beaten. If a person is well the drum is beaten. If prosperous in the chase the drum is beaten; and if death has snatched a member from the community the drum is beaten to prevent his spirit from returning to torment the living.

The drumbeat is often accompanied with singing which is the most discordant of all sounds supposed to be harmonious.

The drums used by the Little Whale river Indians (Fig. 152, No. 3223) differs greatly in construction from those made by the Ungava Indians. The size is rarely so great, seldom exceeding 22 inches. These drums have two heads or membranes fitted on the barrel and secured by means of a single hoop for each head. The two hoops are then connected by the tightening strings.

The membranes are invariably made of deer skin in the parchment condition and not of tanned skins. The snares or thongs across the heads are finer and have pieces of wood instead of quills as "rattlers."

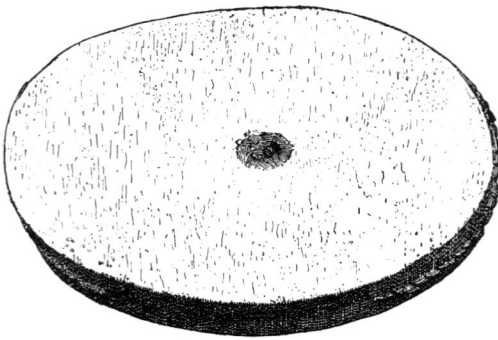

FIG. 153.—Rattle, Nenenot.

The drumstick is a piece of reindeer horn cut as before described; or else, as if to add to the din, a gun-cap box is pierced through from side to side and a few pebbles or shot placed within. A stick is then inserted in the hole through the box and the whole covered with buckskin to prevent separation of the lid and box. This makes a distracting noise.

Rattles for the children (Fig. 153) are made of a hoop of wood bent to a circular form and covered with two heads or membranes. Within it are placed a few pebbles or shot, to produce a rattling sound when

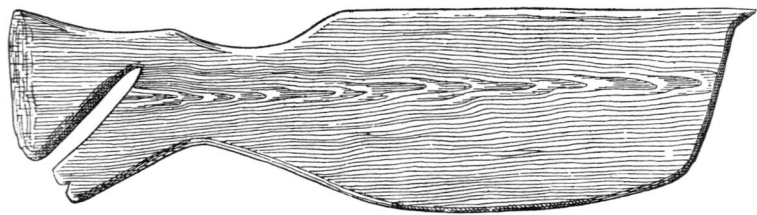

FIG. 154. —Target, reindeer, buck.

the membranes are dry. A cord attached to the circumference enables the rattle to be suspended from the tent-pole in front of the child for whose amusement it is intended. Other toys are made for the children,

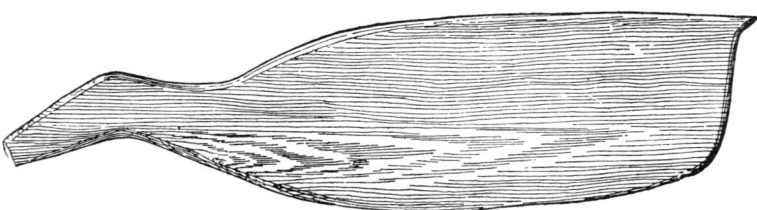

FIG. 155.—Target, reindeer, doe.

but they were not easy for us to obtain. Pl. XLIII represents a doll, dressed in a woman's full suit of clothes. The boys amuse themselves by shooting with blunt arrows at images of reindeer, bucks, does, and fawns, cut out of flat boards stuck up in the snow (Figs. 154, 155).

DOLL, INDIAN WOMAN, FULL DRESS, NENENOT.

FOLKLORE.

During the long winter nights or during the periods of cold or inclement weather in which the Indians may not venture out, they sit
around the fire and relate stories intended for the instruction as well
as entertainment of the younger people. The older men have a great
stock of these stories, and many of the women are noted for their ability
in entertaining the children, who sit, with staring eyes and open mouth,
in the arms of their parents or elders.

The following stories came to me directly and not through the
medium of another white person, and probably I am the only white
person who has heard some of them. I have endeavored to give them
as nearly in the form of the original as the differences between the
English and the Indian languages will permit.

Story of the wolverene and the brant.—A wolverene calling all the birds
together addressed them thus: "Do you not know that I am your
brother? Come to me and I will dress you in feathers." After having
dressed them up he made wings for himself and said: "Now, brothers,
let us fly." The brant told the wolverene, "You must not look below
while we are flying over the point of land when you hear a noise
below. Take a turn when we take a turn."

The first turn they took the wolverene did not look below, but at the
second turn they took, when they came over the point of land, the
animal looked below when he heard the noise of the shouting Indians
and down he came like a bundle of rags.[1]

All the Indians ran up to him and exclaimed "There is a brant fallen
down." One of the old Indian women got hold of him and began to
pluck his feathers off, then to disembowel him. She of course smelled
the horrible stench and exclaimed, "This goose is not fit to eat as it is
already rotten!" She gave the carcass to one of the children to throw
away. Another old woman came up and inquired, "Where did you
throw the brant goose to? How could it be rotten? It is not long
since it was killed." The former old woman replied to her, "Go and
see, if you do not believe." She went and found nothing but the dead
wolverene.

Story of the wolverene.—A wolverene was running along the seashore and perceived a number of geese, brant, ducks, and loons sitting
in the water a short distance off. The wolverene addressing them said,
"Come here, brothers. I have found a pretty bees' nest. I will give it
to you if you will come on shore and have a dance." All the birds
went on land. The wolverene said, "Let us have a dance and I will
sing. Shut your eyes and do not open them until we are done dancing.
He began to sing, "A-ho'u-mu-hou-mu'-mu'-hŭm'." The last word was

---

[1] When the Indians perceive a flock of these brant they make a loud clamor, which frightens the
birds so much that they lose their senses, fall to the ground and are thus killed. These birds are
only seen in the spring migrations and then in great multitudes, while in the fall it is rare to see even
a single individual, as they have a different return route than in spring.

so often repeated (accompanied with the act of the wolverene snipping off the heads of the birds) that the loon opened one eye and saw the headless ducks kicking. The loon ran to the water and exclaimed, "Our brother has killed us!" The wolverene ran after the loon but the loon dived under the water and came up a distance off and cried out, "A ho ho ho ho ho ho!" The wolverene screamed, "Hold your tongue, you red-eyed fowl." The wolverene returned to where the ducks had been killed; plucked their feathers off and cleaned them; put them into a large kettle and boiled them.

While attending to the cooking he saw a whisky-jack (Us' ka tcon) (*Perisoreus canadensis*) flying about. The wolverene took a firebrand and threw it at the bird, exclaiming, "You will be telling on me, you long-tongued bird!" The jay flew away and told the Indians that "Our brother (wolverene) has killed a lot of ducks and has them cooked," adding, "I think he is sleeping. I'll show you where he is if you will come." The Indians replied, "We will go, for we are very hungry." They went and found the wolverene asleep alongside the pot. The Indians ate all of the meat of the ducks. After they had finished the meat they put the bones back into the kettle and went away. The wolverene awakened after a time, took his dish and said to himself, "Now, I shall have my dinner." He poured all the broth into his dish and found nothing but the bones remaining. In his surprise he said, "Surely, I have been sleeping a long time; the meat is all boiled away." The jay told him that he had told the Indians. The wolverene said, "Why did you tell? you stupid bird; I was keeping a nice piece of fat for you.[1] You will not, now, get it for your impudence."

The deer and the squirrel.—A reindeer called all the mammals and birds together and announced that he would give names to all of them. When he came to name the squirrel he inquired of the little creature what name it would prefer. The squirrel replied that it would like to have the same name as the black bear. The reindeer smiled and informed the squirrel that it was too small to have the name of the bear. The squirrel began to cry and wept so long that his lower eyelids became white.

The young man who went to live with the deer.—A young man one morning told his old father that he had dreamed the night before that a deer had asked him to come and live with them. The old father replied, "That is a good sign; you will kill many deer after that dream." The young man went away to hunt, and while out he saw a large herd of deer. A young doe from the band ran up toward him, and he was about to fire at her when she said to him, "Do not fire, for my father has sent me to you. Please put up your arrows." She came nearer and informed him that her father had sent her to ask him to come and live with the deer forever.

---

[1] The jay is well known to be particularly fond of fat of any kind, hence the tempting morsel withheld was a source for future reflection.

The young man inquired, " How could I live with you when it is upon deer that I live? I live in a tent and can not live outside. I can not live without fire. I can not live without water." The doe replied, " We have plenty of fire, water, and meat; you will never want; you will live forever. Your father will never want, as there will be enough deer given to him." The man consented to go with them. The doe pointed to a large hill and said, " That is our home." She told him to leave his deerskin mantle, snowshoes, and arrows on the ground, but to keep the bow. As they were walking along they came to a big valley. She informed him that that was their path. The two went toward the steep hillside and found the ground to be covered with deer. Some of the deer were frightened when they saw the man coming, and started to run. The doe's father said to the frightened deer, " Do you not pity the poor Indians who have to hunt for their living while we do not?" When the young man and the doe came up, the father of the doe addressed the young man, asking if he was hungry. The man replied, " Yes." The father then gave him a piece of nice meat and some fat. After the man had finished eating the father inquired, " Is your father also hungry?" The son replied, " Yes. "

The old buck informed the young man that they would give the son's father some deer to-morrow. After the young man had slept out one night his father, in the morning, went out to look for his son, but found only his mantle, snowshoes, and arrows, which had been cast aside the day before, and also found the tracks in the valley leading to the home of the deer under the hill. The old man returned to his tent and told the other Indians that his son had gone away to live with the deer. The old man then said, " Let us make snares and we will yet take him, as he can not run as fast as the deer." The Indians prepared a number of snare nooses and went to the valley to set them among the bushes on the path. The father of the young doe saw what was going on in the valley and told the rest, " Let us go and give the old man some deer." He told the young man to come with them. The man replied that he could not accompany them, as he would be left behind in no time while they were running. The old buck instructed the young man to keep among the rest of the deer and he would not be left behind them. All the deer then went out to the valley. The young man kept among them; and as they were going through the bushes he heard the shouts of the Indians who were concealed behind them. The deer saw the snares and some of the animals fell into the nooses and were caught. The remainder, with the young man, were soon beyond the snares. The Indians began to kill the deer which had been taken in the nooses, and when they had finished they found they had not captured the young man. They consulted together and decided to search among the tracks of the escaped deer to ascertain whether his foot-prints were among them. They found his track and also the mark of his bow as he had dragged it along in the snow.

The young man's father then said, "Let him go if he thinks he is able to live with the deer;" and the people returned to their tents.

The wolf's daughter going to seek her lover.—An old mother wolf one morning said to her daughter, "You must go and look for your lover or else we shall all starve to death, as your brothers can not kill any deer." The daughter inquired of her mother, "Who is my lover?" The mother replied, "The otter is your lover. He lives in the water. If you go to the narrows of the lake you will find him." The daughter said she would go. So early in the morning she started off, and as she was going along the shore of the lake she saw an open hole in the ice, and in the water the otter was sitting. The wolf went up to the otter, but the otter swam away and was going to dive, when the wolf said, "Do not dive and go away. My mother says you are my lover." The otter asked, "How can I be your lover when I live in the water?" The wolf replied, "You can live on the land as well as in the water." The otter answered back, "I will not live on the land." The wolf retorted, "You will have to live on the land, and if you do not come out I shall smother you in the water." The otter said, "You can not smother me, for I have a number of holes made in the lake ice." The otter dove into the water and disappeared. The wolf began to howl dismally when the otter vanished. The wind began to blow and drifted the snow furiously. The snow fell into the otter's breathing holes and filled them with slushy snow, which soon froze and completely stopped all the holes in the ice but one where the wolf was sitting. This hole was kept clear of snow and ice by the wolf scraping it out as fast as it collected. Soon she heard the otter going to the holes for breath, but when he came near the hole where the wolf was sitting she could hear him snuffing for air, and she stood with open jaws ready to seize him when he should appear. The otter was nearly exhausted, so the wolf went off a little distance, and the otter came up to the surface of the water nearly out of breath. He crept out of the water and rolled himself in the dry snow to take the water off of his coat of fur and exclaimed to the wolf, "I will live with you; I will live with you." The wolf then addressed her lover and said, "Did I not tell you I would smother you?" The otter did not reply to this, but asked her, "Have you got a piece of line? Give it to me, and I will go to catch some fish for you if you will go and prepare a tent." The wolf drew out a piece of fishing line and handed it to the otter. The otter went down into the same hole in the ice whence he had come. He was gone some time, and in the meantime the wolf was busy making the tent, which was completed before the otter returned. Soon after, however, the otter came back to the hole with a long string of fish which he had killed and had them all strung on the line. He left the string of fish in the hole in the ice with one end of it fastened to the ice. The otter rolled himself in the snow to remove the water from his fur, and then went to the tent to tell his wife to go and get the fish which he had left in the hole in the ice.

The wolf went and hauled up the line, which was full of fish, and began to devour so many that soon she could scarcely move. She hauled the remainder of the fish home to the tent.

The otter was sleeping when she returned. She proceeded to clean the fish and put on a large kettle full of the fish to boil for supper. She then crept into bed with her husband, and the next morning she was delivered of a young otter and a young wolf. After the father and mother had taken their breakfast the latter sat with her head hanging down and seemed to be in a miserable mood. The otter inquired of the wife wolf, "What is the matter with you that you sit so quietly?" The wolf answered: "I wish I had some deerskins with which to make clothing for the children. How nicely I should dress them!" The otter replied: "Open the door and I will show you where I get the deer." It was yet early, and the otter went away to seek the deer. The otter saw a band of thirty deer, but had no gun with which to kill them, so he frightened them, and as they were running away he sprang at them each, and jumped through them from end to end. He killed all of them in this manner and then rolled in the snow to cleanse himself. After that was done he wended his way home, and on arriving informed his wife (for it was then a little after sunset) that on the morrow she should go to bring home the deer he had killed, adding that she could follow his track, and thus find them. The wife had a big pot of fish cooked for him when he returned, and when he had finished his supper he went to bed. As soon as the wife suspected her husband to be asleep she went after the deer, and by hauling four at a time she soon had them all brought, and laid them before the tent. When that was finished she went to bed. In the morning the otter told her to get up and make a fire, as she would have to go for the carcasses of the deer which he had killed the day before. The wife replied: "I have already brought them all home." The otter asked her: "How could you bring them home in the dark?" The wife answered: "Look out through the door if you do not believe me." The otter looked and saw the thirty deer all piled up before the door. He turned and looked at his wife, but made no remark. The wolf asked him: "Why do you look at me, so hard?" The otter said: "I was wondering how you could get them home in such a short time." The wolf said: "Come, and take your breakfast, for you will have to help me skin the deer." After they had finished eating their breakfast they began to skin the deer, and soon had them done. The wolf told her husband to make a stage or scaffold for the meat, adding that she would clean the skins. The otter prepared the stage, which in a short time was completed. The meat was placed on the stage and the skins hung up to dry around the tent. They then went in to take their supper. The wife was not in a talkative mood, and soon went to bed. The next morning the wolf hung her head down, and the otter seeing her again in such mood, inquired what was the matter with her that she should be so quiet.

The wolf replied: "I am thinking of my poor father and mother and brothers; I suppose they will all be starved to death. My old father told me to tell you to put a mark on the middle of the lake so they would know where I am." The otter went to the middle of the lake and erected a pile as a mark by which the wolf's relations should know it. The brothers of the otter's wife were on the hill looking for the mark set up by their sister's husband, and when they saw it they exclaimed: "Our sister has saved us! our sister has saved us!" and ran back to their old father's home to give him the joyful intelligence that they had seen the mark put up by the husband of their sister. The old wolf then told his family that they would go and seek their sister and daughter to live with her and her husband. They all went to the hill by the lake, and from the top of it they saw the mark, and from it they followed the track of the otter until they saw the tent in the edge of the woods. They exclaimed : "There is our sister's tent, for the deerskins are hanging outside." They raised such a joyful shout at the prospect before them, that the noise frightened some young otters (for the family had now become larger) which were playing outside. The little ones scampered in and hid themselves behind their father's back. The father inquired, "What is the matter, that you are so frightened?" The little ones replied : "We are running from the Hunger" (for that was the name they applied to the wolves). The mother replied : "Perhaps they see my father, mother, and brothers coming." The otter told his wife to go out and see. She complied, and when she opened the door they saw a row of gaunt wolves; nothing but skin and bones. The newcomers immediately fell to, and began to devour the meat which was on the stage. The otter's wife remonstrated, and said : "Do not be so greedy ; my husband is not a stingy man. I take my meals when he is sleeping, and pretend not to eat much during the day." They all went into the tent and the otter soon went to bed. When they thought he was asleep, they began to eat all the raw meat and fish, and soon finished it. In the morning when the otter had awakened, he remarked to his wife : "I think your brothers will make a fool of me." The wife asked : "What makes you think so?" The otter replied : "They look at me so hard, that I do not know where to turn my eyes." After breakfast the otter and his wolf brothers went away to look for deer. They soon came upon a band of them, and the otter told the wolves to go and kill them. The wolves ran after the deer, but got only one of them. After the deer were frightened by the wolves, the otter sprang after the deer and soon killed every one of them in the same manner he had killed the others. He then cleaned himself in the dry snow and returned home. The wolves had started for the tent before the otter, so when the latter returned they asked the otter : "How many deer did you kill?" The otter replied : "I killed all that were in the band," adding, "In the morning you will have to go for the

deer." So everything was got ready for an early start and they all retired to bed. When they awakened in the morning, one of the wife's
brothers said to another: "Look at our otter brother; he has a white
mouth." The otter turned to his wife and said to her: "Did I not
tell you that your brothers would make a fool of me?" The otter then
took his two otter children in his arms, and told his wife that she
would have to make her living as best she could, as he would not live
with her any more, that he was going away to leave her. He darted
off to the lake, and disappeared under the ice, and was never seen
again.

The devil punishing a liar.—A bear (mackwh) had two young cubs
which she did not want to let know that summer had come, but kept
them in the den and would not let them go out. The young ones continually inquired if the summer had come, and repeated the question
every time the mother returned from the outside. She invariably answered, "No." Some days after she fell asleep, when she had returned
from one of her trips, and while sleeping her mouth opened wide. The
young ones said to each other: "Surely the summer is come, for there
are green leaves in our mother's mouth." The mother had told her
children how beautiful was the summer time, how green the trees, how
juicy the plants, and how sweet the berries; so the cubs, impatient,
while longing for summer that they might enjoy what was outside of
their den, knew by the leaves in their mother's mouth that she had de-
ceived them. The older cub told the younger that they would slip out
at the top of the den and go out while their mother was yet sleeping.
They crept out and found the weather so fine and the surroundings so
pleasant that they wandered some distance off by the time she wakened
from her sleep. She ran out and called loudly for her children, seemingly surprised, and exclaimed: "My sons, the summer has come; the
summer has come." The cubs hid when they heard their mother's
voice. She called to them until nightfall. The older cub said to his
brother: "I wish the devil (A-qan') would hear her and kill her for
telling us the summer had not come, and keeping us in the house so
long when it was already pleasant outside."

The mother bear soon screamed to her sons: "The devil has heard
me and is killing me."

The cubs heard the devil killing their mother with a stone, pounding
her on the head.

They became frightened and ran away.

A wolverene destroys his sister.—A wolverene having wandered far,
for several days without food, suddenly came upon a bear. The former,
feeling very hungry, conceived the plan of destroying his larger prey
by stratagem. The wolverene cautiously approached the bear and exclaimed: "Is that you, sister?" The bear turned around and saw the
wolverene, but in a low tone, which the wolverene did not hear, said to
herself: "I did not know that I had a brother," so ran quickly away.

The wolverene continued to scream: "Come here, sister, our father has sent me to look for you. You were lost when you were a little girl out picking berries." Thus spoken to, the bear approached the supposed brother, who informed her that he knew of a place, on the hill there, where a lot of nice berries were ready for eating, saying: "Do you not see the berries growing on that hill, sister?" The bear answered: "I can not see so great a distance." So the two went up the hillside where the berries grew. When they arrived at the place, and it was some distance off, the bear asked: "How is it that your eyes are so good?" The wolverene replied: My father mashed a lot of cranberries into my eyes and put me into a sweat house." The bear said: "I wish my eyes were as good as yours." The wolverene answered: "I will make your eyes as good as mine if you will gather a lot of cranberries while I prepare a sweat house." The bear went to gather berries while the other prepared the house during her absence. The wolverene selected a stone having a sharp edge, which she concealed under the moss in the sweat house, while she procured a larger stone for the pillow.

After the sweat house was completed the wolverene cried out: "Sister, the sweat house is finished!" The bear returned, bringing a quantity of berries. They both went into the sudatory, whereupon the wolverene instructed the bear to lie with her head upon the stone pillow, while he prepared the crushed berries to put in her eyes. He then said to her: "Now, sister, do not move; you may find the berries will hurt the eyes and make them very sore, but they will be better soon." The wolverene filled the bear's eyes full of the sour berries, which made her exclaim: "Brother, they are making my eyes very sore." The wolverene answered: "You will find them the better for that. After I get your eyes full of the berries I will blow my breath on them." After the eyes of the bear were full of berries the wolverene said: "You are too good to be a sister," so he struck her on the head with the sharp-edged stone and cleft her skull between the eyes and killed her.

The rabbit and the frog.—One day a rabbit was wandering among the hillsides, and at a short distance from him he observed a tent belonging to some Indians. Being timid he crept up to the side of the tent and peeped through a small hole, and saw inside of it a frog sitting near the fire. The rabbit seeing no danger accosted the frog thus: "Brother, what are you doing?" The frog replied: I am playing with the ashes. My brothers have gone off hunting and I am here as I have a very sore leg and can not go far." The rabbit rejoined, "come with me and I will keep you?" The frog answered, "I can not walk as my leg is too sore." The rabbit offered to carry the frog on his back. The rabbit took the frog and giving him a toss threw him on his back and said: "This is the way I will carry you." So they started for the home of the rabbit, where, upon arriving, the rabbit placed the frog inside of the tent while the former went out to look for something to eat. While seeking food the rabbit suddenly spied a smoke curling from among the willows which grew along the branch of the creek. He became frightened and started to run homeward exclaiming. "I have forgotten my crooked knife and I must go quickly to get it." (This part, or what the rabbit says to himself, is sung as a song; with an attempt at imitation of the rabbit's voice.) The rabbit ran hurriedly home and sprang into the tent, whereupon the frog observing the fright of the other inquired, "Brother, what is the matter that you are so excited?" The rabbit answered, "I saw a large smoke." "Where is it?" inquired the frog. The rabbit replied, "It is from among the willows along the creek that runs near by." The frog began to laugh at the foolish fear of the rabbit and answered him that the smoke proceeded from the lodge of a family of beavers, and taunted the rabbit for being afraid of such a timid creature as a beaver when they are good to eat, adding that his own (frogs) brothers often carried him to the beavers' houses to kill them when they were out of food; although his brothers could never kill any of them.

The rabbit was pleased to hear the frog was such a great hunter, and gladly offered to carry the frog to the lodge of the beavers that some food could be procured. The frog accepted the offer and was carried to the creek bank. The rabbit then built a dam of stakes across the stream and below the lodges in order that the beavers should not escape. The frog then directed the rabbit to break into the top of the lodge so that the frog might get at the beavers to kill them. While the rabbit was breaking into the lodge of the beavers, the frog purposely loosened some of the stakes of the weir below in order to allow the beavers to escape, hoping that the rabbit would become angry at him for so doing. When the rabbit saw what mischief the frog had done, he took the frog and roughly shoved him under the ice into the water. This did not harm the frog as it could live under water as well as on land, but the rabbit did not know that, so he believed he had drowned his brother the frog. The rabbit then returned to his home, regretting he had acted so harshly and began to cry for his brother, The frog in the meanwhile, killed all of the beavers and tied them together on a string, then slowly crawled to the rabbit's home with his burden on his back. The frog crept up to the tent but was afraid to enter so he began to play with the door flap of the tent to make a noise to attract the attention of the rabbit within. Finally he cried out to the rabbit, "Brother, give me a piece of fire for I am very cold." The rabbit did not recognize the tired, weak voice of his brother frog, and, afraid lest it be some enemy endeavoring to entice him from his home, picked up a piece of dead coal which had no fire on it and flung it outside. The frog then said, "Brother, there is no fire on this piece and I can not cook my beavers with it." The rabbit then ran out quickly and tenderly carried the frog inside, and immediately the latter began to moan and appear to suffer so much that the rabbit inquired what was the matter and asked if the beavers had bitten him. The frog said, "No, it was you who gave me such a hard push that you have hurt me in the side." The rabbit assured the frog that the injury was unintentionally caused. The frog then directed the rabbit to prepare and cook the beavers. The rabbit went out to fetch them but he began to eat and did not stop until they were all devoured. After having finished eating them the rabbit went for a walk. Ere long he noticed a huge smoke curling from the farther end of a valley and becoming greatly frightened he exclaimed, "I have forgotten my crooked knife and I must go quickly to get it." He dashed into his door in a terrible state of mind. The frog coolly inquired, "What is the matter that you are so scared?" The rabbit said, "I have seen a great smoke at the farther end of the valley through which the creek runs." The frog laughed loudly at his fear and said, "They are deer; my brothers often had me to kill them, as they could not kill any, when we had no meat." The rabbit was delighted at that so he offered to carry the frog toward the place. The frog directed the rabbit to make a snow-shoe for the one foot of the frog. The rabbit soon had it made and gave it to his brother. The frog then said, "Carry me up towards the smoke." The rabbit slung the frog on his back and away they went in the direction of the deer. The frog then told the rabbit to stand in one place and not to move while he (the frog) would work at the deer, and when he had finished he would call him up to the place.

The frog killed all the deer in a very short time, skinned them, and stuck the head and neck of one of the deer into the snow so that it would be looking toward the place whence the rabbit would come. The frog then took the lungs of one of the deer and put it out to freeze. The cold turned the lungs white as tallow. The frog shouted for his brother rabbit to come quickly. When the rabbit came bounding near he saw the eyes of the deer's head staring at him in a queer manner; he was so much alarmed that he exclaimed to the frog, "Brother, he sees me." The frog smiled and said, "I have killed him; he is dead; come on; I have a nice piece of fat saved for you." (It was the frozen lungs of the deer.) So he gave the rabbit a large piece and told him to eat it all and quickly, as it was better when frozen and fresh from the deer's back. The rabbit greedily swallowed large portions and did not observe the deception. After a time they built a lodge or tent for the night. Some few hours after the tent was made the frozen deer lungs which the rabbit had eaten began to thaw and it made the rabbit so violently ill that he vomited continually the entire night. The frog had served him this trick as a punishment for having eaten all of the beaver meat two days before.

The wolverene and the rock.—A wolverene was out walking on the hillside and came upon a large rock. The animal inquired of the rock, "Was that you who was walking just now?" The rock replied,

"No, I can not move; hence I can not walk." The wolverene retorted that he had seen it walking. The rock quickly informed the wolverene that he uttered a falsehood. The wolverene remarked, "You need not speak in that manner for I have seen you walking." The wolverene ran off a little distance and taunted the rock, challenging it to catch him. The wolverene then approached the rock and having struck it with his paw, said, "See if you can catch me." The rock answered, "I can not run but I can roll." The wolverene began to laugh and said, "That is what I want." The wolverene ran away and the rock rolled after him, keeping just at his heels. The animal finally began to tire and commenced to jump over sticks and stones until at last the rock was touching his heels. At last the wolverene tripped over a stick and fell. The rock rolled over on him and ceased to move when it came upon the hind parts of the wolverene. The animal screamed, "Get off, go away, you are hurting me; you are breaking my bones." The rock remained motionless and replied, "You tormented me and had me run after you, so now I shall not stir until some one takes me off."

The wolverene replied, "I have many brothers and I shall call them." He called to the wolves and the foxes to come and remove the rock. These animals soon came up to where the rock was lying on the wolverene and they asked him, "How came you to get under the rock?" The wolverene replied, "I challenged the rock to catch me and it rolled on me." The wolves and foxes then told him that it served him right to be under the rock. They endeavored, after a time, to displace the rock but could not move it in the least. The wolverene then said, "Well, if you can not get me out I shall call my other brother, the lightning and thunder." So he began to call for the lightning to come to his aid. In a few moments a huge dark cloud came rushing from the southwest, and as it hurried up it made so much noise that it frightened the wolves and foxes, but they asked the lightning to take off the coat of the wolverene but not to harm his flesh. They then ran away. The lightning darted back to gather force and struck the rock, knocking it into small pieces and also completely stripped the skin from the back of the wolverene, tearing the skin into small pieces. The wolverene stood naked, but soon began to pick up the pieces of his coat and told the lightning, "You need not have torn my coat when you had only the rock to strike."

The wolverene gathered up his pieces of coat and said he would go to his sister, the frog, to have her sew them together. He repaired to the swamp where his sister dwelt and asked her to sew them. She did so. The wolverene took it up and told her she had not put it together properly and struck her on the head and knocked her flying into the water. He took up the coat and went to his younger sister, the mouse. He directed her to sew his coat as it should be done. The mouse began to sew the pieces together and when it was done the wolverene carefully examined every seam and said, "You have sewed it very well; you will live in the tall green grass in the summer and in grass houses in the winter." The wolverene put on his coat and went away.

Creation of people by the wolverene and the muskrat.—As a wolverene was wandering along the bank of a river he saw a muskrat swimming in the edge of the water. He accosted the latter animal with the inquiry, "Who are you? Are you a man or a woman?" The muskrat answered, "I am a woman." The wolverene informed her that he would take her for a wife. The muskrat replied, "I live in the water; how can I be your wife?" The wolverene told her that she could live on the land as well as in the water. The muskrat went up on the bank to where the wolverene was standing. They selected a place and she began to prepare a home for them. They ate their suppers and retired. Soon after a child was born. The wolverene informed his wife that it would be a white man and father of all the white people. When this child was born it made a natural exit. In due time a second child was born which the wolverene decreed should be an Indian and the father of their kind. This child was born from its mother's mouth. After a time a third child was born, and the wolverene announced it to be an Eskimo and father of its kind. This child was born *ab ano*. In the natural course of events a fourth child was born, and the wolverene decided it to be an Iroquois and father of its kind. This child was born from its mother's nose. After a time a fifth child was born and the wolverene decreed it should be a Negro and father of its kind. This child was born from its mother's ears. These children remained with their parents until they grew up. Their mother then called them together and announced to them that they must separate. She sent them to different places of the land, and, in parting, directed them to go to the white men whenever they were in need of anything, as the whites would have everything ready for them.

Origin of the whitish spot on the throat of the marten.—A man had a wife whom a marten fell in love with and endeavored to possess. Whenever the man would go away from his home the marten would enter, sit by the woman's side, and endeavor to entice her to leave her husband and go to live with him. One day the man returned unexpectedly and caught the marten sitting by the side of his wife. The marten ran out. The man inquired of his wife what the marten wanted there. The woman replied that the marten was striving to induce her to desert him and become his own wife.

The next time the man went off he told his wife to fill a kettle with water and put it on the fire to boil. The man went outside and secreted himself near the house. He soon saw the marten go into the house.

The man stole quietly to the door of the house and listened to the marten, which was talking to his wife. The man sprang into the house and said: "Marten, what are you doing here, what are you trying to do?" The man seized the kettle of hot water and dashed it on the breast of the animal. The marten began to scratch his burning bosom and ran out into the woods; and because he was so severely hurt he now keeps in the densest forests, away from the sight of man.

The Indian and his beaver wife.—One day an Indian was hunting along the bank of a stream and in the distance saw a beaver's house. In a moment he perceived a beaver swimming toward him. He drew up and was on the point of shooting it when the animal exclaimed, "Do not shoot, I have something to say to you." The Indian inquired, "What is it you have to say?" The beaver asked him, "Would you have me for a wife?" The Indian replied, "I can not live in the water with you." The beaver answered, "You will not know you are living in the water, if you will follow me." The Indian further remarked that he could not live on willows and other woods like a beaver. The beaver assured him that when eating them he would not think them to be willows. She added, "I have a nice house to live in." The man replied, "My brother will be looking for me if I come in and he will not know where I am. The beaver directed the man to take off his clothing and leave them on the bank and to follow her. The Indian did as he was instructed. As he was wading through the water he did not feel the water touching him; so they presently began to swim and soon reached the home of the beaver. The beaver told him as she pointed ahead, "There is my home, and you will find it as good and comfortable as your own tent." They both entered and she soon set before him some food which he did not recognize as willow bark. After they had slept two nights his brother became alarmed and went to search for him, and soon found his track. In following it up his brother came to where he had left his clothing on the bank of the stream.

The brother was distressed at finding such things, so went sorrowfully back to the tent thinking that his brother had been drowned, and so told the other Indians when he arrived. With a heavy heart he went to bed and in the morning he awakened and told his wife that he had dreamed his brother was living with a beaver. He told his wife to make some new clothing for the lost brother as he would go and seek the haunts of the beavers to discover his brother. The man occupied himself in making a pair of snowshoes, while the wife prepared the clothing. The next day she had the clothing done and he directed her to make them into a small bundle as he would start on the search early the next morning. Other young men desired to accompany him on the search, but were advised to remain at home as their presence would prevent him from reaching the beaver's retreat. Early in the morning he started off, taking the clothes and snowshoes with him. After some time he found the place where the beaver had her house and in which he suspected his brother to be living. He went to work to make a dam across the stream so as to decrease the depth of water around the beaver's house. The wife had borne two children to the husband by this time, and when the father had seen the water going from their house he told the children: "Your uncle is coming and he is certain to kill you." The water had soon gone down sufficiently to enable the man to cross the stream to where the house was situated.

On arriving there he began pounding at the mud walls. The father told the children to go out or else the house would fall on them. The man outside quickly killed the two young ones. The wife knew she would soon be killed also, and after they had heard the deathblows given to their children she said to her husband, "If you are sorry that I am killed and ever want to see me again, keep the right hand and arm of my body; take off the skin and keep it about you." In a few minutes the brother had begun again to tear out the sides of the lodge. The husband told her to go out, and that his love for her would make him keep her right hand. She then went out and was quickly killed with a stick. When this was done and the husband had heard it all he was very sorry for his wife. Again the man began to destroy the rest of the house and soon had a large hole in the wall of one side. The husband then said to him, "What are you doing? You are making me very cold." The brother replied, "I have brought some warm clothing for you and you will not feel cold." "Throw them in," said the husband, "for I am freezing." He put on the clothes, and while he was doing it the brother noticed the hairs which had grown on the other's back, but said nothing about it. The husband then sat in his house until the other was near freezing to death. The brother then said to him, "Come with me; you can not stay here." The husband demanded, as a condition of returning, that the brother should never say anything to him to make him angry if he went back. The brother promised him not to do so. They then started to return, the brother taking the bodies of the children and mother on his back, the husband walking ahead. They soon arrived at the home of their people. The brother threw down the beavers and directed his wife to skin them. The husband of the beaver asked for the right hand and arm of the beaver who had been his wife. It was given to him. He got one of the other women to skin it, and told her to dry the skin and return it to him. Three nights after their return to their people a great many beavers were killed and a large kettle full of flesh was boiled for food. The people pressed the runaway brother to eat of the flesh of the beavers. He informed them that if it was the flesh of a female beaver he would not eat it. They told him that the flesh of the male beavers was all finished long ago. They forced him to eat a large piece of meat, and when he had swallowed it they gave him more of it. The second piece was no sooner down his throat than a large river gushed from his side. The Indian jumped into the river, while the rest ran away in terror and, as these latter looked down the river, they saw the man swimming by the side of his wife who had been a beaver.

The venturesome hare.—A hare, which had lost his parents, lived with his grandmother. One day, feeling very hungry, for they were extremely poor, he asked his grandmother if he could set a net to catch fish. The old woman laughed at the idea of a hare catching fish, but to humor him, she consented, for she was indulgent to him because he was her only charge and looked forward to the time when he should be able to support her by his own exertions, and not to rely on the scanty supplies which she was able to obtain. These were very meager, as she was infirm, and dreaded exposure. She then told him to go and set the net, but added that she had no fire to cook them with, even if he should catch any. The hare promised to procure fire if he caught the fish. He went to set the net in a lake where he knew fish to be plentiful. The next morning he went to the net and found it to be so full of fish that he was unable to take it up. He lifted one end and saw there was a fish in every mesh of the net. He shook out some of the fish and then drew out the net. Part of the fish were buried, and a large load taken home. He put the fish down outside of the tent, and went in. He told the old woman to clean the fish and that he would go across the river to the Indians' tent and get the fire with which to cook them. The old woman was speechless at such proposed rashness, but as he had been able to catch so many fish she refrained remarking on his contemplated project of obtaining fire in the face of such danger. While the old woman was cleaning the fish he went back after the net which he had put out to dry on the shore of the lake.

He folded it up, placed it under his arm, and ran to the edge of the river which was far too wide to jump over. He used his cunning and assembled a number of whales. These animals came puffing up the stream in obedience to his command. He ordered them to arrange themselves side by side across the stream so that he could walk across on their backs. He most dreaded the Indians, but jumped into the water to wet his fur. This being done he sprang from one whale to another until he was safe on the opposite shore. He then laid down in the sand and bade the whales to disperse. Some Indian children soon came playing along the sandy bank and saw the hare lying there. One of the children picked up the hare and started home with it. When the boy arrived and told how he had obtained the hare he was directed to put it in the iron tent (kettle) where there was a bright fire crackling.

The child put down the hare, upon which an old man told the boy to kill the hare. The hare was terribly frightened, but opened a part of one eye to ascertain whether there was any place of exit beside the door. In the top of the tent he observed a large round hole. He then said to himself: "I wish a spark of fire would fall on my net." Instantly the brands rolled and a great spark fell on the net and began to burn it. The hare was afraid of the fire, so he sprang out of the hole in the apex of the tent. The Indians saw they had been outwitted by a hare, and began to shout and pursue the animal, which attained such speed that when he came to the bank of the river he had not time to recall the whales. He gave an extraordinary leap and cleared the entire expanse of the water. He examined the net and found the fire smouldering. On arrival at his own home he said to his grandmother: "Did I not tell you I would get the fire?" The old woman ventured to inquire how he had crossed the river. He coolly informed her that he had jumped across.

The spirit guiding a child left by its parents.—An Indian and his wife had but one child, which was so infested with vermin that when the parents contemplated going to the tents of some distant friends the father advised the mother to leave the child behind. The next morning after the mother had taken down the tent the little boy asked her "Mother, are you not going to put on my moccasins?" the mother replied, "I shall put them on after I have put on my snow-shoes." The little boy said, "Surely you are not going to leave me!" She said, "No;" but took hold of her sled and started off. The little boy cried out, "Mother, you are leaving me," and endeavored to overtake her in his bare feet; but the mother soon was out of sight. The little boy began to cry and retraced his steps to the tent place. There he cried until the spirit of a dead man came to him and asked, "Where is your mother?" The boy replied, "She has gone away and left me." "Why did she leave you?" asked the old man. "Because I was so covered with lice," replied the boy. The spirit said it would remove all of the lice but three. So it began to pick them off. After this was done the spirit asked, "Where did your mother go?" The boy pointed out her track. The spirit then said to the boy, "Would you like to go to your mother?" The boy answered, "Yes." The spirit put the boy on his back and started in the path made by the sled of his mother. After a while they came to a tree and in looking at it the boy saw a porcupine sitting among the branches. The boy greatly desired to have the animal. So he said, "Grandfather, I wish you would kill the porcupine." The old man answered, "It will make too much smoke for me to kill it." After a time they came across a hare which the boy again desired to have. To this the man assented. So he put the boy down in the snow and soon caught the hare and killed it. It was now becoming dark, so they made their camping place for the night. The spirit gave the boy the hare and told him to cook it. After the meat was cooked the boy asked the old man what parts of the animal he preferred. The old man said "Give me the lungs and kidneys." The boy gave him those parts and consumed the remainder himself. They laid down to sleep and in the morning they again started on the sled track. About noon they came to the tents of the Indians, and among them was the tent of the father and mother of the little boy. The spirit placed the boy down on the outside near the door of the mother's tent and told him to go in. The boy entered and saw his father and mother sitting near the fire. The mother in astonishment said, "Husband, is this not our little boy whom we deserted at our late camp?" The husband asked the boy, "Who brought you here?" The little boy answered, "My grandfather." The mother inquired, "Who is your grandfather?" The father asked, "Where is he now?" The boy replied, "He is sitting outside." The father asked his wife to look outside and see if any one was there. The woman did so and informed him that "I see some one sitting there, but I do not know who it is." The spirit replied, "You should call *me* somebody when you are *no one* to leave your child to perish." The husband directed his wife to invite the old man into the tent.

The spirit declined to enter. The father then asked the son to tell him to come in. The boy went out and conducted the old man within the tent. The latter seated himself across the fire (this is intended to mean opposite the door but on the other side of the fire). They slept in the tent that night, and when the little boy awakened he found all the people preparing to snare deer. The people asked the little boy to accompany them. He did so, and when he was ready to start he asked the old man what part of the deer he should bring home for him. The old man replied that he would enjoy the lungs better than any other part. The boy promised to bring a quantity for him on his return in the evening. Toward evening the boy returned loaded with choice bits for the old man who had conducted him to his father and mother. While outside of the tent he called to the old man, saying that he had brought home some food for him. Hearing no reply he entered the tent, and not seeing the man he inquired of his mother where the person was. The mother announced that he had departed, but did not know where he had gone. It was late, but the boy resolved to rise early and follow his track. He was up at daybreak, and finding the track followed it until he observed the spirit crossing a large lake which was frozen over. The boy cried out to the old man to wait for him. The spirit awaited his approach. The boy said to him, "Why did you go away when I had promised you some choice food?" The spirit replied that it could not dwell among living people, as it was only a spirit and that it was returning to its abode. The old man advised the boy to return to his people. The boy did so, but the next morning the desire to see the good old man seized the boy, and again he started to find him. The other people then tied the boy to a tree and he soon forgot his benefactor.

Fate of two Indian men.—Two Indian men who had gone off for the fall and winter's hunt were living by themselves. They were very unsuccessful in procuring furs and food, so that when the depths of winter had approached and the cold was intense they resolved to seek the camp of their friends. They were provided with nothing but bows and arrows. The next morning they started off and tramped all day without seeing a living thing. They made their camp and lamented they had no food. They finally prepared to sleep, when one of them remarked to the other, "To-night I shall dream of porcupines." They slept, and in the morning the one related that he had seen a lot of porcupines around the tent while he was dreaming. They determined to proceed, but the one finally thought if they would stop there for the day and succeeding night they would have all the porcupine meat they would want. They remained there that day, and in the middle of the night they were aroused by a noise which proved to be porcupines gnawing the bark from the tent poles. The one man said, "Slip out and kill some with a stick;" but added, "Go out in your bare feet." He went out barefooted and killed two or three, and dashed back into the tent with his feet nearly frozen. He stuck his feet into the hot ashes and told the other man to bring in the animals. The other man did so, and began to prepare the flesh for cooking. They ate one of the porcupines, and by daylight were ready to begin their journey. They went idly along, shooting their arrows in sport at anything they could see. They continued this amusement until near sunset, when one exclaimed, "My arrow has struck something; see, it is moving." The other replied, "What can it be, when it is sticking only in the snow?" The other said he would try and find out what it was. He cautiously examined, and found when he began to dig it out that the arrow had entered the den of a bear. So they scratched away the snow and soon saw a long, black hair sticking out of the hole. He jumped back and exclaimed, "It is some sort of animal with black hair." The other replied, "Let us try and get it out. It may be good to eat." They finally drove the bear out and soon killed it. They began to skin it, which was soon done. One of the men then said, "It is too big and ugly to eat; let us leave it." The other, however, cut off a large piece of fat and put it on the sled. They then prepared their camp, and when morning came they started off and traveled all day. When night came they made their camp and soon had a huge fire burning. One of the men hung the piece of fat over the fire and the oil soon dripped into the fire. It created such a nice smell that one of them said, "Let us taste the fat; it may be good to eat." They tasted it and found it so good that they rated each other soundly for being so foolish as to leave such nice flesh so far behind them. They resolved to return for it. So they returned for the carcass of the bear, which was far behind them, and as it had tasted so good they determined to lose no time in starting. They went immediately, although it was now dark and very cold. They came to the place where it had been left and discovered that the wolves and foxes had eaten all the meat, leaving nothing but the bones. They were very angry, and began to lay the blame each on the other for having left it. They regretted they had left such meat for wolves and foxes. They determined to proceed to where they had camped the third time. On the way they became very thirsty, and, stopping at a creek to drink, they drank so long that their lips froze to the ice of the water hole, and they miserably perished by freezing.

The starving wolverene.—On the approach of winter a wolverene, which had been so idle during the summer that he had failed to store up a supply of provisions for himself, his wife, and children, began to feel the pangs of hunger. The cold days and snowstorms were now at hand. The father one day told his wife that he would go and try to discover the place where his brothers, the wolves, were passing the winter and from them he would endeavor to procure some food. The wife desired him not to remain away long, else the children would starve to death. He assured her that he would be gone no longer than four days, and made preparations to start early on the succeeding morning. In the morning he started and continued his journey until near nightfall, when he came to the bank of a river. On looking at the ice which covered its surface he descried a pack of wolves ascending the river at a rapid rate. Behind these were four others, which were running at a leisurely gait. He soon overtook the latter group, and was perceived by one of these old wolves, which remarked to the others, "There is our brother, the wolverene, coming." The animal soon joined the wolves and told them that he was starving, and asked for food. The wolves replied that they had none, but that the wolves in advance were on the track of some deer and would soon have some. The wolverene inquired where they would camp for the night. They told him to continue with them on the track of the others until they came to a mark on the river bank. The wolves, accompanied by the wolverene, continued their way until one of the old wolves called attention to the sign on the bank and proposed they should go up to it and await the return of the others. They went up and began to gather green twigs to make a clean floor in the bottom of the tent. This was no sooner done than the young wolves (the hunters) returned and began to put up the tent poles. The old wolves said they themselves would soon have the tent covering in place. The wolverene was astonished at what he saw and wondered whence they would procure the tenting and fire. The old wolves laughed as they observed his curiosity, and one of them remarked, "Our brother wonders where you will get the tent cover from." The wolverene replied, "I did not say that; I only said my brothers will soon have up a nice and comfortable tent for me." The wolves then sent him off to collect some dry brush with which to make a fire. When he returned the tent was already on the poles. He stood outside holding the brush in his arms. One of the wolves told him to bring the wood inside the tent. He entered and gave the brush to one of the young wolves (the leader of the hunters). The leader placed the brush in position to create a good fire, and while that was being done the wolverene wondered how they would start the fire. One of the old wolves remarked, "Our brother wonders where and how you will get the fire." He made no reply, as one of the young wolves (the leader) took up a kettle and went outside to get some snow to melt for water, and returned with it full of snow. He set the kettle down and sprang quickly over the pile of brush and it started into a blaze in an instant. It was now an opportunity for the wolverene to wonder whence should come the supply of meat to boil. One of the old wolves said, "Our brother wonders where you will get some meat to cook for supper." One of the young wolves went out and brought in a brisket of deer's meat. As soon as the wolverene saw the meat he asserted that he did not wonder about the source of the supply of meat, but that he only wished there was some meat ready for cooking. The meat was cut up and placed in the kettle and when it was ready it was served out. The choicest portions were selected for the wolverene and placed before him with the injunction to eat all of it. He endeavored to consume it, but the quantity was too great even for him. He, having finished his meal, was about to place the remainder on one of the poles when a wolf, observing his action, told him not to place it there or else the meat would change into bark. He then laid it down on a piece of clean brushwood and when he suspected the eyes of the wolves were not turned toward him he stealthily inserted the portion of meat between the tenting and the pole. The wolves saw his action and in a few minutes the wolverene became very sleepy and soon retired. One of the wolves carefully displaced the meat from the pole, where the wolverene had put it, and thrust in its stead a piece of bark. In the morning when the wolverene awakened his first thought was of the remnant of food. He reached up for it and found nothing but the piece of bark. The wolves were on the alert and one of them said, "Did I not tell you it would change into bark if you put the meat in that place?" The wolverene hung his head and answered, "Yes," and again laid down to sleep. By the time he awakened the wolves had a second kettle of meat cooked. They desired the wolverene to arise and eat his breakfast. The leader told him to hasten with his meal, as he had discovered some fresh deer tracks. The wolverene thought he would watch how they broke camp and see where they put the tentings. He went off a few steps and while his back was turned the tent disappeared and he failed to discover where it was secreted. The animals then started off, the young ones taking the lead while the four old ones and the wolverene followed leisurely behind. After they had crossed the river the wolverene began to wonder where they would halt for the night. One of the old wolves told him they must follow the track of the leader and they would come to the sign made for the site of the camp. They continued for the entire day, but just before sundown they came across the bones of a freshly killed deer from which every vestige of meat had been removed, apparently eaten by wolves; so the wolverene thought he would stand a poor chance of getting a supper if that was the way they were going to act. The party continued on the track and soon came upon the mark for the tent site.

The wolverene was glad to rest, but sat down and began to look ahead in the distance for the returning hunters. After a few minutes he looked around and saw the tent standing there. The wolves then sent the wolverene for dry brush, while they gathered green branches for the tent floor. He brought so small a quantity that it would not suffice. The young wolves returned at the same time and they directed him to again procure some brush. When he returned he found they had stripped all the fat off of the deer meat, although, he had not seen them bring any when they returned, and placed it around the inside edges of the tent. The brush was put down and again the leader jumped over it and a bright, crackling fire started up. The wolves then said to themselves in a low tone of voice: "Let us go outside and see what our brother will do when he is left alone with the fat." They went outside and immediately the wolverene selected the nicest and largest piece of fat and began to swallow it. The wolves at the same moment inquired of him: "Brother, are there any holes in the tent cover?" His mouth was so full, in his haste to swallow the fat, that it nearly choked him. They repeated their inquiry and the wolverene gasped out the answer, "yes." The wolves then said: "Let us go inside." The wolverene sprang away from the fat and sat down by the fire. They put on a large kettle of meat and soon had their supper ready. They gave the wolverene all the fattest portions they could find. Having eaten so much of the frozen fat he became so violently ill, when the hot food melted the cold fat in his stomach, that he vomited a long time, and was so weak that he became chilly and shivered so much that he could not sleep. He asked for a blanket, but one of the wolves placed his own bushy tail on the body of the wolverene to keep him warm. The wolverene shook it off and exclaimed: "I do not want your foul-smelling tail for a blanket." So the wolf gave him a nice and soft skin blanket to sleep under. When he awakened he announced his intention to return to his family, as they would soon be dead from hunger. One of the old wolves directed the younger ones to make up a sledload of meat for the wolverene to take home with him. The wolf did so, but made the load so large and long that the wolverene could not see the rear end of the sled. When it was ready they told him of it, and, as he was about to start, he requested they would give him some fire, as he could not make any without. The leader asked how many nights he would be on the journey homeward. He answered, three nights. The wolf told him to lie down in the snow. He did so and the wolf jumped over his body three times, but strictly enjoined upon him not to look back at the sled as he was going along. The wolverene promised he would comply with his instructions. After the animal had started and got some little distance from the camp of the wolves he thought of the peculiarly strange things he had witnessed while among those animals; and, to test himself, he concluded to try the method of making a fire. He stopped, gathered a quantity of dry brush and placed it as he had seen the wolves arrange it. He then sprang over it and a huge blaze gave evidence of the power within him. He was so astonished that he resolved to camp there. He melted some snow and drank the water and retired to rest, without having looked at the sled. The next morning he started early and made his camp before sunset, as he was very tired. He gathered some brush and made the fire by jumping over the pile of fuel. His supper was only some melted snow which he drank and retired. In the morning he started to continue his journey homeward and still had not seen the sled which he was dragging. As he was ready to start he was so confident of his ability to create fire that he threw away his flint and steel. He traveled all day until toward sunset he was so fatigued that he concluded to make his camp for the night. He was so elated with his newly acquired faculty of making fire that he eagerly gathered a great quantity of dried twigs and branches, until a large heap was before him. He jumped over it, and turned round to see the flames creep up and watch the sparks fly. There was not a sign of a blaze or a spark to meet his gaze. He again jumped over it, and again, until he was so exhausted that he could not clear the top of the pile, and at last he knocked the top of it over, as his failing strength did not enable him to avoid it. The only thing left for him to do was to return for his flint and steel, which he had so exultingly thrown aside. The animal berated himself soundly for having done such a silly trick. Not having seen the sled he was surprised to find how quickly he regained the site of the camp of the previous night. Having recovered his flint and steel he returned, and soon had a fire started; but it was now near daylight. He resolved to start on his journey as soon as he had some water melted for a drink. He began to think how quickly he had made the trip for his flint and steel, and concluded that the great length of the sled had been purposely made to cause him unnecessary fatigue, as it could not be so very heavy, or else that he must be extraordinarily strong. He determined to examine it, and did so. He could not see the farther end of the load. He flattered himself that he was so very strong, and concluded to continue his journey. He attempted to start the sled, and found he could not move it in the least. He upbraided himself for permitting his curiosity to get the better of his sense. He removed a portion of dry meat and a bundle of fat, and made them into a load to carry on his back. He placed the remainder on a stage, and was about ready to start homeward to his wife and children, whom he believed must be by this time nearly dead from starvation.

He put the pack of meat on his back and set out. That evening he arrived at his home, and as soon as his wife heard him her heart was glad. He entered and informed the family that he had brought home a quantity of meat and fat, and had procured so much as to be unable to carry it all at once. His wife begged him to fetch her a piece of meat, as she was nearly starved. He went out and brought in a large piece of fat. The wife devoured such a quantity of it that she became very ill, and suffered all through the night. In the morning the wol-verene stated he would return for the meat which he had stored away the previous day. He started in the early morning, so as to return by daylight.

As soon as the wolverene looked upon the sled loaded with meat the spell was broken. One of the old wolves ordered the young wolves to go and destroy the meat and fat which the wolverene had left on the stage. They eagerly set out on the track of the sled, and soon saw the staging where the wolverene had stored the remainder of the food. When they came up to it they fell to and devoured all but a few scraps of it. The wolves then went away, and in a few hours the wol-verene returned. He saw what had happened and exclaimed : "My brothers have ruined me! My brothers have ruined me!" He knew it had been done because he had looked back at the sled, although strictly enjoined upon not to do so under any circumstance. He gath-ered up the fragments which the wolves had left and returned home. When he arrived there he informed his wife that his brothers had ruined him, because they had eaten all the meat which he had stored away while out hunting.

The starving Indians.—A band of Indians, who had neglected to store away a supply of food for a time of scarcity, were upon the point of starvation. An old man who lived at a little distance from the camp-ing place of the band, had wisdom to lay by a good store of dry meat and a number of cakes of fat, so that he had an abundance while the other improvident people were nearly famished. They applied to him, begging for food, but they were refused the least morsel. One day, however, an old man came to him asking for food for his children. The man gave him a small piece of meat. When the man's children ate this food they began to cry for more. The mother told her little boy to stop crying. He persisted in his clamor until his mother asked him: "Why do you not go to the old U' sets kwa nĕ po?" (the name means One whose neck wrinkles into folds when he sits down). This old man heard the mother tell her child to go to him, and muttered to him-self, "That is just what I want."

The little boy went to the old man's tent door, and lifting aside the flap, said: "I want to come in." He went in and the old man addressed the boy by his own name, saying: "What do you want, U' sets kwa nĕ po?" in such a kindly voice that the boy felt assured. The boy said: "I am very hungry and want some food." The old man inquired in an astonished voice: "Hungry? and your meat falling down from the stage?" The old man bade the boy sit down, while he went out to the stage and selected some choice portions and brought them into the tent and gave them to the boy. The old man then asked the boy if he had a sister. The boy said that he had a father, mother, and one sister.

After the boy had finished eating, the old man directed the boy to come with him and see the meat stages. They went out and the old man said: "Now, go home and tell your father that all of this food will belong to you if he will give me his daughter." The little boy went home and repeated what the old man had said. The father signified his willingness to give his daughter in marriage to the old man. The boy returned to the old man and stated that his father was willing to give away his daughter. The old man immediately went out, took some meat and fat from the stage, and then cooked three large kettles of food. When this was done he selected a suit of clothing for a man and two suits for women. He placed the nicer one of the latter near his own seat, and the other two suits directly on the opposite side of the fireplace (the place of honor in the tent). He then told the little boy to call all the Indians, adding: "There is your father's coat, your mother's dress, and your sister's dress. Tell your parents to sit where they see the clothing," pointing to the clothes intended for them, and the sister to sit near the old man, pointing to his own place. The boy ran out and apprised the people, together with his own relations. The boy returned to the old man's tent before the guests arrived. The boy's father came first, and the boy said: "Father, there is your coat." The mother then entered, and the boy said: "Mother, there is your dress." The sister then entered, and the boy pointed to the dress, saying: "Sister, there is your dress." All the other Indians then came in and seated themselves. They took two kettles of meat and broke the fat into pieces and feasted until all was consumed. The old man helped his wife, her father, mother, and brother to the contents of the other kettle. When all the food was finished the old man said to the boy, "U′ sēts kwa nĕ po, go and set your deer snares." The old man went with him to find a suitable place. They could find only the tracks of deer made several days previously. They, however, set thirty snares and returned home. The next morning they all went to the snares and found a deer in each one. The people began to skin the deer and soon had a lot of meat ready for cooking. They began to feast, and continued until all was done. By this time a season of abundance had arrived.